Drug and British Drug Policy

Critical Analysis of the Misuse of Drugs Act 1971

Edited by

Ilana Crome, David Nutt and Alex Stevens

With a Foreword by The Rt Honourable Norman Baker

≋ WATERSIDE PRESS

Drug Science and British Drug Policy
Edited by Ilana Crome, David Nutt and Alex Stevens

ISBN 978-1-914603-26-6 (Paperback)
ISBN 978-1-914603-27-3 (EPUB ebook)
ISBN 978-1-914603-28-0 (PDF ebook)

Copyright © 2022 This work is the copyright of Drug Science UK. All intellectual property and associated rights are hereby asserted and reserved by that organization in full compliance with UK and international law. No part of this book may be copied, reproduced, stored in any retrieval system or transmitted in any form or by any means without the prior written permission of the publishers to whom all such rights have been assigned worldwide.

Cover design © 2022 Waterside Press. Main cover image Pete Fowler: www.petefowler.co.uk

Main UK distributor Gardners Books, 1 Whittle Drive, Eastbourne, BN23 6QH. Tel: (+44) 01323 521777; sales@gardners.com; www.gardners.com

North American distribution Ingram Book Company, One Ingram Blvd, La Vergne, TN 37086, USA. Tel: (+1) 615 793 5000; inquiry@ingramcontent.com

Cataloguing In-Publication Data A catalogue record for this book can be obtained from the British Library.

Printed by Severn, Gloucester, UK.

Published 2022 by
Waterside Press Ltd
Sherfield Gables
Sherfield on Loddon, Hook
Hampshire RG27 0JG.

Telephone +44(0)1256 882250
Online catalogue WatersidePress.co.uk
Email enquiries@watersidepress.co.uk

All royalties from the sale of this book go to Drug Science.

Table of Contents

Foreword xi
    The Rt Hon Norman Baker

About the author of the Foreword *xiii*
Publisher's note *xiv*
Dedication *xv*
About the editors *xvi*

Introduction 17
    Ilana Crome, David Nutt and Alex Stevens

    Chapter Outline *18*
    Acknowledgments *20*

PART I: THE IMPACT OF DRUGS 21

1 At the Frontiers of Psychiatry 23
    Ilana Crome and David Nutt

    Background *23*
    The MDA 1971 *26*
    Recent Research *29*
    Protecting and Facilitating Research *31*
    New Strategy — New Policy? *32*
    References and Extra Reading *34*

2 **A Forensic Science Perspective** 39
Leslie A King

Generic Legislation *39*
General Problems with Generic Control *43*
Capture of Inactive Substances *44*
Effect on the Pharmaceutical Industry *44*
Analytical Issues *45*
Specific Concerns with Generic Control *45*
Classification *48*
Undefined Terms *50*
References and Extra Reading *52*
Statutory Provisions *53*

3 **Fifty Years of MDMA** 55
Val Curran, Fiona Measham, David Nutt and Anne Katrin Schlag

Proactive Prohibition in the UK *55*
The Tragic Case of Leah Betts *57*
The Scientific Risk Assessment of MDMA *58*
A Case of Using Science Selectively to Demonise a Drug? *58*
Negative Perceptions Impact Research Funding *60*
History of MDMA: Timeline *62*
Moving Forward as a Medicine *64*
What Are the Ways Forward with MDMA? *64*
References and Extra Reading *66*

Ilana Crome, David Nutt and Alex Stevens (eds)

4 **Displacement, Adulteration and Innovation** 69
   How the MDA 1971 Failed to Control NPS
   Fiona Measham and Michael Pascoe

   The High Hopes of Prohibition   *69*
   Legal Highs: The Eagle Has Landed   *71*
   Ending the Game of Cat and Mouse   *72*
   Drug-related Deaths: A Temporary Reprieve   *73*
   Monitoring Prevalence: The Paradox of Demand and Use   *76*
   Diversion   *78*
   Drug checking and Surveillance: The Poverty of Policy   *79*
   NPS in Custodial Institutions: A Microcosm of UK Drug
        Policy   *80*
   Conclusion   *81*
   References and Extra Reading   *82*

5 **Cannabis: Past, Present and Future** 85
   Anne Katrin Schlag and David Nutt

   A Summary of the Past 50 years   *86*
   Medical Cannabis   *91*
   Present Progress   *93*
   Continuing Controversies   *94*
   Conclusions and Future Avenues   *95*
   References and Extra Reading   *96*

6 **Narratives of Drug-related Harm** 99
   Anna Ross and Anne Katrin Schlag

   Stories in Policy: The Personal is Political   *99*
   The Master Narrative — The 'Problem' Drug User   *100*
   Conclusion   *108*
   References and Extra Reading   *109*

PART II: IMPACT ON THE MEDICAL, PHARMACY AND VETERINARY PROFESSIONS 111

7 Chronic Pain 113
Brigitta Brandner and Maximilian Dewhurst

Section 1: Chronic Pain and the Epidemic of Opioids   *113*
Section 2: The Role of Legislation for Controlled Drugs   *114*
Section 3: Drugs Used in Practice   *116*
Section 4: The Burden of Opioid Prescribing in Chronic Pain: Does Addiction in Chronic Pain Patients Really Exist?   *123*
Section 5: When Does Opioid Prescribing in Chronic Pain Become a Problem?   *124*
Section 6: Is there Room for Improvement in the MDA 1971 in the Context of Pain Management?   *126*
In Summary   *127*
References and Extra Reading   *128*

8 The Impact of the MDA 1971 on the Veterinary Profession 131
Polly Taylor

Background   *132*
Therapeutic CDs Used in Veterinary Medicine   *133*
Veterinary Surgeons and Suicide   *144*
Conclusions   *144*
References and Extra Reading   *146*

9 Enabling Access to Essential Medicines and Devices 149
Rosalind Gittins

Harm Reduction   *150*
Medical Psychedelics   *153*
Medical Cannabis   *154*
Access to Prescription Medication   *156*
References and Extra Reading   *158*

Ilana Crome, David Nutt and Alex Stevens (eds)

PART III: LEGACIES OF THE DRUG LAWS 163

10 How States Have Adapted Their Drug Laws 165
Emily Crick and Adam Holland

The UN Drug Conventions *166*
De Jure Decriminalisation in Portugal *167*
De Facto Decriminalisation in The Netherlands *169*
Harm Reduction in Switzerland and Across Europe *171*
Drug Policy in the UK *172*
Conclusion *174*
References and Extra Reading *175*

11 The Sixties, Barbara Wootton and the Counterculture 183
Revisiting the Origins of the MDA 1971
Toby Seddon

Origins and Development of the MDA 1971 *184*
Conclusion *189*
References and Extra Reading *191*

12 The Ongoing Impact on the Racialised Policing of Black Communities..193
Bisola Akintoye, Amal Ali and Alex Stevens

Quantifying Disparities *194*
The Intersectional Experience of Being Policed for Drugs *198*
The Effect of Drug Policing on Relationships Between Black
    Communities, Police and the State *201*
Reducing Disparities, Increasing Trust *203*
Conclusion *205*
References and Extra Reading *206*

vii

PART IV: PERSPECTIVES AND APPROACHES 209

13 Challenging Stigma, Changing Minds 211
Jane Slater and Mary Ryder

The MDA 1971: Harming Not Protecting Families *213*
Reframing Drug Policy to Protect Child Wellbeing: Storytelling From the Front Line of the UK's Drug War *217*
Dialogue With Policymakers: Speaking Truth to Power *218*
Conclusion *221*
References and Extra Reading *222*

14 The MDA 1971: No Education 225
Patrick Hargreaves

Personal Social and Health Education in Practice *227*
Models of Drug Education *228*
A New Strategy for Drug and Alcohol Education *231*
A Realistic Role for PSHE *232*
The Family and Other Influences *234*
Media *235*
Conclusion *236*
References and Extra Reading *238*

15 The Impact of Drug Legislation on Climate Change 241
Rosalind Gittins, Steve Rolles and Katherine Watkinson

Drug Use Paraphernalia *241*
Prescribed Interventions *242*
Nitrous Oxide *243*
Safe Spaces for Using Substances *244*
Illicit Production and Supply *244*
References and Extra Reading *246*

Ilana Crome, David Nutt and Alex Stevens (eds)

16 **An Application of Decision Conferencing and Multi-criteria Decision Analysis** 249
   Lawrence D Phillips

The Beginnings *249*
The 2010 *Lancet* Paper *250*
What is MCDA? *252*
What is Decision Conferencing? *254*
Other Drug Harm Studies *258*
Nicotine Delivery Products *259*
Drug Policy *260*
References and Extra Reading *261*

17 **The MDA 1971: Missteps and Misunderstandings** 263
   Rudi Fortson KC

The MDA 1971: A Regulatory Regime *263*
'Designated Drugs' May Have Medicinal Value *266*
A Flexible Regime — Subject to the Will of Government *268*
The MDA: An Enduring Regime *271*

PART V: CHANGING POLICY 273

18 **Regulating the Legal: Minimum Unit Pricing of Alcohol in Scotland** 275
   Eric Carlin

Alcohol — No Ordinary Commodity *276*
Population-level Measures, Including Pricing Policies to Reduce Harm Due to Alcohol Consumption *278*
Alcohol in Scotland *279*
Summing-up — Broad Lessons for Drug Policy *287*
References and Extra Reading *288*

19 **A Modest Proposal to Decriminalise the Simple Possession of Drugs** 293
Kirstie Douse, Niamh Eastwood and Alex Stevens

    The Harms of Criminalisation   *294*
    The Relevant Sections of the MDA 1971   *295*
    Comparison With the Psychoactive Substances Act 2016   *296*
    Our Modest Proposal   *297*
    Counter-arguments   *298*
    Conclusion   *300*
    References and Extra Reading   *301*

20 **The Legal Regulation of Drugs in the UK** 303
James Nicholls and Steve Rolles

    What is Legal Regulation?   *303*
    Risk-based Models of Control   *304*
    Types of Regulation   *305*
    Profit-making Versus Public Health   *307*
    Supporting Previously Impacted Communities   *308*
    Balancing Autonomy and Intervention   *309*
    Regulated Versus Residual Markets   *310*
    Acknowledging the Limits of Regulation   *311*
    References and Extra Reading   *312*

Index   *315*

Foreword

The Rt Hon Norman Baker

The Misuse of Drugs Act 1971 (MDA 1971) is one of the worst pieces of social legislation passed by the British Parliament in my lifetime. It is a tragedy that it remains on the Statute Book more than 50 years on.

It never helps to pass legislation as a sort of panic measure. Think of the Official Secrets Act 1911—a panic about what the Germans were doing—or the Dangerous Dogs Act 1991—a panic after several nasty attacks by dogs on children. Before long, neither law looked very good.

The 1971 Act represented a slow-burning panic by the Establishment at how the rigidly controlled 1950s had given way to the 'let it all hang out,' flower power of the late 1960s. It was part of an attempt to clamp down on the freedom, colour and individuality that had sprung up, to turn back the clock. And so the swinging sixties turned into the swingeing seventies. The entirely false premise behind the MDA 1971 was that by choking off the supply of hitherto legally obtainable drugs, such as heroin prescribed under controlled conditions by doctors, and by increasing penalties for possession, including through imprisonment, the use of recreational drugs could be put back in its tin with the lid pressed down.

A cursory consideration of the failed era of alcohol prohibition before the war in the USA should have been enough to dissuade the powers-that-be from this futile course of action. It wasn't. Instead, we have had half a century of the 'war on drugs' which has seen recreational drug use climb inexorably. It has been a bonanza for dealers and pushers. It is a sign of institutional madness to increase the dose of a medicine that is proving harmful, but that is what we have had from most politicians down the years. And the more the public has begun to question the official line, the shriller have become the voices of

Home Secretaries, frightened that drug use was running away from them and fearful of being labelled 'soft on drugs.'

The official response to cannabis, in particular, has verged on the absurd. Not only has this relatively harmless substance been elevated into the status of some Great Evil, so as to demonise it further, but the substance's beneficial health properties, which have been recognised for centuries, have been denied. Cannabis, we were told, had no medical value whatsoever, which made it almost impossible for those medical entities that wanted to test its properties even to get a licence to do so.

When I became Crime Prevention Minister in the UK Government in 2013, with drug policy within my portfolio, I was determined to bring some evidence-based sanity to drugs policy. The following year I published an international comparator of drug policies. This demonstrated very clearly that treating drug use as a health issue rather than one of law and order was not only more humane and compassionate, but it is an approach that actually reduces drug use. By contrast those countries that crack down hard end up with all sorts of extra social problems, such as the spread of HIV through shared needles. True to form, the reaction of the Home Secretary of the day, Theresa May, was not to learn from the report but to try to bury it. Orthodoxy could not be allowed to be challenged. I began to understand how Galileo must have felt when his peers blanked out his evidence that the earth went round the sun.

I am not in any way advocating the use of any drugs. But I am advocating that the country bases its drug policy on what works in reducing harms rather than on mantras that politicians feel safe with. Take cannabis for instance. Unlike alcohol or tobacco, both legally available of course, cannabis is not a killer. But the arrival of skunk has meant that the natural substance, grass or resin, is harder to find. Yet skunk undoubtedly does pose risks to mental health. If the Government were to establish a legal route to obtain cannabis as has happened in places like Uruguay, it could control the type of cannabis available including its strength and purity. People are unlikely to want to seek out a harmful illegal variety from a back street dealer if they can access something with quality guaranteed legally. How many people seek out illegally distilled spirits? Such an approach would also have the advantages of removing business from pushers and providing an income stream for the Government.

It is time to see the MDA 1971 for what it is: a bad law that has the opposite effect to that which was intended. The so-called war on drugs is lost. It could never be won. Let us replace this knee-jerk law with something rational, something evidence-based, something more humane.

About the author of the Foreword

Elected Liberal Democrat Member of Parliament for Lewes in 1997, Norman John Baker was Home Office Minister of State for Crime Prevention from 2013 to 2014 and Parliamentary Under Secretary for Transport from 2010 to 2013. He established the Home Office Ministerial Expert Panel on New Psychoactive Substances (see *Chapter 4*) and his Coalition Government policy paper for the Home Office, 'Drugs: International Comparators' mentioned in the Foreword above was published in 2014.[1] He was appointed to the Privy Council in 2014.

---

1. See: www.gov.uk/government/publications/drugs-international-comparators

Publisher's note

The views and opinions in this book are those of the individual authors/contributors and not necessarily shared by the publisher. Whilst every effort has been made to ensure the accuracy of the information contained in the text, readers should draw their own conclusions concerning the possibility of alternative views, accounts, descriptions or explanations.

We would like to dedicate this book to those who suffer from the damaging effects of drugs and drug laws; to those colleagues who aspire to understand and alleviate the impact of drugs; and to our families and friends who support our involvement in this compelling and challenging endeavour.

Ilana Crome, David Nutt and Alex Stevens

About the editors

Professor Ilana B Crome MD, FRCPsych is Professor Emerita of Addiction Psychiatry, Keele University and Honorary Consultant Psychiatrist, Midlands Partnership NHS Foundation Trust. She is currently Chair of Trustees, Drug Science and has contributed widely to research, training and policy in addiction. She is lead editor for two textbooks on *Substance Use and Older People* (2015, Wiley) and *Substance Use and Young People* (2020, Routledge).

Professor David Nutt DM, FRCP, FRCPsych, FMedSci, DLaws is Professor of Neuropsychopharmacology at Imperial College London. He is the Founding Chair of the charity Drug Science, and Chair of PAREA Europe.[2] From 2000–2009 he served on the Advisory Council on the Misuse of Drugs. He has published extensively with over 500 research papers and 36 books including *Drugs Without the Hot Air* (2021, UIT Cambridge) and his autobiography *Nutt Uncut* (2021, Waterside Press).

Professor Alex Stevens is Professor in Criminal Justice at the University of Kent. He was a member of the Advisory Council on the Misuse of Drugs (2014–2019) and President of the International Society for the Study of Drug Policy (2015–2019). He is currently a board member of Harm Reduction International and Chair of Drug Science's Enhanced Harm Reduction Working Group. His publications include *Drugs, Crime and Public Health* (Routledge, 2011) and *Drug Policy Constellations* (Policy Press, forthcoming).

---

2. Psychedelic Access and Research European Alliance: see https://parea.eu/

Introduction

Ilana Crome, David Nutt and Alex Stevens

The 27 May 2021 marked 50 years since the Misuse of Drugs Bill received Royal Assent to become an Act of Parliament. To mark the anniversary, several charities focused on reducing the harms of drugs banded together to demonstrate their united opposition to 50 years of failing drug policy. The reason for our opposition was documented and signed by over 50 Members of Parliament:

> 'The Misuse of Drugs Act 1971[1] is not fit for purpose. For 50 years, it has failed to reduce drug consumption. Instead, it has increased harm, damaged public health and exacerbated social inequalities. Change cannot be delayed any longer. We need reform and new legislation to ensure that future drug policy protects human rights, promotes public health, and ensures social justice.' (Transform Drug Policy Foundation[2])

Every year, billions of pounds are wasted, several thousands of lives lost, and tens of thousands of people needlessly criminalised, due to this outdated and ineffective legislation. This must stop. Our families, friends and communities deserve drug policies that promote public health, human rights and social justice. Our drugs laws were created when the world was very different. Society, politics, technology and the economy today differ in many respects to how they were in the 1970s. Patterns of drug consumption, availability and production have also changed dramatically. Our drug laws will not be the same in another 50 years' time, so it is a matter of when policies change, not if. While the world changes around us, we need drug policies that are no longer shackled

---

1. Throughout this book Misuse of Drugs Act 1971 is abbreviated to MDA 1971 or 'the 1971 Act.'
2. See https://transformdrugs.org/mda-at-50/parliamentary-support

to the past. This book analyses the inflexible system of prohibition from a multidisciplinary perspective. Written by a team of experts, all of whom agree that the current regulatory framework must change, the book also suggests a range of opportunities for improvement.

Chapter Outline

The book brings together experts in the field who have been working on a wide assortment of methodologies and it captures their considered insights on this complex, important and so often emotive area. Many of them are also members of the Drug Science Scientific Committee, which endeavours to deliver, review and investigate scientific evidence relating to psychoactive drugs. The book is in five parts covering the impact of drugs, their impact on the medical, pharmacy and veterinary professions, legacies of the drug laws, perspectives from education and legal professionals, and conclusions with regard to changing policy.

Part I covers the enormous possibilities as well as the enigmas and dilemmas surrounding psychedelic drugs: MDMA (ecstasy), new (or novel) psychoactive substances (NPS) and cannabis. *Chapter 1*, 'At the Frontiers of Psychiatry' by Crome and Nutt, reviews recent developments on psychedelic drugs, which have the potential to revolutionise the treatment of some psychiatric disorders. However, they draw attention to how these advances in research for patient benefit have been — and are still being — hampered because of the status of psychedelics in the MDA 1971. In *Chapter 2*, King, a forensic drugs scientist, explains how in the 1971 Act there is little relationship between classification of drugs (i.e. the A, B, C system) and the harmfulness of substances even though it was ostensibly founded on that basis. By charting the prohibition, medicalisation and future regulation of MDMA (the UK's most popular 'party drug'), Curran, Measham, Nutt and Schlag undertake a fascinating exploration of 'Fifty Years of MDMA' in *Chapter 3*. NPS are then reviewed by Measham and Pascoe in *Chapter 4* where they skilfully tease out the deficiencies of the 1971 Act that drove displacement in both NPS supply and use.

In *Chapter 5*, 'Cannabis: Past Present and Future,' Schlag and Nutt discuss how despite the fact that medical cannabis was legalised in 2018, which marked the most recent shift from absolute prohibition to a regulated medical model, this has come with many challenges so that the clinical impact has been extremely limited within the National Health Service. To complete Part I, in *Chapter 6* Ross and Schlag movingly draw our attention to how the MDA 1971 has impacted the lives of millions of people in the UK. Their analysis of drug narratives also highlights unintended outcomes of poorly designed policy.

Part II focuses on the impact of the MDA 1971 on the medical, pharmacy and veterinary professions. Brandner and Dewhurst (*Chapter 7*, 'Chronic Pain') cover the tricky problem of finding a balance between pain management and overuse of opioid medications. Although the 1971 Act has limited the overprescription of opioid medications, the restrictions imposed mean that is has been more difficult to develop clinical trials to explore effective interventions with drugs such as cannabis and psilocybin. In *Chapter 8*, Taylor emphasises how drugs controlled under the MDA 1971 are vital treatments for animals and illustrates how drug control inevitably affects the veterinary profession. To close Part II, Gittins stresses the importance of 'Enabling Access to Essential Medicines and Devices' (*Chapter 9*).

In Part III the legacies of drug laws and their repercussions are discussed by Crick and Holland in 'How States Adapted Their Drug Laws Within United Nations Drug Convention to Improve the Health and Welfare of Their Citizens' (*Chapter 10*). They examine three UN drug conventions and the subsequent impact on their signatory nations, demonstrating how several of the signatories are now adapting their national laws within the flexibility of the conventions in response to failures of prohibition and increasing levels of drug-related harm. Next, Seddon considers 'The Sixties, Barbara Wootton and the Counterculture,' an historical analysis in which he outlines how the 1971 Act came to be enacted and how its implementation has morphed into a political tool since its inception (*Chapter 11*). In *Chapter 12*, Akintoye, Ali and Stevens examine 'The Ongoing Impact on the Radicalised Policing of Black Communites' through a critique of discriminatory enforcement.

Part IV brings together views from families and carers, educators, practising lawyers and activists. In *Chapter 13*, 'Challenging Stigma, Changing Minds: The Role of Families in Drug Policy Reform,' Slater and Ryder highlight how prohibition and criminalisation promote the devastating effects of stigma, shame and discrimination on people who use drugs. This may be partly related to the limitations in the strategies provided by educators, families and the media to teach children and young adults (and their families) about drugs which allow them to make educated and informed choices about the relative harms of drug use as explained by Hargreaves in *Chapter 14*. Then Gittins, Rolles and Watkinson draw attention to the often overlooked consequences of 'The Impact of Drug Legislation on Climate Change' in *Chapter 15*. Part IV rounds off with Phillip's contribution which describes 'An Application of Decision Conferencing and Multi-criteria Decision Analysis' (*Chapter 16*) (as he explains, MCDA is emerging as a modern methodology for tackling drug policy, the gold standard to guiding decisions) and *Chapter 17*, in which Fortson, a member of King's Counsel, looks at legal 'Missteps and Misunderstandings' concerning the 1971 Act following a comprehensive review of the legal relationship between the MDA 1971, the Psychoactive Substances Act 2016, Medicines Acts and other aspects of drug legislation.

'Changing Policy' is the subject matter of Part V, which deals with potential ways in which the law could be reformed. Carlin (*Chapter 18*) describes the real-life social experiment of minimum unit pricing of alcohol in Scotland as a model of evidence-based policy and compares this with the attempts of the MDA 1971 to control and prohibit substances. If the 1971 Act is failing to achieve its stated goals, other options are discussed by Douse, Eastwood and Stevens in 'A Modest Proposal to Decriminalise the Simple Possession of Drugs' (*Chapter 19*). Finally, in *Chapter 20*, Nicholls and Rolles examine 'The Legal Regulation of Drugs in the UK' and related matters.

Acknowledgments

In addition to the authors of each of the above chapters, we would like to thank the various charities who have been working tirelessly to improve drug policy, including Transform Drug Policy Foundation, Release, LEAD UK, Anyone's Child, Crew, Kaleidoscope, Black Sox and the All-Party Parliamentary Group on Drug Policy Reform.

We would also like to acknowledge James Bunn who has provided extraordinary support from conceptualisation through to culmination of this book. It provides a rich mix of thought-provoking observations and analyses which we hope provides compelling evidence to underpin, motivate and inspire the next crucial steps.

PART I
THE IMPACT OF DRUGS

CHAPTER 1

At the Frontiers of Psychiatry

Ilana Crome and David Nutt

Background

The current policy ambition in the United Kingdom is to reduce harms by reducing drug use. The evidence base for harms, examined scientifically, resulting from the diverse range of substances is referred to throughout this book.

In the UK, the number of deaths due to substances is staggering. It far exceeds other preventable deaths such as melanoma, suicide, road traffic accidents and AIDS, which total around 10,000 per annum. Alcohol is responsible for approximately 25,000 deaths each year and is now the leading cause of death in men under 50 years old. Deaths from liver disease rose steeply between 1970 and 2006, 80% of which are alcohol-related and 20% due to viral hepatitis. Tobacco still leads to 80,000 deaths each year although tobacco consumption has decreased. The death rate due to drugs in the UK is now the highest in Europe: opiate and cocaine deaths are at an all-time high (Crome and Nutt, 2021).

Harmful use of alcohol, a legal drug, causes more than 5% of the disease burden worldwide (WHO, 2018). Alcohol is the leading risk factor for the overall burden of disease in men, and tobacco and alcohol are in the top five in the global burden of disease (ibid). Alcohol consumption has increased as it became more affordable and sales from corner shops and supermarkets became legal and has doubled over the last 50 to 60 years. The pattern of drug use, too, has changed markedly over the last 100 years. Between 1920 and 1960 drug use was very low and mostly by people with other conditions (MacGregor, 2010). The Drugs (Prevention of Misuse) Act 1964 prohibited the sale of drugs without a medical prescription to addicts, which was only permitted as a last resort. Now over three million adults reported using drugs in England and Wales in the last year and one in three 15 year olds said they took drugs in 2018 (Office for National Statistics (ONS), 2020). In the latest ONS survey, Drug Misuse in England and Wales Year Ending March 2020 (ONS, 2021) an estimated:

- One in eleven adults aged 16 to 59 years had taken a drug in the last year (9.4%; approximately 3.2 million people); this is the same as the year ending March 2019 but with an increase from 8.6% in the year ending March 2010.

- 3.4% of adults aged 16 to 59 years had taken a Class A drug in the last year (approximately 1.1 million people); this was similar to the previous year (3.7%).

- Around one in five adults aged 16 to 24 years had taken a drug in the last year (21%; approximately 1.3 million people); this was similar to the previous year (20.3%).

- 7.4% of adults aged 16 to 24 years had taken a Class A drug in the last year (approximately 467,000 people); this was not significantly different from the previous year (8.7%).

Addictions, often a cause or consequence of mental illness, exact a high price in preventable illness, disability, and deaths, and are a marker of deprivation and inequality: improved treatment options are urgently needed (Case and Deaton, 2015). Other consequences of substance use are peppered throughout this book and include physical illness, injury, family adversity, crime, direct and indirect economic costs to the country, community decline, and environmental damage. Some of these are compounded by attempts to control drugs. Risks and causes thus encompass social, biological, psychological and pharmacological factors. Moreover, certain patient populations face higher risks and greater likelihood of developing these problems. Adolescents, for example, are at higher risk due to being at a vulnerable stage of development, whereas in older people depression and cognitive impairment are the most common conditions (Crome and Williams, 2020; Royal College of Psychiatrists, 2018; Crome et al, 2015).

Substances may lead to intoxication, withdrawal symptoms, and other psychiatric problems such as psychosis from amphetamine or cocaine, or depression resulting from alcohol consumption. The combination of mental illness and substance misuse disorders is a critical challenge for research, practice and policy. These interactions are common, particularly at high levels of use, and they are often intricate and difficult to disentangle. However, this population are often even more stigmatised and excluded than people suffering from one disorder alone. An understanding of these inter-relationships may enhance greater appreciation of some common mechanisms which lead to addiction and psychiatric disorder, with improved treatments for both conditions. Compounding matters is the current national and international mental health crisis (WHO, 2018) that has been exacerbated by the Covid-19 pandemic resulting in a rapid escalation of addiction and mental health problems.

In the 1980s, a public health approach embracing harm reduction emerged initially as a response to AIDS driven by the fear of needle sharing by heroin users and to an expansion of treatment programmes combined with a criminal justice approach. Unfortunately, subsequent political shifts towards crime reduction have eclipsed the public health approach of harm reduction. However, the health, social and Criminal Justice Systems currently in place are not able to provide the flexible response in which the public can have confidence and to which they can adhere. In addition, current vindictive policies which criminalise people with substance dependence are unlikely to yield positive outcomes as addicts are suffering from a clinical disorder which requires treatment and support rather than indiscriminate sanctions.

Concurrently a greater understanding of the psychology and the biology underlying addiction unfolded. The concept of 'dependence' emerged, i.e. a set of criteria by which to diagnose what was described as 'addiction'. In due course, dependence came to be regarded as a chronic relapsing brain disorder (Leshner, 1997). This new conceptualisation, along with novel imaging technologies, has catalysed a contemporary era in understanding (Nutt and McLellan, 2013). However, as the current prevalence rates demonstrate, there is increasing use, and resultant mental, physical and social harms, including deaths, so the conclusion must be that the policy ambition has not been achieved. How can this be explained?

The MDA 1971

The revision of the Dangerous Drugs Act 1964 led to the MDA 1971. The 1971 Act has two separate dimensions: classes and schedules.

Classes define the penalties for illegal possession. Within each class, penalties intending to serve as deterrents differ in severity, depending on whether they are for possession, for personal use, dealing, supply or importation. These penalties are meant to indicate the relative harms of the different drugs and act as a deterrent to use or supply. Severity of penalties is related to the potential of each drug for individual harm rather than cumulative social harm, which arguably would be more rational. They reflect the predominant UK policy of prohibition of recreational drug use that has been in place for nearly a century.

Within the classes we can identify three categories of drugs:

- those continuing to enjoy recognition as medically useful but also associated with abuse (e.g. opioids, amphetamine) and currently in Schedules 2 or 3;

- those that lost recognition as medicines and continued to be associated with abuse (e.g. lysergic acid diethylamide (LSD), MDMA (ecstasy), psilocybin); and

- those that had never enjoyed recognition as medicines and continued to be associated with abuse (e.g. crack cocaine and ketamine analogues).

All the drugs in the latter two categories are in Schedule 1. Schedule 1 contains all drugs that are considered to have no recognised medical use. Schedules 2 to 5 define the degree of safekeeping that different medicines require because of the therapeutic benefits of many 'misused' or recreational drugs.

Some 'drugs of abuse' are used therapeutically, for example opioids, benzodiazepines, amphetamines, and constituents of cannabis, so the regulations make allowance for these. However, other drugs such as psychedelics (e.g. psilocybin) and MDMA which have lesser harms and, as will be described later, with therapeutic potential for managing a range of conditions such as alcohol dependence, depression and post-traumatic stress disorder (PTSD), are not currently available legally for treatment (Nutt et al, 2013).

As the costs of prohibition—in the hope that this will deter substance use and social and personal damage—are not inconsequential, there is a case for considering the proportionality of the penalty to the evidence of the harms that may accrue both socially and individually. When the MDA 1971 was introduced, it included understanding of the perceived harms caused by drugs, but they were not as well understood then as now. The Advisory Council on the Misuse of Drugs (ACMD) was established to

'keep the drug situation under review and to advise ministers on the measures to be taken for preventing the misuse of drugs or for dealing with problems connected with their misuse.'

One of its key objectives was (and is) to decide on the relative harms of drugs, and so locate them within the Classes A, B and C.

Since 1971 there has been some movement of drugs between classes. Ketamine and GHB (gamma hydroxybutyrate) have come newly under the control of the 1971 Act. Methamphetamine has moved from Class B to Class A. Magic mushrooms have been categorised as Class A and benzylpiperazine as Class C. Cannabis has moved from Class A/B to C and then back to Class B. Until 2009, all Governments had followed the advice of the ACMD, but then, for the first time, their recommendations about cannabis and ecstasy were not heeded (Stevens and Measham, 2014).

Probably the most important example of the divergence between science and policy is in the classification of what constitutes a 'legal' or 'illegal' drug. Alcohol, which is, of course, widely and lawfully available, produces considerable harm. Tobacco too, is highly addictive and harmful, but legal. Cannabis, on the other hand, remains illegal in many countries, but does relatively little harm (Weissenborn and Nutt, 2012). Comparative levels of harm show that alcohol and tobacco were among the most lethal, while some Class A drugs, such as MDMA, LSD, and psilocybin (magic mushrooms), were among the least harmful (Nutt et al, 2010).

Substances are now commonly consumed in combination, and some combinations are more dangerous than others. New drugs emerge, and sometimes if a particular drug becomes difficult to obtain either because of a change in the law or reduced supply, a more potent drug develops. Examples of this are cannabis and heroin which have been supplemented by synthetic cannabinoids or fentanyl. Very often users are not aware of what precisely is contained in the drugs they are using, and so are not aware of the risk to which they are exposing themselves. Laws and policies need to take account not only of the type of drug and extent of use but these changing profiles of both drug and user and particularly socio-economic factors.

Thus, what half a century has shown us is that, overall, deaths from substance use have risen. People who use illicit opioids have excess risk of death from all major causes of death (Lewer et al, 2022). There are a broad range of factors that contribute to this sad situation. There has been an increasing use of warnings and out-of-court disposals for low level drug offences and the moving of cannabis-based medicinal prescriptions to Schedule 2. However, the last years can be characterised as having seen prohibitionist developments in UK drug laws. These strategies have failed to achieve their goal, and sometimes have even led to the development and use of more harmful substances (Nutt, 2019). Particularly disturbing perhaps is that the Schedule 1 controls make it very difficult to use certain drugs for medical research for many banned drugs do have potential as treatments (Nutt et al, 2013). Examples include the use of cannabis for pain, anxiety, insomnia (Nutt, 2022; Sarris et al, 2021); MDMA for PTSD and alcohol dependence (Sessa et al, 2021; Mitchell et al, 2021); ketamine for alcohol use (Grabski et al, 2021); psilocybin for depression (Carhart-Harris et al, 2021; Rucker et al, 2021); psilocybin for anorexia nervosa (Spriggs et al, 2021) and ayahuasca for depression (Palhan-Fontes et al, 2019). Those evidence-based policies that could reduce the use of alcohol, especially minimum unit pricing, have not been introduced universally. Scotland, and recently Wales, have introduced these changes and preliminary data is encouraging (see *Chapter 18* by Eric Carlin).

Addiction is a complex, multifaceted enduring state in which different behavioural, psychological, social and molecular mechanisms operate. Over the last few years, new imaging technologies have been used to study brain molecular mechanisms and their relationship to psychological effects. We now know the possible neurotransmitters that medications for substance misusers target and which help reduce substance use and achieve abstinence. Antagonists such as naltrexone blocks heroin getting to binding site; opioid antagonists such as nalmefene and naltrexone can be used for alcohol; and methadone and buprenorphine can be substituted for heroin, baclofen and sodium oxybate for alcohol and varenicline for tobacco.

However, it is a fairly consistent finding that only about 30% of patients with alcohol dependence are abstinent after one year of treatment (Anton et al, 2006) with lower success for opioid and cocaine, and drop-out rates from treatment are 30% (Lappan et al, 2020). It goes without saying that medications are prescribed within the context of the individual's behaviour, psychology and social environment. Hence our objective is not just to detoxify patients, or maintain them on substitute medications, but to sustain use reduction or abstinence. Prevention of relapse is key. In the next section we reflect on recent studies which use a novel approach to treatment for addictive behaviours and some mental illnesses which combines both pharmacological and psychotherapeutic methodologies.

Recent Research

As a result of the frustration of the poor outcomes due to limitations in available treatment options, over the last few years there has been renewed interest in the use of several substances such as psychedelic drugs and cannabis. The use of psychedelic drugs has a long history, with about 1,000 papers being published between 1940 and the 1960s. However, in the 1970s research was stopped since these compounds were placed in Schedule 1 in the Controlled Substances Act in the US, and the Misuse of Drugs Regulations in the UK, which effectively ended routine clinical use and research because these drugs were deemed not to have any medical use. 'Classic' psychedelics—agonists of the serotonin 2A (5-HT 2A) receptor—include psilocybin, LSD, mescaline, and dimethyltryptamine (DMT), as well as DMT-containing ayahuasca.

These substances are low in physical toxicity and non-addictive (Nutt et al, 2010). Classic administration and naturalistic studies have provided preliminary evidence that these could be beneficial in various psychiatric disorders and substance use disorders (tobacco, alcohol, opioids, cocaine, methamphetamine and cannabis) and lead to recovery (Garcia-Romeu et al, 2020; Agin-liebes et al, 2021)). Such studies have complemented epidemiological and observational studies. The possibility arises that these substances target an underlying mechanism that is effective across drugs of addiction. In addition, they also have utility in other psychiatric disorders especially depression (Carhart-Harris et al, 2021) and end of life anxiety (Griffiths et al, 2016).

Psychedelics have also been used in a treatment trial on alcohol on the basis of very early evidence that ketamine and MDMA may be beneficial for alcohol use disorders, and aid psychological therapy. Sessa et al (2021) conducted the UK's first clinical study with MDMA-assisted therapy for the treatment of alcohol dependence. Grabski et al (2021) have examined 96 patients with severe alcohol disorder in a double-blind placebo controlled clinical trial. Ketamine and mindfulness-based relapse prevention psychological therapy were the active components, whilst saline and alcohol education were controls. Patients were allocated to four treatment groups. Ketamine was well tolerated, and patients who had received ketamine had more abstinent days in the six months post treatment though relapse did not differ significantly between the groups.

In addition to psychedelics, medicinal cannabis is increasingly a focus of research with growing evidence of efficacy in many brain disorders. To facilitate this research the charity Drug Science set up their Project TWENTY21 (T21) initiative which arranges medical cannabis prescriptions at cost price from a variety of suppliers through a portal that also collects efficacy and adverse effects data. So far over 2,000 patients have joined the project and first results on them are emerging (Nutt, 2022).

Protecting and Facilitating Research

Despite the promotion of medication assisted treatment, cognitive behavioural therapy (CBT) and contingency management over the last two decades, access to substance use disorder treatments is bedevilled by obstacles such lack of availability of services and rigidity of treatment regimes (Drummond, 2017). These complex yet fascinating areas for future research described above have great potential to re-invigorate psychiatric enquiry and practice. Interdisciplinary researchers are working together to design trials, taking account of patient expectations and reservations in undertaking these therapies (Spriggs et al, 2021; Mitchell et al, 2020; Sarris et al, 2021). More holistic relational aspects of care rather than a focus on purely the 'drug treatment' are being explored. Even after regulatory approval has been granted, the idea of using new technologies to monitor safety and efficacy is being suggested. The intriguing proposal is that psychedelics could be compatible with 12 step programmes (Yaden et al, 2020), given that many individuals—two million worldwide—seeking addiction treatment also engage with 12 step models of care (Kelly et al, 2020).

While the US has embraced drug law reform to some degree, the UK still has a 'zero-tolerance' policy. Some of the drugs which could be used as medications, for example psychedelics, are still illegal and classified as Schedule 1 drugs (the most severely restricted category) under the UK MDA 1971 and UN conventions. This schedule is reserved for drugs that are thought to have no therapeutic value and therefore cannot be lawfully possessed. Schedule 1 drugs may be used for the purposes of research but a Home Office licence is required. This category is increasingly inappropriate for psychedelics which have been continually proved to be both safe and effective. Under experimental and clinical conditions these drugs are carefully monitored in that they are delivered in very small doses, i.e. micro and controlled doses.

If control on the use of drugs currently banned was eased, research into the power of psilocybin and other similar compounds, for example MDMA and ketamine, could greatly accelerate. For example, medical cannabis was moved down to Schedule 2 in 2018, which has led to more treatment and research possibilities. Thus, if more drugs with therapeutic benefit were rescheduled from Schedule 1 to Schedule 2, they could be researched more easily and thus accelerate knowledge in both clinical and laboratory settings. Banned compounds are stigmatised, thus making it even more difficult to obtain funding for research. Licensing to undertake the research is costly, thus further hindering organizations in the implementation of such work. The twin burden of restrictions on research and lack of funding has thwarted this work.

New Strategy — New Policy?

Mental illness and substance misuse constitute a massive public health challenge, so that countless individuals have major unmet needs. There have been limited novel treatments in the last 50 years, while simultaneously there has been a rapid development of experimental techniques and understanding generated by modern neuroscience research. This has catalysed an accumulating evidence base for the effectiveness and safety of psychedelics which have limited abuse potential. The drugs act fast and are lasting therapeutically. Recent studies indicate that in combination with psychotherapy they could be beneficial for the millions of people who suffer from addictive problems, depression, anxiety, anorexia, obsessive compulsive disorder (OCD), thus bridging the gap between pharmacology and psychotherapy. Despite a multitude of obstacles, it is encouraging that the research that has been undertaken more recently has begun to be funded by academic institutions and commercial investment.

The clinical and research initiatives into 'banned' drugs as treatments over the last decade are some of the most important and stimulating in the modern history of psychiatry. In order to drive this promising work forwards, and to further progress therapeutic and research activity, it is vital that restrictions imposed by the current MDA 1971 into undertaking research with those drugs with therapeutic potential are lifted. Initially the drug laws were thought to act by deterrence, but this has not led to reduction in drug use and harms. It has, overall, we believe, led to an increase in usage, in health harms and an increase in deaths. It would be shameful and morally indefensible if the potential for developing effective medications for millions of people suffering from addiction and mental illness are impeded by an out of date, misguided and uninformed policy. Although some exemptions may be issued in certain circumstances, for example scientific research, this is extremely time-consuming, protracted, cumbersome and expensive.

Thus a review would be timely as reform will help reverse the damaging and costly consequences of the 50 years of the current regulatory system which has achieved quite the opposite of what it appeared to set out to do. As is the case in many countries now, policy regarding substances is best placed within healthcare departments rather than the Home Office. For example, in The Netherlands testing of substances via hospital-based laboratories appears to have reduced deaths from some new recreational drug products according to a recent European Monitoring Centre for Drugs and Drug Addiction (EMCDDA, 2017) report

In Portugal the provision of appropriate comprehensive treatment interventions and facilities had a profound impact (Tiago, 2017). It significantly reduced opioid deaths from 2004 to 2011 and now Portugal has the lowest death rates from opioid overdose in Europe. Prescription of medicinal cannabis is an alternative to opioid analgesics, and there has been the development of safer overdose prevention centres (OPCs) (often previously called drug consumption rooms (DCRs): see *Chapter 10*) where people can inject in sterile conditions.

Although there were high hopes for the new drug strategy (HM Government, 2021), it still does appear to favour a criminal justice approach, despite comparatively increased levels of investment in services. A dramatically fresh approach which favours treatment over punishment is what is needed. It is certainly the case that treatment can be effective in reducing drug-related deaths — see the Portuguese experiment mentioned above and the UK data during the 2000–2010 Labour Government years when treatment was prioritised.[1] The public, policymakers and scientists need to act in unison to produce an evidence-informed, balanced and workable response as substance use and misuse remains a feature of everyday life in the UK today.

Professor Ilana B Crome MD, FRCPsych is Professor Emerita of Addiction Psychiatry, Keele University and Honorary Consultant Psychiatrist, Midlands Partnership NHS Foundation Trust. She is currently Chair of Trustees, Drug Science and has contributed widely to research, training and policy in addiction.

---

1. See www.ons.gov.uk/peoplepopulationandcommunity/birthsdeathsandmarriages/deaths/bulletins/deathsrelatedtodrugpoisoninginenglandandwales/2020

She is lead editor for two textbooks on *Substance Use and Older People* (2015, Wiley) and *Substance Use and Young People* (2020, Routledge).

Professor David Nutt DM, FRCP, FRCPsych, FMedSci, DLaws is Professor of Neuropsychopharmacology at Imperial College London. He is the Founding Chair of the charity Drug Science, and Chair of PAREA Europe.[2] From 2000-2009 he served on the Advisory Council on the Misuse of Drugs. He has published extensively with over 500 research papers and 36 books including *Drugs Without the Hot Air* (2021, UIT Cambridge) and his autobiography *Nutt Uncut* (2021, Waterside Press).

References and Extra Reading

Agin-liebes G, Haas T F, Lancelotta R et al (2021), Naturalistic Use of Mescaline is Associated with Self-reported Psychiatric Improvements and Enduring Positive Life Changes, *ACS Pharmacology and Translation Science,* 4 543–552. DOI: 10.1021/acsptsci.1c00018

Andersen K A A, Carhart-Harris R and Nutt D J (2021), The Therapeutic Effects of Classic Serotonergic Psychedelics: A Systematic Review of Modern Era Clinical Studies, *Acta Psychiatrica Scandinavica*, 143:101–108. DOI: 10.1111/acps.13249

Anton R F, O'Malley S S, Ciraulo D A et al (2006), Combined Pharmacotherapies and Behavioural Interventions for Alcohol Dependence: The COMBINE Study: A Randomised Control Trial, *Journal of the American Medical Association*, 295: 2003–2017.

Carhart-Harris R, Giribaldi B and Watts R (2021), Trial of Psilocybin Versus Escitalopram for Depression, *New England Journal of Medicine*, 384: 1402–1411. DOI: 10.1056/NEJMoa2032994

Case A and Deaton A (2015), Rising Morbidity and Mortality in Midlife Among White Non-Hispanic Americans in the 21st Century, Proceedings of the National Academy of Sciences USA, 112(49): 15078–83. DOI: 10.1073/pnas.1518393112

Crome I B and Nutt D J (2021), Drugs, Drug Harms and Drug Laws in G Ikkos and N Bouras, *Mind, State and Society*, 239–250, Cambridge: Cambridge University Press.

Crome I B and Williams R (2020), *Substance Misuse and Young People: Critical Issues*, London: Routledge.

---

2. Psychedelic Access and Research European Alliance: see https://parea.eu/

Crome I B, Wu I-T, Rao R and Crome P (2015), *Substance Use and Older People*, West Sussex: Wiley Blackwell.

Dale O, Haigh R, Blazdell J and Setthi F (2020), Social Psychiatry, Relational Practice and Learning from COVID-19, *Mental Health Review Journal,* 25:4 297–300.

Dangerous Drugs Act 1964: www.parliament.uk/about/living-heritage/transformingsociety/private-lives/relationships/collections1/parliament-and-the-1960s/dangerous-drugs-act-1964/

Drummond C (2017), Cuts to Addiction Services Are a False Economy, *British Medical Jourtnal*, 357: j2704. DOI: 10.1136/bmj.j2704

European Monitoring Centre for Drugs and Drug Addiction (EMCDDA) (2017), Drug Checking as a Harm Reduction Tool for Recreational Drug Users: Opportunities and Challenges.

Garcia-Romeu A, Davis A K, Erowid E et al (2020), Persisting Reductions in Cannabis, Opioid and Stimulant Misuse After Naturalistic Psychedelic Use: An Online Survey, *Frontiers in Psychiatry,* 10: 955.

Grabski M, McAndrew A, Lawn W et al (2021), Adjunctive Ketamine with Relapse Prevention Based Psychological Therapy in the Treatment of Alcohol Use Disorder, *American Journal of Psychiatry,* 00.1–12. DOI: 10.1176/appi.ajp.2021.21030277

Griffiths R R, Johnson W J, Carducci M A et al (2016), Psyilocybin Produces Substantial and Sustained Decreases in Depression and Anxiety in Patients with Life Threatening Cancer: A Randomized Double Blind Trial, *Journal of Psychopharmacology,* 30: 12, 1181–1197. DOI: 10.1177/0269881116675513

Gukasyan N, Nayak S M (2021), Psychedelics, Placebo Effects, and Set and Setting: Insights from Common Factors Theory of Psychotherapy, *Transcultural Psychiatry.* DOI: 10.1177/1363461520983684

Home Office (2021), From Harm to Hope: A 10 Year Drugs Plan to Cut Crime and Save Lives, London: Home Office.

Kelly J F, Humphreys K, Ferri M (2020), Alcoholics Anonymous and Other 12-step Programs for Alcohol Use Disorder, Cochrane Database of Systematic Reviews.

Lappan S N, Brown A W and Hendricks P S (2020), Dropout Rates of In Person Psychosocial Substance Use Disorder Treatments: A Systematic Review and Meta-analysis, *Addiction,* 115(2): 201–217.

Lepow L, Morishita H and Yehuda R (2021), Critical Period for Plasticity as a Framework for Psychedelic Assisted Psychotherapy, *Frontiers in Neuroscience,* 15: 710004. DOI: 10.3389/fnins.2021.710004

Leshner, A I (1997), Addiction is a Brain Disease, and It Matters, *Science*, 278(5335): 45–47. DOI: 10.1126/science.278.5335.45

Lewer D, Brothers T D, Van Hest N et al (2022), Causes of Death Among People Who Used Illicit Opioids in England, 2001–18: A Matched Cohort Study, *Lancet Public Health*, 7 e126–35. DOI: 10.1016/S2368-2667(21)00254-1

MacGregor S (2010), Policy Responses to the Drug Problem in S MacGregor (ed.), *Responding to Drug Misuse*, 1–19, London: Routledge.

Misuse of Drugs Act 1971: www.legislation.gov.uk/ukpga/1971/38/contents

Mitchell J M, Bogenschutz M, Lilienstein A, et al (2021), MDMA Assisted Therapy for Severe PTSD: A Randomized, Double Blind, Placebo Controlled Phase 3 Study, *Nature Medicine*, 1025–1033. DOI: 10.1038/s41591-021-01336-3

Noorani T and Martell J (2021), New Frontiers or a Bursting Bubble? Psychedelic Therapy Beyond the Dichotomy, *Frontiers in Psychiatry*, 12, 727050. DOI: 10.3389/fpsyt.2021.727050

Nutt D J (2022), Why Doctors Have a Moral Imperative to Prescribe and Support Medical Cannabis, *British Medical Journal*, 376: n3114. DOI: 10.1136/bmj.n3114

Nutt D J, King L A and Phillips L D (2010), Drug Harms in the UK: A Multi Criteria Decision Analysis, *The Lancet*, 376(9752): 1558–1565.

Nutt D and McLellan A T (2013), Can Neuroscience Improve Addiction Treatment and Policies? *Public Health Review*, 35: 5. DOI: 10.1007/BF03391704

Nutt D J, King L A and Nichols D E (2013), Effects of Schedule I Drug Laws on Neuroscience Research and Treatment Innovation, *Nature Reviews Neuroscience*, Aug;14(8): 577–85. DOI: 10.1038/nrn3530

Nutt D J, Erritzoe D and Carhart-Harris R (2020), Psychedelic Psychiatry's Brave New World, Cell 181: 24–28. DOI: 10.1016/j.cell.2020.03.020

Nutt D J (2019), New Psychoactive Substances: Pharmacology Influencing Practice, Policy and the Law, *British Journal of Clinical Pharmacology*, x: 1–8.

Office for National Statistics (ONS) (2020), Drug Misuse in England and Wales: Year Ending March 2020.

Office for National Statistics (ONS) (2021), Adult Substance Misuse Treatment April 2020 to March 2021.

Palhan-Fontes F Barreto D Onias H et al (2019), Rapid Antidepressant Effects of the Psychedelic Ayahuasca in Treatment Resistant Depression: A Randomised Placebo-controlled Trial, *Psychological Medicine*, 49(4): 655–633. DOI: 10.1017/S0033291718001356

Royal College of Psychiatrists (2018), College Report 211, Invisible Addicts, London: Royal College of Psychiatrists.

Rucker J, Jafari H Mantingh T et al (2021), Psilocybin Assisted Therapy for Treatment of Major Depressive Disorder: A Protocol for a Randomised, Placebo Controlled Feasibility Trial, *British Medical Journal,* Open 11.e056091. DOI: 10.1136/bmjopen-2021-056091

Sakal C Lynskey M Schlag A K et al (2020), Medical Cannabis Improves Quality of Life by 50%: Preliminary Results From Project 2021: www.drugscience.org.uk/medical-cannabis-improves-quality-of-life-by-over-50-percent-results-from-project-twenty21/

Schlag A K, O'Sullican S E Zafar R et al (2021), Current Controversies in Medical Cannabis: Recent Developments in Human Clinical Applications and Potential Therapeutics, Neuropharmacology, 191: 108586. DOI: 10.1016/j.neuropharm.2021.108586

Sarris J, Sinclair J, Karamacoska D, Davidson M and Firth J (2020), Medicinal Cannabis for Psychiatric Disorders: A Clinically Focussed Systematic Review, *BMC Psychiatry,* 20.24: https://doi/10.1186/s12888-019-2409-8

Sessa B, Higbed L, O'Brien S et al (2021), First Study of Safety and Tolerability of 3,4-methylenedioxymethamphetamine-assisted Psychotherapy in Patients with Alcohol Use Disorder. Journal of Psychopharmacology, 35:4, 375–383. DOI: 10.1177/0269881121991792

Spriggs M, Douglass H M, Park R J et al (2021), Study Protocol for Psilocybin as a Treatment for Anorexia Nervosa: A Pilot Study, *Frontiers in Psychiatry.* DOI: 10.3389/fpsyt.2021.735523

Stevens A and Measham F (2014), The 'Drug Policy Rachet': Why Do Sanctions for New Psychoactive Drugs Typically Go Up, *Addiction,* 109: 1226–1232. DOI: 10.1111/add.12406

Tiago S C (2017), The 15th Anniversary of the Portuguese Drug Policy: Its History, Its Success and Its Future, *Drug Science Policy and Law,* 3: 1–5.

Yaden D B, Berghella A P, Regier P S et al (2021), Classic Psychedelics in the Treatment of Substance Use Disorder. Potential Synergies with Twelve Step Programs, *International Journal of Drug Policy,* 98, 103380. DOI: 10.1016/j.drugpo.2021.103380

Weissenborn R. and Nutt D J (2012), Popular Intoxicants: What Lessons Can be Learned From the Last 40 Years of Alcohol and Cannabis Regulation? *Journal of Psychopharmacology,* 26(2): 213–220.

World Health Organization (2018), Global Status Report on Alcohol and Health 2018, Geneva: World Health Organization.

CHAPTER 2

A Forensic Science Perspective

Leslie A King

The forensic drugs examiner determines if items such as powders, tablets, capsules, used syringes and vegetable matter submitted by law enforcement agencies contain a controlled substance for the purposes of the MDA 1971. That apparently simple objective can be confounded by analytical issues. A more significant problem surrounds the interpretation of results because of the extensive use of generic definitions even though that legislation is usually designed by forensic scientists and implemented by them in their day-to-day work. In addition, there are a number of undefined words in the 1971 Act such as 'derivative' and 'homologue.' Finally, in the MDA 1971 there is little relationship between classification (i.e. the A, B, C system) and the harmfulness of substances even though it was ostensibly founded on that basis.

Generic Legislation

Generic legislation is not new; examples long pre-date the MDA 1971, although the Home Office Advisory Council on the Misuse of Drugs (ACMD) has taken the concept to an extreme level.

The early period: 1920s–1930s
The essence of generic control is that a group of substances are defined by their chemical structure so that there is no need to list every controlled substance by

name. The second International Opium Convention, which came into force in 1928 included specific control of morphine and diacetylmorphine (heroin). Within a short time, other, non-controlled, esters of morphine started to appear (Delavingne, 1935). They were intended as direct substitutes for heroin without any specific medical advantage. The most commonly-manufactured were dibenzoylmorphine and acetylpropionylmorphine; both could be easily converted back into morphine, and both could be used as drugs of misuse in their own right. This problem was addressed by the League of Nations Convention (1931). That convention includes the phrase 'Diacetylmorphine and the other esters of morphine and their salts.' That was sufficient to stop the production of morphine variants. Those words are still recognisable today in the Single Convention on Narcotic Drugs (UN, 1961) as well as the MDA 1971. The UN (1961) convention extended the use of generic controls to 'Ecgonine, and any derivative of ecgonine which is convertible to ecgonine or to cocaine', 'Lysergide and other N-alkyl derivatives of lysergamide' and 'morphine methobromide, morphine N-oxide and other pentavalent nitrogen morphine derivatives'.

Structure-specific control of phenethylamines in the 1960s

Meanwhile, in the, UK an attempt was made to group a large number of central nervous system stimulants into a single definition. The Drugs (Prevention of Misuse) Act 1964 contained the following definition (with certain named exceptions):

> 'Any synthetic compound structurally derived from either α-methylphenethylamine or β-methylphenethylamine by substitution in the side chain, or by ring closure therein, or by both such substitution and such closure...'

Although this captured compounds such as phentermine, methylphenidate and other prescription anorectics common in those days, it soon became clear that a refined interpretation included many drugs that were not stimulants. It was even argued that some barbiturates such as phenobarbitone were also captured. Difficulties then arose with interpretation when multiple bonds were present in the side chain or substitution by oxidation occurred in the side chain. That generic control was repealed by the Drugs (Prevention of Misuse) Act 1964, Modification Order (1970).

Structure-specific control of ring-substituted phenethylamines in 1977

Following this early failure, it would be some years before generic control of phenethylamines again entered the legislation, this time in the MDA 1971. The focus would be on ring-substituted phenethylamines (Modification Order, 1977) and it would be followed by generic controls for many other groups. That control of phenethylamines reads as follows:

> 'any compound (not being methoxyphenamine or a compound for the time being specified in sub-paragraph (a) above) structurally derived from phenethylamine, an N-alkylphenethylamine, α-methylphenethylamine, an N-alkyl-α-methyl-phenethylamine, α-ethylphenethylamine, or an N-alkyl-α-ethylphenethylamine by substitution in the ring to any extent with alkyl, alkoxy, alkylenedioxy or halide substituents, whether or not further substituted in the ring by one or more other univalent substituents.'

This rather daunting statement is efficient in capturing a large number of ring-substituted phenethylamines such as MDMA, 2C-B and indeed many of the 179 substances later listed in PiHKAL (Shulgin and Shulgin, 1991). But the statement also raises the next problem with generic control; apart from organic chemists, few others can understand it. Perhaps the most depressing part about generic control is the sheer difficulty in getting it right. The example of how the 1964 attempt failed was mentioned earlier. But the recent history of attempts by the ACMD to get it right shows many more failures.

The expansion of generic control after 1977

Table 1 below lists controlled drug groups now subsumed within the MDA 1971 by generic definitions.

Table 1: Chemical groups for which generic controls operate under the MDA 1971, showing their year of first introduction and classification.

Group	Year	Class
Anabolic/Androgenic steroids	1996	C
Barbiturates	1984	B
Benzofurans and related compounds (*)	2014	B
N-Benzylphenethylamines (*)	2014	A
Cannabinols	1971	B
Cathinones and related compounds	2010	B
Ecgonine derivatives	1971	A
Fentanyls	1986	A
Lysergide and derivatives of lysergamide	1971	A
Pentavalent derivatives of morphine	1971	A
Pethidines and alphaprodine derivatives	1986	A
Phenethylamines	1977	A
Phenyl- and benzylpiperazines	2009	C
Phenylcyclohexylamine derivatives	2013	B
Pipradrol derivatives	2012	B
Synthetic cannabinoid receptor agonists (SCRAs)	2009	B
Tryptamines	1977	A

Substances shown as (*) had been subject to earlier temporary control. The original generic definition of tryptamines was introduced in 1977 but revised in 2014. The original generic definition of synthetic cannabinoid receptor agonists (SCRAs) was introduced in 2009 but has been revised numerous times. Cannabinols and cannabinol derivatives were originally in Class A, but later moved to Class C and finally Class B in 2008. The definition of cathinone derivatives was revised in 2011.

General Problems with Generic Control

Amsterdam et al (2013) suggested that drugs prohibited by generic legislation will be quickly replaced by new substances falling outside the definition. While this is true, it applies equally to a system where substances are listed by name. Secondly, they suggested that substances defined via generic legislation will capture useful medicines. However, those authors gave the example of GBL (γ-butyrolactone), but neither GBL nor any related compounds fall within the scope of any known generic control. They also stated that:

> 'The introduction of generic legislation violates the principle of legality, the rule that nothing is punishable without penalty provision and the associated accountability to citizens. Citizens need to understand what exactly is punishable according to law.'

However, the principle of generic control causes no legal difficulties in the UK and, furthermore, unlike analogue control, what is controlled is set out precisely in the scope of the generic definitions.

The use of generic control in other jurisdictions has increased rapidly over the past ten years, largely in response to the appearance of new psychoactive substances (NPS). The European Monitoring Centre for Drugs and Drug Addiction Annual Report for 2018 (EMCDDA, 2018) shows that until 2010 there were only two countries in Europe that used generic control, but by 2017 this had increased to 16. According to the United Nations Office on Drugs and Crime (UNODC, 2021), there are now 22 member states of the UN that have generic control in their drug legislation.

Capture of Inactive Substances

Because the MDA 1971 relies on the concept of actual or potential social harm, rather than the specific pharmacological or toxicological properties of a controlled drug, no great difficulty arises from the introduction of generic control. This would be more of concern in those jurisdictions and the UN itself where there is an *a priori* need to review the pharmacological and toxicological properties of every substance considered for control. It is quite certain that amongst the essentially infinite number of generically defined substances there will be compounds that have no useful properties and will not be used as drugs of misuse. However, this blurs the principle that penalties associated with drug offences should correlate with the harmful properties of that drug.

Effect on the Pharmaceutical Industry

Drug development in the pharmaceutical industry is a commercially sensitive area and it may not be possible to know how drug legislation has had an impact. As discussed later, there is an example where careless drafting of the generic definitions of SCRAs inadvertently captured existing therapeutic agents. It might be argued that if the pharmaceutical industry did wish to develop substances that were covered by generic controls, it should be a simple matter to either issue licences or modify the legislation. Unfortunately, experience shows that changing legislation, particularly the Misuse of Drugs Regulations (MDR), is less easy.

Following a consultation exercise in 2020, a report (ACMD, 2021) described the problems relating to the legal status of SCRAs faced by academia, the pharmaceutical industry and contract research organizations. Those compounds, which are in Schedule 1 of the MDR, require a licence to produce, possess or supply within the UK and an import/export licence to take them across the UK border. Apart from the cost of such licences, respondents to the consultation reported on the difficulty of comprehending the generic definitions, the long delays in obtaining licences (typically a year), the highly bureaucratic process of obtaining licences and the fact that licences are restricted to activities at a single site thereby inhibiting external collaboration. The ACMD recommended that the Home Office should define the term 'research organization,' and that the MDR should be amended to allow domestic research using up to 100mg without licence and allow a similar amount to be imported or exported except where the SCRAs are controlled internationally.

Analytical Issues

Most forensic science laboratories are equipped with gas chromatography-mass spectrometry, the technique of first choice for examining controlled drugs. Nevertheless, good laboratory practice requires that analytical findings on questioned substances should be compared with results obtained using pure reference compounds. In a defined list system, it is possible, at least in principle, to synthesise samples of every controlled drug. But generic control theoretically covers an unlimited number of compounds. In the early 1990s, the Forensic Science Service encountered an unknown substance that was not included in any mass-spectral or chromatographic library. NMR spectroscopy enabled the chemical structure to be identified as MBDB, a close relative of MDMA (ecstasy). At the time, MBDB had not been seen anywhere else. Yet its identification was important since it was a Class A controlled drug by virtue of the generic definition of phenethylamines. The same difficulty of having no reference material still happens today.

Specific Concerns with Generic Control

Mephedrone
A number of cathinone derivatives including mephedrone were controlled in 2010, but the Amendment Order (2010) was badly drafted. It added 4-methylmethcathinone and a group of generically-defined cathinone (2-aminopropan-1-one) derivatives to Part II of Schedule 2. However, this generated confusion for forensic scientists and legal practitioners. In creating the legislation, a decision had been made by the Home Office to mention mephedrone specifically, perhaps to make it clear that this substance was being controlled. But experience had shown that a normal feature of generic definitions is that

they avoid mentioning any specific controlled substance by name, although substitution patterns in an uncontrolled nucleus are used. Thus, one isomer of mephedrone was listed in one sub-paragraph, while all isomers of mephedrone (i.e. the 2-, 3- and 4-positional isomers) were absorbed within a generic definition in another sub-paragraph. This amounted to double entry. To distinguish those different isomers is a challenging task for a laboratory. Yet without that absolute identification, it would not be clear under which sub-paragraph of the Act 4-methylmethcathinone was controlled. Eventually, following many discussions between the forensic science community and the Crown Prosecution Service, a legally acceptable, but temporary, workaround was concocted. The problem was formally addressed in the following year with a subsequent Amendment Order (2011), which removed specific reference to 4-methylmethcathinone, such that all three isomers (2-, 3- and 4-methylmethcathinone) were covered by the generic definition and there was no longer a requirement to identify a specific isomer.

Benzofuran and related compounds

A number of compounds structurally derived from 1-benzofuran, 2,3-dihydro-1-benzofuran, 1*H*-indole, indoline, 1*H*-indene or indane, some of which were previously subject to temporary control in 2013, were later placed under permanent control as Class B drugs (Amendment Order, 2014). The generic definition reads as follows:

> 'Any compound (not being a compound for the time being specified in paragraph 1(ba) of Part 1 of this Schedule) structurally derived from 1-benzofuran, 2,3-dihydro-1-benzofuran, 1*H*-indole, indoline, 1*H*-indene, or indane by substitution in the 6-membered ring with a 2-ethylamino substituent whether or not further substituted in the ring system to any extent with alkyl, alkoxy, halide or haloalkyl substituents and whether or not substituted in the ethylamino side-chain with one or more alkyl substituents.'

The definition refers to 'the ethylamino side-chain.' While that term is not ambiguous, it cannot mean what was intended; an ethylamino substituent in a ring would have the nitrogen atom directly attached to the ring. So, the definition succeeded in controlling compounds which were of no interest, but failed to control those that were. The legislation of the Bailiwick of Guernsey introduced a Modification Order (2014) which avoided this problem by using the more precise term '2-aminoeth-1-yl' for the ring substituent. No correction has been made to the error in the MDA 1971, even though the ACMD was made aware of it. But like so many NPS, the benzofurans and associated compounds have long since disappeared from the illicit market and that piece of legislation has been quietly forgotten.

The phenidate group

Aside from errors of commission, the ACMD has been inconsistent in the use of generic legislation. In 2017, 12 analogues of the existing Class B methylphenidate were added by name to the MDA 1971 as Class B drugs (Amendment Order, 2017). It is not clear why they were not incorporated into a generic definition since all are based on the core structure methyl(piperidin-2-yl)acetate. Although the original report (ACMD, 2017) expressed some uncertainty about the possible legitimate use of these drugs, and thus a possible reason for the lack of generic control, a subsequent circular (Home Office, 2017) noted that they would all be added to Schedule 1 of the MDR '... since they have no recognised medicinal use outside of research in the United Kingdom.'

Synthetic cannabinoid receptor agonists (SCRAs)

These substances mimic the effect of cannabis by interacting with the same neurochemical receptors that are targeted by tetrahydrocannabinol (THC), the active principle of cannabis. SCRAs first came to notice in Europe around 2008 and have since become the most frequently reported compounds in Europe. To date, over 200 different SCRAs have appeared and represent by far the largest group of NPS. They were first controlled under the MDA 1971 by an Amendment Order (2009). However, within two years, clandestine manufacturers had moved on to an entirely new series of structures. The MDA 1971 caught up with this development by an Amendment Order (2013), but within a year the scene had changed again. The SCRAs were becoming ever more numerous and complex in their chemical structure. A new attempt (ACMD, 2014) sought to control these so-called third generation substances, but this attempt suffered from serious problems. Following that report, four addenda were produced over the next 18 months, each to update and correct the previous issue. One of the major problems with the 2014 definition was that it inadvertently captured 12 pharmaceutical products. These were effectively removed by a revised definition (Amendment Order, 2016). Secondly, the ACMD report of 2014 provided a 19-page annex setting out how the definition should be interpreted. That set a precedent since no other generic definitions had been treated in this way. More significantly it raised a constitutional question, namely it is not the role of the executive to interpret legislation; that is a matter for the courts.

The definition of 2016 soon had to be updated (Amendment Order, 2019), but, soon after, the ACMD were discussing how to deal with what they were now calling the fourth generation compounds (ACMD, 2020). Many observers have recognised this never-ending story as a triumph of hope over experience; one that has tested the concept of generic control to near destruction. It might be asked why the Psychoactive Substances Act 2016 (PSA 2016) was not sufficient. The latest definition of SCRAs in the Act runs to over 700 words and makes that apparently complex definition of phenethylamines mentioned earlier seem rather elementary. More importantly, it raises the question as to whether generic definition really is the best way of dealing with these substances. It might be easier and a lot more comprehensible if substances were to be specifically named. For comparison, the US Controlled Substances Act has 43 named SCRAs in Schedule I, the UN Convention (UN, 1971) lists 18 and the European Union lists just five.

SCRAs arose as a response to the control of cannabis. In the early days, these compounds, especially many of the so-called JWH compounds, had been well-studied and there were few reports of users coming to harm. As successive controls were implemented, clandestine manufacturers of these substances moved to ever more exotic compounds, about which little was known. Evidence now indicates that SCRAs have become among the most toxic of all NPS (King and Corkery, 2018).

Classification

It is unclear why a three-class system was adopted in the MDA 1971. Anecdotal accounts from the late 1960s, when the Misuse of Drugs Bill was being debated, suggest that the Government's plan was to have a two-class approach. Although the terms are largely obsolete, the idea may have arisen because there was a commonly-held view that drugs of abuse could be divided into 'hard drugs' and 'soft drugs', a concept that is currently used in the Opium Law of The Netherlands. However, the question of where to place cannabis and cannabis resin in this structure is said to have caused so much debate that a compromise was reached whereby cannabis became Class B such that 'hard drugs' were placed in Class A and the 'soft' substances were distributed between Class B and a new Class C. Whatever the truth, when the MDA 1971 came into force, Class B contained only 14 named entries and Class C contained ten. By contrast, there were over 90 named substances in Class A. It should be noted that the classification system is entirely independent of scheduling under the UN (1961) and UN (1971) conventions; movements between classes is a purely domestic issue.

In a statement by the Home Secretary (James Callaghan) in 1970, the purpose of introducing drug classes was:

> '…to make, so far as is possible, a more sensible differentiation between drugs. It will divide them according to their dangers and harmfulness in the light of current knowledge and it will provide for changes to be made in the classification in the light of new scientific knowledge.'

Considerable time and energy have been expended in the UK, particularly since 2002, on the classification of cannabis, and to a lesser extent MDMA. The irony is, that despite four reviews by the ACMD, the first of which was in 1979 and all of which recommended that cannabis should be a Class C drug, it is now back to where it was in 1971 as a Class B drug. If that were not of sufficient concern, there is evidence of a disconnect between *de jure* and *de facto* in how cannabis offenders are treated. In other words, law enforcement agencies and the lower courts often treat cannabis as if it were a Class C drug. Whatever one's views on cannabis, this situation is unsatisfactory; justice is not best served by allowing law enforcement agencies to determine penalties when there is a wide geographical disparity particularly in the use of out-of-court disposals such as community resolutions.

Not only have few substances been reclassified, but almost all that have changed their status have been moved to a higher class. This effect has been described as the 'drugs ratchet' (Stevens and Measham, 2014). The only substances to have been permanently moved down in their classification are nicodicodine, cannabinol and cannabinol derivatives. And only two substances have been permanently removed from control, namely prolintane (in 1973) and propylhexedrine (in 1995).

Undefined Terms

Homologues

A particular type of derivative is known as a homologue. This term is used to describe a compound belonging to a series which differ from each other by a repeating unit. Thus methane, ethane, propane, *n*-butane etc. are part of a homologous series where the constant difference between adjacent members is a methylene (CH2) moiety. It is therefore correct to say, for example, that ethane, propane, *n*-butane etc. are the higher homologues of methane and that methane and ethane are the lower homologues of propane. The definition of a homologue has a long history of proving a troublesome concept in legislation. The Pharmacy and Poisons Act 1933 referred to 'Ergot, alkaloids of; their homologues', but it was never established what was meant by 'homologue' and in particular whether it included lysergide (LSD).

The MDA 1971 defines cannabinol derivatives as

> '…the following substances, except where contained in cannabis or cannabis resin, namely tetrahydro derivatives of cannabinol and 3-alkyl homologues of cannabinol or of its tetrahydro derivatives.'

It was the intention of the late Professor Geoff Phillips, the author of many of the early generic definitions in the MDA 1971, that 'homologue' should mean only higher homologues. In other words, a controlled substance arises if, in a tetrahydrocannabinol (THC) derivative, the original pentyl (five-carbon) side chain substituent is modified to contain six or more linear or branched carbon atoms. Unfortunately, that curious definition of a homologue was never documented. If it is maintained that only the higher homologues are included, then tetrahydrocannabivarin (THCV), with a three-carbon side chain, is not covered by the definition of a controlled cannabinol derivative. However, it is generally accepted that 'homologue' means both lower and higher homologues in which case THCV is a controlled drug. The significance of this debate arises because it has been suggested that THCV might have some therapeutic value, but research on substances in Schedule 1 of the Misuse of Drugs Regulations proves difficult (Nutt et al, 2013).

Derivatives

While a homologue is a type of derivative, the word derivative itself can lead to even more problems. In some places in the MDA 1971, derivative is defined and used unambiguously such as in the generic definition of phenethylamines mentioned earlier where the phrase 'structurally derived from' was clarified in a legal judgment and is not contentious. Elsewhere, 'derivative' can be found in two of the generic definitions mentioned earlier, namely 'Ecgonine, and any derivative of ecgonine which is convertible to ecgonine or to cocaine' and 'Lysergide and other *N*-alkyl derivatives of lysergamide.' In both cases, there are different opinions as to what is controlled. In the former it can be argued that the word 'convertible' is the stumbling block. Thus 2-carbomethoxytropinone, a substance with no intrinsic misuse potential becomes a controlled drug because it can be converted in two steps to cocaine. That conclusion makes little sense since almost anything can be converted into almost anything else. In the second example, it is quite unclear if the non-hallucinogen 2-bromo-LSD (BOL-148), a substance that has been used to treat cluster headaches, is a controlled derivative of lysergamide. An extensive review of this area has been provided by King et al (2013).

Dr Leslie A King is now retired. He was a forensic scientist for 29 years, a member of the ACMD for 15 years and an advisor to the EMCDDA. He is the author of *Forensic Chemistry of Substance Misuse: A Guide to Drug Control* (2nd edn, 2022, Royal Society of Chemistry).

References and Extra Reading

Advisory Council on the Misuse of Drugs (2014), 'Third generation' Synthetic Cannabinoids, London: Home Office: www.gov.uk/government/publications/third-generation-synthetic-cannabinoids (accessed September 1, 2021).

Advisory Council on the Misuse of Drugs (2017), Further Advice On Methylphenidate-Related NPS, London: Home Office: https://assets.publishing.service.gov.uk/government/uploads/system/uploads/attachment_data/file/598494/ACMD_s_further_advice_on_methylphenidate-related_NPS_Mar_17.pdf (accessed September 1, 2021).

Advisory Council on the Misuse of Drugs (2020), Synthetic Cannabinoid Receptor Agonists (SCRAs), Final Report, London: Home Office: www.gov.uk/government/publications/synthetic-cannabinoid-receptor-agonists (accessed September 1, 2021).

Advisory Council on the Misuse of Drugs (2021), Consideration of Barriers to Research. Part 1. Synthetic Cannabinoid Receptor Agonists (SCRAs), London: Home Office: www.gov.uk/government/publications/consideration-of-barriers-to-research-part-1 (accessed September 1, 2021).

Amsterdam J van, Nutt, D and van den Brink, W (2013), Generic Legislation of New Psychoactive Drugs, *Journal of Psychopharmacology*, 27(3): 317–324. DOI: 10.1177/0269881112474525 (accessed September 1, 2021).

Delavingne, M (1935), Some International Aspects of the Problem of Drug Addiction, *British Journal of Inebriety (Alcoholism and Drug Addiction)*, 32(3): 125–151. DOI: 10.1111/j.1360-0443.1935.tb05021.x (accessed September 1, 2021).

European Monitoring Centre for Drugs and Drug Addiction (2018), Annual Report, EMCDDA: www.emcdda.europa.eu/publications/edr/trends-developments/2018_en (accessed July 5, 2022).

Home Office (2017), Home Office Circular 008/2017: A Change to the Misuse of Drugs Act 1971 to Control U- 47,700, Twelve Methylphenidate Related Substances and Sixteen 'Designer' Benzodiazepines: https://assets.publishing.service.gov.uk/government/uploads/system/uploads/attachment_data/file/616781/misuse_of_drugs_act_circular_008_2017.pdf (accessed September 1, 2021).

King, L A, Ujváry, I and Brandt, S (2013), Drug Laws and the 'Derivative' Problem. *Drug Test Analysis*, 6(7–8): 879–883. DOI: 10.1002/dta.1523 (accessed September 1, 2021).

King, L A and Corkery J M (2018), An Index of Fatal Toxicity For New Psychoactive Substances, *Journal of Psychopharmacology*, 32(7): 793–801. DOI: 10.1177/0269881118754709 (accessed September 1, 2021).

League of Nations Convention (1931), Publications of Treaties and International Engagements Registered with the Secretariat of the League of Nations, No. 3219. Convention for Limiting the Manufacture and Regulating the Distribution of Narcotic Drugs, and Protocol of Signature. Signed at Geneva, July 13, 1931: http://treaties.un.org/doc/Publication/UNTS/LON/Volume%20139/v139.pdf (accessed September 1, 2021).

Nutt, D J, King, L A and Nichols, D E (2013), Effects of Schedule I Drug Laws On Neuroscience Research and Treatment Innovation, *Nature Reviews Neuroscience*, 14: 577–585. DOI: 10.1038/nrn3530 (accessed September 1, 2021).

Shulgin, A and Shulgin, A (1991), *PiHKAL: A Chemical Love Story*, Berkeley: California, Transform Press.

Stevens, A and Measham, F (2014), The 'Drug Policy Ratchet': Why Do Sanctions For New Psychoactive Drugs Typically Only Go Up? *Addiction*, 109(8): 1226–1232. DOI: 10.1111/add.12406 (accessed September 1, 2021).

United Nations (1961), UN Single Convention on Narcotic Drugs, International Narcotics Control Board: www.incb.org/incb/convention_1961.html (accessed September 1, 2021).

United Nations (1971), UN Convention on Psychotropic Substances 1971, International Narcotics Control Board: www.unodc.org/unodc/en/treaties/psychotropics.html (accessed September 1, 2021).

United Nations Office on Drugs and Crime (UNODC) (2021), Country List: www.unodc.org/LSS/Country/List (accessed September 1, 2021).

Statutory Provisions

Drugs (Prevention of Misuse) Act 1964: www.parliament.uk/about/living-heritage/transformingsociety/private-lives/relationships/collections1/parliament-and-the-1960s/dangerous-drugs-act-1964/ (accessed September 1, 2021).

Drugs (Prevention of Misuse) Act, 1964, Modification Order (1970): www.legislation.gov.uk/uksi/1970/1796/pdfs/uksi_19701796_en.pdf (accessed September 1, 2021).

Misuse of Drugs Act 1971: www.legislation.gov.uk/ukpga/1971/38/contents

Misuse of Drugs Act 1971 (Modification) Order (1977), (SI 1243): www.legislation.gov.uk/uksi/1977/1243/made (accessed September 1, 2021).

Misuse of Drugs Act 1971 (Amendment) Order (2009), (SI 3209): www.legislation.gov.uk/uksi/2009/3209/made (accessed September 1, 2021).

Misuse of Drugs Act 1971 (Amendment) Order (2010), (SI 1207): www.legislation.gov.uk/uksi/2010/1207/made (accessed September 1, 2021).

Misuse of Drugs Act 1971 (Amendment) Order (2011), (SI 744): www.legislation.gov.uk/uksi/2011/744/made (accessed September 1, 2021).

Misuse of Drugs Act 1971 (Amendment) Order (2013), (SI 239): www.legislation.gov.uk/uksi/2013/239/contents/made (accessed September 1, 2021).

Misuse of Drugs Act 1971 (Ketamine etc.) (Amendment) Order (2014), (SI 1106): www.legislation.gov.uk/uksi/2014/1106/contents/made (accessed September 1, 2021).

Misuse of Drugs (Guernsey)(Modification) Order (2014), (SI No. 79).

Misuse of Drugs Act 1971 (Amendment) Order (2016), (SI 1109): www.legislation.gov.uk/uksi/2016/1109/contents/made (accessed September 1, 2021).

Misuse of Drugs Act 1971 (Amendment) Order (2017), (SI 634): www.legislation.gov.uk/uksi/2017/634/article/5/made (accessed September 1, 2021).

Misuse of Drugs Act 1971 (Amendment) Order (2019), (SI 1323): www.legislation.gov.uk/uksi/2019/1323/contents/made (accessed September 1, 2021).

Psychoactive Substances Act 2016: www.legislation.gov.uk/ukpga/2016/2/contents (accessed September 1, 2021).

CHAPTER 3

Fifty Years of MDMA

Val Curran, Fiona Measham, David Nutt and Anne Katrin Schlag

In 1967, a medical student in San Francisco introduced Alexander ('Sasha') Shulgin to MDMA (3,4-methylenedioxymethamphetamine; 'ecstasy'). Shulgin re-synthesised the substance and explored its psychoactive properties personally with several friends, including some psychotherapists who then examined its effects on their patients. One of those therapists, Ann (who later married Shulgin), described MDMA as 'penicillin for the soul.' Psychotherapists commented that MDMA enhanced their patients' communication in treatment sessions and seemed to allow them to achieve greater insights into their problems.

MDMA developed as both a therapeutic and recreational drug in the US during the 1970s and early 1980s and, despite opposition from therapists, was prohibited as a Schedule 1 drug there in 1985. Schedule 1 meant that MDMA was seen to have no currently accepted medical use and (in the US) a high potential for abuse.

Proactive Prohibition in the UK

The story of the prohibition of MDMA in the UK is, however, more complex and perhaps more surprising. MDMA was prohibited in 1977 in an act of 'proactive prohibition' in the first generic legislation of its kind, through a broad ranging amendment to the MDA 1971. This type of legislative control was later revived to address the appearance of new psychoactive substances

(NPS). MDMA was one of several hundred chemicals which were prohibited in a broad ranging generic amendment to the MDA 1971 in 1977, despite there being evidence of neither prevalence of use nor problems associated with its use. Therefore, MDMA was banned both before it became popular and before it became a problem. This is a remarkable case study of how the inclusion of a drug in the 1971 Act abjectly failed in its aim of effectively deterring use.

Becoming a Class A, Schedule 1 controlled drug in the UK in 1977 did not stop its subsequent popularity. A good ten years *after* prohibition, MDMA was adopted as the new dance drug of choice for the emergent acid house, rave and dance club scenes from the 'decade of dance' of 1988–98 onwards (Fisher and Measham, 2018). Initially gathering in disused warehouses and isolated fields, after a clamp-down on 'illegal' parties, the rave scene gravitated towards indoor and licensed premises in the early 1990s. This accelerated after the 1994 Criminal Justice and Public Order Act, with more legal, licensed dance clubs and 'super clubs' developing from the mid 1990s onwards, and MDMA continuing to be the drug of choice inside them. A study conducted in Manchester dance clubs in the late 1990s, for example, found that over 36% either had taken and/or planned to take MDMA that evening and concluded that it was 'the most popular drug of choice outside of cannabis' (Measham et al, 2001).

MDMA has remained one of the most popular party drugs in the UK, across a range of nightclub, dance and festival contexts. Use has fluctuated but remained fairly buoyant for over three decades, with the main annual national household survey finding that more frequent club and festival goers are more likely to report taking MDMA (Home Office, 2020). In the UK, MDMA was initially sold in tablet form, most usually as round white tablets. This changed in the mid 2000s with the appearance of MDMA in crystalline form sold as a higher priced, higher purity 'premium' product, resulting in a new two-tier market (Smith et al, 2009). In the 2010s this changed again with alterations in precursor ingredients and after a global drought around 2008–10, tablets became shaped, branded and coloured. There was also a large increase in their MDMA content, and the emergence of these 'super strength' tablets reportedly containing up to and over 350mg of MDMA or three adult doses. Alongside the increased MDMA content of tablets and more sophisticated manufacturing, the drug-related death rate also increased in the UK, from ten deaths in 2010 to a peak of 92 deaths in 2018 (Office for National Statistics (ONS), 2021). Many of these deaths were notable for being of teenagers with relatively little experience of, or tolerance for MDMA, inadvertently taking very large doses in hot, crowded conditions in nightclubs and summer festivals. The large variations in strength, colour and the form of consumption (in tablet, crystal and capsule form) have all helped to facilitate adulteration of the illicit MDMA market and with only very limited drug checking available in the UK (Measham and Turnbull, 2021) have added to the risks of consumption.

The Tragic Case of Leah Betts

One of the first and most enduringly high-profile UK MDMA-related deaths did not happen in a nightclub or festival, however. Leah Betts died at home at her 18th birthday party in 1995, after taking one tablet. Her parents issued a photograph of their daughter lying in a hospital bed just before she died, an image which spawned a poster campaign, schools drugs education programme and a generation of teenagers hearing the new mantra that 'one pill can kill'. Dr John Henry, a toxicologist at a West London hospital emergency department and a pioneer in MDMA research, gave evidence at Betts' inquest. Henry had dealt directly with MDMA-related hospital admissions and published papers in the early 1990s on the subject of why otherwise healthy young people died from this new dance drug. Henry identified the importance of overheating, dehydration and delayed kidney functioning in MDMA-related complications. He gave evidence to Betts' inquest that she died from drinking too much water—hyponatremia—rather than drinking too little water or consuming an adulterated tablet or having a toxic reaction to the drug itself. Her consumption of seven litres of water in under 90 minutes in a non-clubbing setting tragically illustrated how misplaced adherence to harm reduction advice to drink liberal amounts of water could lead to increased harm. Thereafter, not only was harm reduction advice subsequently tempered to highlight the nuances of hydration, informed by the risks of both excessive and inadequate fluid intake after taking MDMA, but Betts herself became the contested 'poster girl' for both prohibitionist and harm reduction lobbies. Her parents, a police officer and nurse, also embodied this duality, propelled by their grief to embark on a very public journey in the late 1990s from prohibitionists to harm reductionists.

The Scientific Risk Assessment of MDMA

Despite these individual tragedies, the overall drug-related death rate remained mercifully relatively low by comparison with other legal and illegal drugs, and by comparison with the numbers taking it each weekend, with some commentators estimating the annual mortality rate to be about seven per million users in the mid 1990s (Saunders, 1997). This led the statutory scientific advisory body to the UK Government, the Advisory Council on the Misuse of Drugs (ACMD), to a review of MDMA. The Final Report published in 2008 made a number of recommendations, many of which were accepted by the Government at that time. Two key recommendations were rejected, however: recommendation Number 6 to reclassify MDMA from Class A to Class B in recognition of its lower relative harm profile; and recommendation Number 12 to establish a national testing scheme for harm reduction and trend monitoring purposes, similar to the Dutch Drugs Information Monitoring Scheme (DIMS) (ACMD, 2008). It was another eight years before drug checking was introduced in the UK, with The Loop's 2016 festival multi-agency safety testing pilot (Measham, 2019).

In 2010, Nutt and his colleagues published their seminal study on drug harms. Using multi-criteria decision analysis (MCDA: see *Chapter 16* for details) they showed that ecstasy ranked relatively low on harms to the individual and to society, not warranting its Class A status. These results were replicated internationally. Nevertheless, when Professor Nutt publicly stated that alcohol is more harmful than ecstasy he was sacked from his role as chair of the ACMD — highlighting the continuation of valuing politics over scientific evidence.

A Case of Using Science Selectively to Demonise a Drug?

Following its legislative control, the numbers of people using MDMA skyrocketed. In the USA in July 2001, New York police confiscated one million ecstasy pills in what was then the single largest ecstasy seizure in history.[1] This in turn prompted Bob Graham, the democratic senator for Florida, to introduce

---

1. See www.justice.gov/archive/ndic/pubs2/2580/odd.htm

the 'Ecstasy Anti-Proliferation Act' in 2000 followed by the stronger 'Ecstasy Prevention Act' in 2001. Graham invited two scientists to speak at the press conference he called to announce this Bill at Congress and the funding being allocated to research on the harms of MDMA. Possible benefits of the drug were not then considered, let alone seen as fundable research topics.

The first scientist to speak was a powerful orator, Professor George Ricaurte, who told the press that MDMA damages the serotonergic system in the brains of non-human primates and rats. By using inter-species scaling, he explained that these neurotoxic effects would likely generalise to humans. Indeed, a widely cited study by Ricaurte's group (McCann et al, 1998) reported that 14 MDMA users showed decreased global and regional brain 5-HT transporter binding compared with 15 non-using controls. Further, decreases in 5-HT transporter binding were positively correlated with the number of times they reported using MDMA (this varied between 70 and 400 times) suggesting an association between extent of use and decreased 5-HTT binding. Interestingly, no correlation was provided with cumulative dose over time or self-reported dose usually taken which varied from 150 to an unimaginable 1,250mg and none of the MDMA users had binding data outside the control group range.

The second speaker was Professor Val Curran who the previous year had published a paper (2000) entitled 'Is MDMA Neurotoxic in Humans?' In this, she concluded that human studies were fraught with multiple methodological problems and evidence was inevitably indirect which made it virtually impossible to draw any causative links between MDMA use and human brain serotonin markers. For example, early animal studies injected 5mg/kg for four days into squirrel monkeys and similar doses in rats. In an average 75kg human that would be a whopping 375mg per day, much higher than oral doses of 80–120mg that most people used to take on just one or two days in a month.

Illicit 'MDMA' pills could contain variable doses of MDMA and also contaminants and adulterants, making it unclear what drug was actually taken and at what dose. Indeed, a recent study of the contents of UK MDMA pills in circulation in festivals in the summer of 2021 found that about 44% contained no MDMA at all (Pascoe et al, 2022). As many UK clubbers are polydrug users (Measham et al, 2001) it is important to understand what other drugs are taken on the same night as MDMA.

Also, how reliable is information on a person's history of drug use? Baseline differences in brain serotonin markers may pre-date MDMA use, as too may many other differences, including cognitive function, impulsivity, and mental health. The time course of MDMA effects is important as the three Es (euphoria, energy and empathy) of MDMA are followed by low mood and exhaustion, probably a combination of the impact of the drug, a night's dancing, lack of sleep, lack of food and dehydration. Many studies tapped such transient, residual effects or neuroadaptations so could infer little about neurotoxicity. Subsequent neuroimaging studies of MDMA users who had stopped using the drug for about a year suggested that brain serotonin markers returned to levels similar to controls over time (see Muller et al, 2019 for a meta-analysis). Thus, rather than neurotoxicity, these again reflected transient neuroadaptive effects which may occur during active MDMA use but are subsequently largely reversible.

People stop using MDMA mainly because they move on in life, stop clubbing, get married, or think the quality of MDMA has dropped; some however stop for mental health reasons (Verheyden et al, 2003). It is unclear to what extent mental health problems pre-dated MDMA use or were caused by it. Regardless, only 12% of users in Verheyden et al's study reported any difficulty in stopping and even fewer started using again. As one would expect with a drug that most users take about once or twice a month, addiction to MDMA was predominantly a myth.

The plot thickened when Ricaurte et al (2002) published a primate study in *Science* suggesting that even one night's recreational use of MDMA may result in *dopaminergic* neurotoxicity and thus increase the risk of Parkinson's disease. Curiously, they cited few other studies which had found normal dopamine (but reduced serotonin) markers in heavy MDMA users. This paper was subsequently retracted (2003) when it emerged that the drug actually given *had not been MDMA* but *methamphetamine*, which is known to have toxic effects on the dopaminergic system in all animal species, including humans.

Negative Perceptions Impact Research Funding

The message being sent out by the media and many Governments was clear. It was put succinctly on 26 September 2002 by Dr Alan Leshner, a highly-respected former director of the US National Institute on Drug Abuse (NIDA): 'Using Ecstasy is like playing Russian roulette with your *brain* function.'

This extreme negative perception of MDMA was also reflected in funding research on MDMA. To quote a funding call from NIDA on Sept 26 2004,

> 'Furthermore, despite scientific evidence of short- and long-term deleterious consequences, such as effects on learning and memory, there appears to be a perception of MDMA as a benign or harmless drug.'

If any impairment was found in the multiple studies exploring MDMA's cognitive effects, memory was the most consistent. A range of cognitive functions (including working memory, episodic memory, verbal learning, and executive functions) was assessed in 109 participants: 25 current ecstasy users, 28 ex-ecstasy users (abstinent for at least one year), 29 polydrug-using controls (matched to both ecstasy-using groups for the use of other recreational drugs) and 27 drug-naïve controls (Hoshi et al, 2007). The results suggest that recreational drug use in general, rather than MDMA use per se, can lead to subtle cognitive impairments and that *recent drug use appears to impact the strongest on cognitive performance.*

In The Netherlands, a prospective study recruited 188 volunteers who were not currently MDMA users but were thought more or less likely to initiate use in the foreseeable future. Extensive baseline neuroimaging and behavioural testing was performed, and participants were followed over time so that in one paper (Schilt et al, 2007), 58 who had started MDMA use were compared with 60 non-users. Level of use, however, was minimal at a mean total of 3.2 (median of 1.5) MDMA tablets. On a recognition memory task, MDMA users scored 29.95 (out of 30) at baseline and 29.66 at follow up; controls 29.88 and 29.93 respectively. Such was the desire to show a drug harm, a novel memory measure was used — the number of participants showing any decline in score was compared in each group — and this produced a significant group difference in favour of controls doing better. A significant MDMA 'harm to human memory' had been dug out from what scientists routinely call a ceiling effect where every group's average performance was 99% correct.

History of MDMA: Timeline

1912 — MDMA first synthesised and patented by the German chemical company Merck.

1953 — US Army experiments with MDMA, possibly as a truth serum.

1967 — Shulgin introduced to MDMA by graduate student.

1977 — Shulgin introduces MDMA to psychotherapist Leo Zeff, who introduces the drug to West coast therapists.

MDMA prohibited under the MDA 1971.

1988 — Ecstasy linked to emergence of acid house and rave music, which spawns 1990s electronic dance music and global club cultures.

MAPS funds animal toxicity studies and human safety studies at Stanford University and Johns Hopkins University (both US).

1990 — Rave has gone mainstream.

1993–98 — Relaxation of laws in Switzerland for five years. Small research group uses MDMA psychotherapy.

1995 — Tragic death of Leah Betts after taking single ecstasy tablet, leading to a media frenzy about the harms of ecstasy.

2008 — ACMD recommendation to reclassify MDMA from Class A to Class B rejected by the UK Government.

2009 — David Nutt sacked as chair of the ACMD for stating that MDMA is less harmful than alcohol.

2010 — Drug Science publishes scientific evidence showing that MDMA is less harmful than many legal drugs.

Val Curran and John Halpern prove to a US court that sentencing for MDMA reflects a distorted and selective use of scientific evidence.

Results of first randomised controlled test (RCT) for MDMA therapy published.

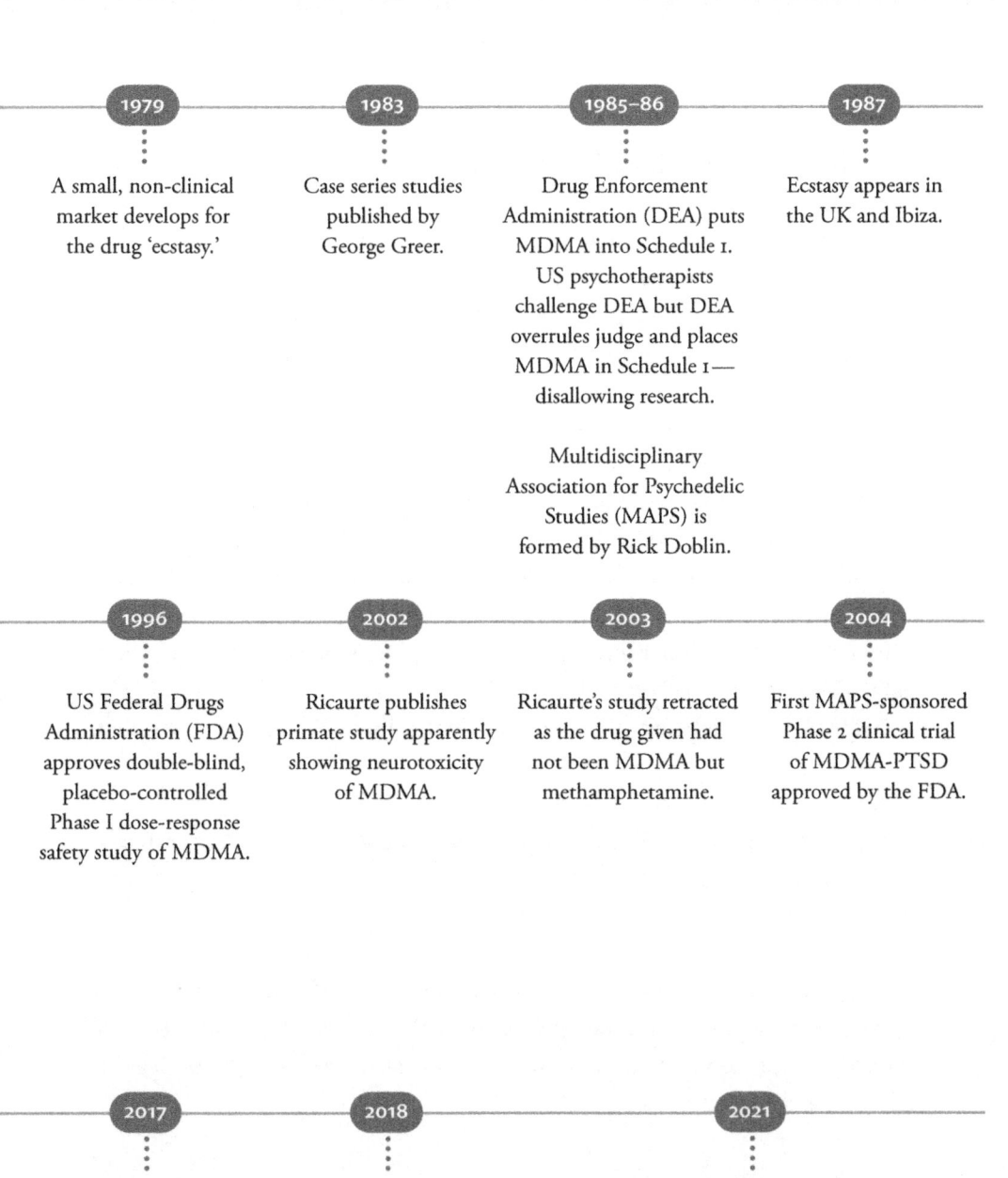

1979
A small, non-clinical market develops for the drug 'ecstasy.'

1983
Case series studies published by George Greer.

1985–86
Drug Enforcement Administration (DEA) puts MDMA into Schedule 1. US psychotherapists challenge DEA but DEA overrules judge and places MDMA in Schedule 1—disallowing research.

Multidisciplinary Association for Psychedelic Studies (MAPS) is formed by Rick Doblin.

1987
Ecstasy appears in the UK and Ibiza.

1996
US Federal Drugs Administration (FDA) approves double-blind, placebo-controlled Phase I dose-response safety study of MDMA.

2002
Ricaurte publishes primate study apparently showing neurotoxicity of MDMA.

2003
Ricaurte's study retracted as the drug given had not been MDMA but methamphetamine.

2004
First MAPS-sponsored Phase 2 clinical trial of MDMA-PTSD approved by the FDA.

2017
FDA grants Breakthrough Therapy status for MDMA.

2018
Drug-related death rate increases in the UK, from ten in 2010 to a peak of 92 in 2018 (ONS, 2021).

2021
MAPS publishes Phase 3 clinical trial results which show that MDMA-assisted therapy is highly efficacious in treating severe PTSD. First study on safety and tolerability of MDMA for alcohol use disorder shows promising results.

Ecstasy remains the favoured club drug and the recent emergence of very high dose tablets continues to lead to deaths that testing or a regulated market would likely reduce.

Moving Forward as a Medicine

Recent empirical findings are returning MDMA into the medical fold, clearly showing that many of the historical fears were overstated. Indeed, 50 years on from Shulgin's psychotherapist friends' MDMA-assisted psychotherapy treatments, MDMA is once again moving forward as a medicine. After a lengthy research hiatus, an increasing number of trials are showing the efficacy of MDMA as a medicine to address a variety of hard to treat conditions. The year 2021 saw Phase 3 trials in both the US and EU of MDMA assisted therapy for PTSD. Mitchell et al (2021) found that, in comparison to manualised therapy with inactive placebo, MDMA-assisted psychotherapy was highly efficacious in individuals suffering from severe PTSD. The treatment was well-tolerated and, importantly, safe — a far cry from the scaremongering which has tainted the drug since decades. Other indications being explored include alcohol dependency (Sessa et al, 2021).

MDMA-assisted therapy represents a potential breakthrough treatment that:

(a) warrants further research; and
(b) clearly shows that this is not the 'evil drug' as portrayed by the media since the late 1980s, which mirrored media representations of psychedelics a couple of decades before.

Far from being a brain-damaging recreational drug, MDMA is increasingly being positioned as a novel therapeutic tool (Nutt and de Wit, 2021). Back to the MDA 1971, 50 years on, it is surely time to facilitate research and legalise MDMA as a medicine.

What Are the Ways Forward with MDMA?

Today, 45 years after prohibition of MDMA as a Class A, Schedule 1, drug, there is no evidence that the MDA 1971 has substantially impacted on the price, purity, availability, or popularity of MDMA in the UK. Ecstasy has remained clubbers' favourite party drug for the past three decades. It seems that the three Es make it an enduringly appealing recreational drug in party settings. Given deaths from very high dose tablets currently being imported from The Netherlands, legalising for recreational use would have advantages if State controlled so that dose and purity can be regulated, and potential harms reduced.

Professor Val Curran is Emerita Professor of Psychopharmacology at University College London where she established the Clinical Psychopharmacology Unit in 1996. She is a founding member of the charity Drug Science and advisor to the UK All Party Parliamentary Group on Drug Policy Reform. Her research includes drugs used medically, drugs used recreationally, and several drugs (e.g. cannabinoids, ketamine, opiates) used in both contexts.

Professor Fiona Measham is Chair in Criminology at the University of Liverpool and founding Director of The Loop, a non-profit harm reduction organization that introduced drug checking in the UK. She is a founding member of Drug Science and member of the Advisory Council on the Misuse of Drugs since 2008. Her co-edited collection on *Young Adult Drinking Styles* (2019, Palgrave Macmillan) won the British Medical Association award for Best Psychiatry Book 2021.

Professor David Nutt DM, FRCP, FRCPsych, FMedSci, DLaws is Professor of Neuropsychopharmacology at Imperial College London. He is the Founding Chair of the charity Drug Science, and Chair of PAREA Europe.[2] From 2000–2009 he served on the Advisory Council on the Misuse of Drugs. He has published extensively with over 500 research papers and 36 books including *Drugs Without the Hot Air* (2021, UIT Cambridge) and his autobiography *Nutt Uncut* (2021, Waterside Press).

Dr Anne Katrin Schlag is a Chartered Psychologist and Head of Research at Drug Science, where she leads research for the Medical Cannabis Working Group, and the Medical Psychedelics Working Group. She holds Honorary Senior Fellowships at both Imperial College London and King's College London, and currently is Chair of the Cannabis Industry Council Research Group.

---

2. Psychedelic Access and Research European Alliance: see https://parea.eu/

References and Extra Reading

Advisory Council on the Misuse of Drugs (2008), MDMA ('Ecstasy'): A Review of Its Harms and Classification Under the Misuse of Drugs Act 1971, London: Home Office.

Curran H V (2000), Is MDMA ('Ecstasy') Neurotoxic in Humans? An Overview of Evidence and of Methodological Problems in Research, *Neuropsychobiology*, 42(1): 34–41. DOI: 10.1159/000026668

Fisher H and Measham F (2018), *Night Lives*, London: All Party Parliamentary Group for Drug Policy Reform (UK), Durham University, The Loop and Volteface: 1–88: http://volteface.me/app/uploads/2018/07/Night-Lives-PDF.pdf

Home Office (2020), Drug Misuse: Findings From the 2018 to 2019 Crime Survey for England and Wales, Report for the Home Office, London: Home Office.

Hoshi R, Cohen L, Lemanski L et al (2007), Ecstasy (MDMA) Does Not Have Long-term Effects on Aggressive Interpretative Bias: A Study Comparing Current and Ex-ecstasy Users With Polydrug and Drug-naïve Controls, *Experimental and Clinical Psychopharmacology*, 15(4): 351–358. DOI: 10.1037/1064-1297.15.4.351

McCann U D, Szabo Z, Scheffel U et al (1998), Positron Emission Tomographic Evidence of Toxic effect of MDMA on Brain Serotonin Neurons in Human Beings, *The Lancet*, 352(9138): 1433–1437. DOI: 10.1016/S0140-6736(98)04329-3

Measham F, Aldridge J and Parker H (2001), *Dancing on Drugs: Risk, Health and Hedonism in the British Club Scene*, London: Free Association Books.

Measham F (2019), Drug Safety Testing, Disposals and Dealing in an English Field: Exploring the Operational and Behavioural Outcomes of the UK's First Onsite 'Drug Checking' Service, *International Journal of Drug Policy*, 67: 102–107. DOI: 10.1016/j.drugpo.2018.11.001

Measham F and Turnbull G (2021), Intentions, Actions and Outcomes: A Follow up Survey on Harm Reduction Practices After Using An English Festival Drug Checking Service, *International Journal of Drug Policy*, 95: 1–10. 103270. DOI: 10.1016/j.drugpo.2021.103270

Mitchell J M, Bogenschutz M, Lilienstein A et al (2021), MDMA-Assisted Therapy for Severe PTSD: A Randomized, Double-blind, Placebo-controlled Phase 3 Study, *Nature Medicine*, 27(6): 1025–1033. DOI: 10.1038/s41591-021-01336-3

Nutt D J, King L A and Phillips L D (2010), Drug Harms in the UK: A Multicriteria Decision Aanalysis, *The Lancet*, 376(9752): 1558–1565. DOI: 10.1016/S0140-6736(10)61462-6

Office for National Statistics (ONS) (2021), Deaths Related to Drug Poisoning in England and Wales: 2020 Registrations, *Statistical Bulletin*.

Pascoe, M, Radley, S, Simmons, H and Measham, F (2022), The Cathinone Hydra: Increased Cathinone and Caffeine Adulteration in the English MDMA Market After Brexit and COVID-19 Lockdowns, *Drug Science, Policy and Law*. DOI: 10.1177/20503245221099209

Ricaurte G A, Yuan J, Hatzidimitriou G, Cord B J and, McCann U D (2002), Severe Dopaminergic Neurotoxicity in Primates After a Common Recreational Dose Regimen of MDMA ('Ecstasy'), *Science,* 297: 2260–3.

Ricaurte G A, Yuan J, Hatzidimitriou G, Cord B J and McCann U D (2003), Retraction, *Science*, 301: 1429.

Schilt, T, de Win M M L, Koeter M et al (2007), Cognition in Novice Ecstasy Users With Minimal Exposure to Other Drugs: A Prospective Cohort Study, *Archives of General Psychiatry*, 64(6): 728–736. DOI: 10.1001/archpsyc.64.6.728

Sessa B, Higbed L, O'Brien S et al (2021), First Study of Safety and Tolerability of 3,4-Methylenedioxymethamphetamine-assisted Psychotherapy in Patients with Alcohol Use Disorder, *Journal of Psychopharmacology*, 35(4): 375–383. DOI: 10.1177/0269881121991792

Smith Z, Moore K and Measham F (2009), MDMA Powder, Pills and Crystal: The Persistence of Ecstasy and the Poverty of Policy, *Drugs and Alcohol Today*, 9(1): 13–19.

Verheyden S, Henry J and Curran H V (2003), Acute, Sub-acute and Long-term Subjective Consequences of 'Ecstasy' (MDMA) Consumption in 430 Regular Users, *Human Psychopharmacology*. DOI: 10.1002/hup.529

CHAPTER 4

Displacement, Adulteration and Innovation
How the MDA 1971 Failed to Control NPS

Fiona Measham and Michael Pascoe

The High Hopes of Prohibition

The MDA 1971 created a regulatory regime that not only classified and controlled contemporary psychoactive substances of concern when the legislation was passed by Parliament but also aimed to address future drug problems. The 1971 Act created a statutory scientific advisory body—the Advisory Council on the Misuse of Drugs (ACMD)—which contained a panel of unpaid scientific advisors who were appointed by the Home Secretary to advise all Government departments on the physical and social harms of drugs. At the heart of the MDA 1971 was a process whereby ACMD gathered and reviewed evidence, deliberated and made recommendations to Government and beyond, which subsequently may (or may not) have been adopted by Government and resulted in legislative change such as amendments to the MDA 1971 classification system. This cycle of reviews and recommendations was challenged by the unexpected and rapid emergence of growing numbers of new psychoactive substances (NPS), notable for the speed and scale of psychoactive innovation, which combined with the development of global and internet supply chains against a backdrop of broader globalisation of legal and illicit markets.

This chapter looks at the emergence of NPS, the attempts to control them through existing and new legislation in the UK and focuses specifically on how the already creaky structure of the 1971 Act responded to NPS. The authors suggest that the infiltration of many 100s of NPS onto the UK drug market from 2008 onwards posed the biggest threat to the successful operation of the MDA 1971 since it was enacted and dealt what history may come to consider one of its death blows.

With a focus on the transformation of synthetic cathinones and synthetic cannabinoid receptor agonists (SCRAs) from desirable 'legal highs' to restricted, problematised and missold psychoactive substances, the chapter teases out the deficiencies of the MDA 1971 that drove displacement in both NPS supply and use. Data on drug use, drug markets and drug checking are used to trace the merging of established and new markets, through the rise and fall of cathinones such as mephedrone, methylone, N-Ethylpentylone and eutylone, and how the Psychoactive Substances Act 2016 (PSA 2016) was a far-reaching patch applied to attempt to repair the flailing MDA 1971.

The early years of the MDA 1971

The MDA 1971 aims, by prohibiting supply, possession and associated activities for specified psychoactive drugs, to discourage those activities for fear of criminal sanction and thereby to reduce associated physical and social harm. The three tiers of classification have three associated levels of severity of criminal sanction with the view that this adds greater deterrent threat to potential offenders. Therefore, promoting deterrence—for people who supply and use drugs—is at the heart of the 1971 Act. The Act's deterrent value has more to do with political idealism than evidence-based policy, however, with a House of Commons Select Committee on Science and Technology review (2006: 52) concluding that they

> 'found no solid evidence to support the existence of a deterrent effect, despite the fact that it appears to underpin the Government's policy on classification.'

Whilst the MDA 1971 focused predominantly on classification and scheduling of individual drugs, even in its first decade there was a recognition of the utility of bringing whole families of chemical cousins under legislative control in one swoop through the use of generic legislation. Generic legislation was introduced through an amendment to the MDA 1971 in 1977 which saw several hundred chemicals controlled, including a number of amphetamine-type drugs such as MDMA (ecstasy), MDEA (3,4-Methylenedioxy-N-ethylamphetamine or Eve), MDA, PMA (para-Methoxyamphetamine) and PMMA. The interesting point here (discussed further in *Chapter 17* by Rudi Fortson KC) is that these drugs were not yet available, used or deemed to be a problem in the UK and therefore the generic legislation could be considered 'proactive prohibition' in that legislative controls were introduced to ban hundreds of drugs before they became a problem, if at all. In fact, it was another eleven years before MDMA appeared in any significant volume in the UK, as the new dance drug of choice in acid house, rave and dance club cultures from 1988 onwards (Measham et al, 2001).

Legal Highs: The Eagle Has Landed

NPS first entered political dialogue during the late 2000s. During this period, NPS fell outside of the purview of national (e.g, MDA 1971, Misuse of Drugs Regulations 2001) and international (e.g. United Nations Conventions 1961, 1971 and 1988) legislation and were widely marketed as 'legal highs', available in high street 'headshops' and from online retailers. Whilst typically sold as research chemicals *not intended for human consumption* or as benign items such as plant food (in the UK) and bath salts (in the US), these substances were purchased primarily by members of the public, rather than researchers or botanists.

NPS can be broadly categorised in relation to their chemical structures and psychoactive effects. Examples include aminoindanes (e.g. MDAI) and synthetic cathinones (e.g. mephedrone), which offer similar effects to entactogens and stimulants such as MDMA, amphetamines and cocaine. Phencyclidines (e.g. methoxetamine) produce dissociative effects similar to ketamine, whilst SCRAs produce similar effects to cannabis, though often with more potent effects related to very high and variable strength.

The initial appeal of NPS related to a mixture of push factors from established street drugs and pull factors to NPS. Prior to legislative control, at least initially, NPS were generally high purity at a time of very low purity in established street drugs, easily available from legitimate outlets (cheap mephedrone cost approximately £10 per gramme until banned in 2010), without legal sanction and additionally had an air of novelty surrounding them (Measham, 2021).

Very quickly, however, policymakers, academics and commentators realised the significance of NPS and the potential problems that could develop. The sheer numbers of different drugs, the potential for almost limitless variations, the globalisation of drug trafficking and the new role of the internet in both legitimate and dark web sales all caused challenges for the existing review process. Scientific advisors to Government therefore recommended a number of legislative solutions to bolster the MDA 1971 and the regulatory framework surrounding psychoactive substances of concern in the UK, which the Government accepted and introduced. These included reviving generic legislation to ban whole families of chemical cousins: SCRAs in 2009, 2013 and 2016, and synthetic cathinones in 2010. Furthermore, and in recognition of the limitations in the speed of operation of the MDA 1971 and the associated review process by ACMD, temporary class drug orders (TCDOs) were introduced in the UK in 2011 for the purpose of temporarily banning importation, exportation, production and supply of a 'legal high' for a number of months whilst ACMD undertook a full assessment and considered whether it should be permanently banned under the MDA 1971. Other countries also realised the limitations of their regulatory systems and bolstered them with legislative solutions such as analogue legislation (in the US), blanket bans on psychoactive substances (in Israel and Ireland) and tiered controls (in the EU).

Ending the Game of Cat and Mouse

The initial optimism of 2008 to 2013 that the MDA 1971 generic legislation, TCDOs and trading standards actions could together control the rapidly expanding NPS trade faded with sustained evidence of 'cat and mouse' responses between legislators and NPS entrepreneurs, whereby successive generic legislation was passed for each new generation of NPS. It became apparent that by the time a fresh NPS was detected, and its use became widespread enough to attract political attention and kickstart the process of review, recommendations and legislative control, many more substances had already been developed and were waiting in the wings to replace their banned chemical associates. A Home

Office Ministerial Expert Panel on NPS, established by The Rt Honourable Norman Baker MP, Minister in the Coalition Government in 2013 (and author of the Foreword to this book), recommended a new legislative approach, a blanket ban, which resulted in the passing of the PSA 2016.

The PSA 2016 sought to achieve a paradigm shift in the ways these substances were regulated, by banning all psychoactive substances by default unless otherwise exempt. The stated aims of the PSA 2016 included:

- firstly, reducing the availability of NPS through ending open sale;

- secondly, reducing drug-related deaths due to NPS consumption; and

- thirdly, ending the aforementioned game of 'cat and mouse' with NPS entrepreneurs (Home Office, 2018).

Whilst open sales had declined prior to the 2016 legislation coming into force and intentional use of NPS decreased, as the purity of established street drugs returned and surpassed their 2008/10 low point (see Measham, 2021 for comparison of self-report surveys in this time), the following section of this chapter outlines notable ways in which the MDA 1971 and PSA 2016 failed in their overarching mandate to reduce physical and social harm.

Drug-related Deaths: A Temporary Reprieve

Prior to the PSA 2016, drug-related deaths (DRDs) for NPS were rising across England and Wales. Major drug groups implicated in these deaths included cathinones (primarily mephedrone), SCRAs and benzodiazepine analogues. Upon coming into force, NPS DRDs dropped substantially in 2017, likely reflecting their reduced access, availability and use (see Figure 1), alongside renewed popularity of established street drugs as their purity increased. Self-reported past year use of NPS by 16 to 59 year olds decreased from 0.7% in 2016 to 0.3% in 2020 (ONS, 2021; Table 1.02). Despite an apparent decrease in use, however, DRDs crept back up and at the time of writing now exceed the level observed prior to the 2016 Act. The increase in deaths since 2017 may reflect the establishment of new supply chains, filling the void left by high street and online retailers, as well as a shift toward the use of NPS which pose greater health risks to individuals, particularly benzodiazepines, as well as the contested nature of which drugs are included in NPS DRD statistics.

It should be noted that DRDs related to stimulant NPS are far exceeded by DRDs related to established stimulant drugs, particularly cocaine. During its 2008 to 2011 heyday, however, mephedrone was a drug of choice for considerable numbers of people who use drugs (Measham et al, 2010). This related not only to the pull factors of mephedrone (cheap, legal to sell and possess, high purity, easily available), but also the push factors of established street drugs (expensive, illegal to sell and possess, low purity, restricted availability), with some of these perceived benefits continuing after legislative control of mephedrone (Wood et al, 2012), leading to its chosen use being characterised as a supplement to low purity established party drugs like cocaine and MDMA, rather than as a substitute for them (Moore et al, 2013).

During this period of very low purity in established street drugs, stimulant-related DRDs decreased substantially for the first time since the early 1990s, nearly halving from 437 (2008) to 240 (2011) (ONS, 2021). In this same period, prevalence of past year stimulant use by 16 to 59 year olds remained relatively stable, from 18.1% in 2007/8 to 18.5% in 2011/12 (Home Office, 2012). Since the 2010 generic ban on synthetic cathinones, stimulant DRDs have increased five-fold, primarily driven by increased deaths involving cocaine and MDMA, in line with their increased purity. The ban on synthetic cathinones in 2010 immediately doubled the street price of mephedrone from £10 to £20 per gramme and the rapid increase in cocaine purity at £40 to £50 per gramme disincentivised a switch from cocaine to mephedrone and its prevalence fell throughout the 2010s.

Figure 1: Drug-related deaths in England and Wales relating to NPS (first graph) and stimulants (second graph) from 2000–2020. 2008–11 period of peak cathinone availability highlighted in grey. The Psychoactive Substances Act came into force in 2016 (dashed lines). (Based on ONS, 2021).

Displacement, Adulteration and Innovation

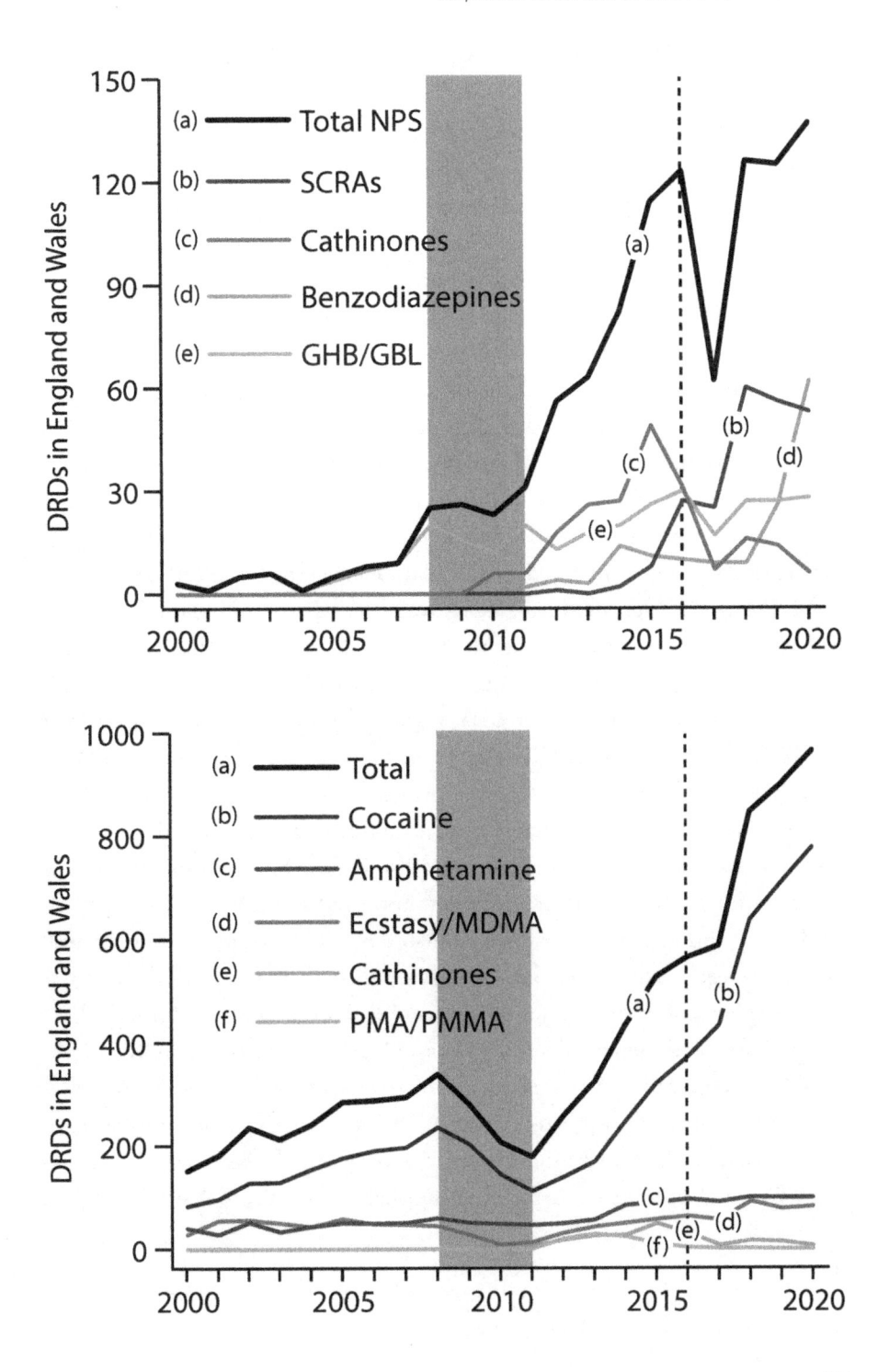

Monitoring Prevalence: The Paradox of Demand and Use

As previously mentioned, self-reported use of NPS in the broader 16 to 59 year old population fell in England and Wales after 2016. It should be noted, however, that self-reported use is unable to capture information on unintentional consumption of NPS, for example through adulteration of established street drugs. Over the years, The Loop (a non-profit, non-Government organization which offers community-based and event-based drug checking services) has tested substances of concern in circulation and collected data on purchase intent.[1] The Loop has detected the presence of synthetic cathinones in samples known or suspected to have been sold as MDMA throughout each year in operation. The emergence of these cathinone adulterants in the UK seemingly mirrors periods of scarcity or low purity in the MDMA supply chain, with a number of different analogues detected year-on-year. For example, following the banning of mephedrone in 2010, methylone (a cathinone analogue of MDMA) was identified missold as MDMA in 2013 to 2015, followed by pentylone and *N*-Ethylpentylone in 2016 to 2018. Following the international ban on *N*-Ethylpentylone in spring 2019, it virtually disappeared as an adulterant for MDMA. In summer 2021, a smörgåsbord of new cathinones was identified in circulation at UK festivals presumed to be missold as MDMA, including clephedrone (4-CMC), metaphedrone (3-MMC) and eutylone (Pascoe et al, 2022). In each of these cases, little information was available at the time of detection regarding the effects and risks posed by each substance. The appearance of each cathinone adulterant appeared to be determined by their availability and legal status overseas, outside of UK legal jurisdiction, as well as by their legal status under the MDA 1971, illustrating how UK legislation is not the only legislative influence on drug supply and possession within the UK. Clephedrone and metaphedrone, for example, were not banned in The Netherlands until October 2021, making them attractive propositions for MDMA adulteration for drug suppliers operating in Dutch markets. Furthermore, in the UK, whilst these cathinones were already banned, their classification as Class B provides an incentive for drug suppliers to substitute them for Class A

---

1. See, generally, www.wearetheloop.org

drugs such as MDMA and cocaine to reduce the risk of criminal sanction and the sentence if apprehended and convicted.

In 2021, in the wake of Covid-19 lockdowns, cathinones were detected in one fifth of MDMA samples analysed by The Loop at English music festivals. At the same festivals, approximately 35% of surveyed festival attendees reported having taken and/or intending to take MDMA that day, whilst under 1% reported having taken and/or intending to take cathinones (Pascoe et al, 2022). In the broader community, similar observations were made by the Welsh Emerging Drugs and Identification of Novel Substances (WEDINOS) project, indicating that MDMA adulteration was a UK-wide phenomenon in 2021, not merely limited to the festival scene. In England and Wales, 1.4% of 16 to 59 year olds report past year MDMA use and 0.3% report past month use (ONS, 2020). During periods of high adulteration, many individuals may unintentionally consume NPS and thus the number of people using these substances may be substantially greater than captured by self-report surveys.

Outside of stimulant drugs, another key example of unintentional NPS consumption can be found with vape liquids purported to contain cannabis, CBD and THC but identified as containing SCRAs, a growing feature of adulteration of the cannabis market tracked by European drug checking services (Oomen et al, 2022). Of 153 samples purchased as cannabis vape products submitted to WEDINOS in 2020–21, over half (56%) were found to contain SCRAs instead (WEDINOS, 2021). SCRAs have been implicated in a string of fatal and non-fatal poisoning incidents in the UK over the past decade. DRDs associated with SCRAs exceeded that of any other NPS until 2020, after which they were overtaken by benzodiazepine analogues. Cannabis is used by around one in 12 adults in England and Wales and poses relatively low physical and social harms (Nutt, King and Phillips, 2010; ONS, 2020). Whilst used by a significantly smaller proportion of the population, SCRAs have been responsible for proportionately many more deaths than cannabis. Little data exists on the extent of the use of cannabis-based vape products, yet demand may be expected to increase in the coming years, particularly amongst younger consumers who favour vape products over smoking. The absence of legal avenues for acquiring such products continues to put these individuals at risk of mis-selling and adulteration with NPS.

Thus, the use of NPS can be characterised as transforming from primarily intentional legal consumption from 2008, to intentional illegal consumption in the early 2010s, and to unintentional illegal consumption from the mid 2010s onwards, with the increased merging of NPS and established street drug markets (Measham, 2021). Unintentional consumption poses additional challenges to protecting public health and monitoring drug use. When taking an unknown substance, the dose, effects and duration can be significantly different from what is expected. In some cases, adulterants pose significantly greater toxicological risks to the individual. In the case of MDMA, cocaine and cannabis, legislative control through the MDA 1971 seemingly incentivised innovation of new drugs to evade detection through the development of cathinones and SCRAs, initially actively promoted as 'legal highs' and, after new legislative controls (generic legislation, TCDOs and the PSA 2016), as illicit adulterants.

Diversion

The emergence of NPS is set against a backdrop of a broader cultural shift away from criminalisation and towards public health responses to drugs in the UK over the last decade, evident in the patchwork of innovative policies and practices at local level, often spearheaded by police and third sector organizations. Perhaps the starkest example of this is the development of a range of local 'diversion' programmes whereby individuals are directed away from the criminal sanctions of the MDA 1971 and towards alternative interventions such as, firstly, arrestee diversion schemes of which the Bristol Drugs Education Programme by Avon and Somerset police was the first, and secondly, drug checking (discussed below), both of which were introduced in the UK in 2016. These pragmatic programmes are expanding across an increasingly wide area of the country and are supported by the Dame Carol Black review and Government Drug Strategy (2021). The local diversion and intervention schemes, framed as pragmatic policing and public health responses to the enduring demand for psychoactive drugs combined with the rising DRD rate, have largely sidestepped overt political posturing and have not been contentious with the electorate. An optimistic reading of this patchwork of initiatives is that there may be an appetite for change which could extend beyond greater support for individuals who use drugs and towards broader policy reform.

Drug checking and Surveillance: The Poverty of Policy

Managing the health risks associated with drug use can be aided by tracking their emergence and prevalence with robust systems of surveillance. Ideally, such a system would be complemented by an early warning system to alert stakeholders, policymakers, clinicians and the public to information highlighting current trends and risks. Success stories in this area include the European Monitoring Centre for Drugs and Drug Addiction (EMCDDA) and the Trans-European Drugs Information (TEDI) network, which pool drug surveillance data from a variety of sources to help inform policy within and across European nations. The lack of a national monitoring system within the UK, however, continues to leave individuals at risk from unknown substances of concern in circulation. The UK Government's Forensic Early Warning System (FEWS) sought to track the emergence of NPS from 2011–2017 and recorded the appearance of many novel benzodiazepine analogues, cathinones and SCRAs. Unfortunately, the FEWS programme ended shortly after the implementation of the PSA 2016, despite the detection of new NPS reaching a zenith in its final year of reporting (Home Office, 2018).

A poignant example of the failure of UK drug policy in this area was the re-emergence of para-methoxy amphetamine (PMA) and para-methoxy methamphetamine (PMMA) in the 2010s. First discovered in the 1970s and banned in the UK through the same generic amendment to the MDA 1971 that covered MDMA in 1977, both drugs can be manufactured from readily available precursors, including aniseed and fennel oils. PMA and PMMA were together responsible for 83 deaths in 2012 to 2015, including a string of four fatalities over the 2014/15 Christmas party season related to 'Superman' tablets containing PMMA missold as ecstasy. Such tragedies might have been avoided if the public had been made aware of the adulterated ecstasy tablets in circulation through a prompt, public, national early warning system, as happened in The Netherlands, with a red alert issued on national television as soon as identified by the Government-funded Drugs Information Monitoring System (DIMS) in December 2014 (Sample, 2015).

UK drug checking services, which combine rapid chemical analysis of substances of concern with individually tailored healthcare consultations delivered directly to service users, have operated in the UK since 2016. The Government has largely followed a laissez faire approach to drug checking whilst The Loop (mentioned above) has operated event-based pilots from 2016 onwards and community-based pilots from 2018 onwards, to build the UK evidence base. These drug checking pilots have reduced the consumption of harmful substances and the dosage/high strength of drugs consumed proving popular with service users, stakeholders and the wider public alike (Measham and Turnbull, 2021). Furthermore, following the closure of the Government-owned Forensic Science Service in 2012, such testing services can provide valuable intelligence on drug market trends and, with drug checking, the opportunity to assess the discrepancies between purchase intent and drugs in circulation.

NPS in Custodial Institutions: A Microcosm of UK Drug Policy

Whilst a more progressive shift has been evident with diversion initiatives at local level, one area which draws together the national prohibitionist response to NPS with regressive prison policy is regarding NPS use by incarcerated offenders. In the broader community, possession of NPS is not included in the MDA 1971 and associated legislation and is not an offence unto itself. Under section 9 of the PSA 2016, however, possession of NPS within custodial institutions (such as prisons and young offender institutions) is an offence carrying a maximum punishment of up to 12 months' imprisonment and/or a fine. Despite the harsher penalties facing institutional residents, NPS use within prisons has increased at a greater rate than in the general population. Use of SCRAs (such as 'spice' and 'black mamba') is particularly widespread, placing an additional burden on emergency responders. Rather than dealing with the root causes driving demand for SCRAs, such as alleviating boredom or self-medicating for mental health issues exacerbated by prison life, use of these drugs has been framed as a disciplinary issue. Instead of developing policies to support prisoners and reduce demand, in stark contrast to the regional initiatives outlined above, the UK Government instead instigated legislation banning possession only for custodial residents (Duke, 2020).

Conclusion

The MDA 1971 had been in existence for nearly 40 years when NPS first appeared, yet this mature piece of legislation was very quickly considered unfit for the purpose of meeting the new challenge of NPS when they first emerged. This legislative failure was evident in the need to introduce and bolster the UK prohibition regime through TCDOs, a slew of generic legislation and the introduction of the PSA 2016, with each change attempting to patch over the gaping holes in the 1971 Act. Whilst the problems with the PSA 2016 have been comprehensively charted, it was the failure of the MDA 1971 that was the driver and precedent for the UK Government to feel cornered into proposing a blanket ban on all except a handful of exempted psychoactive substances. This is because the MDA 1971 alone was no match for the profit-driven ingenuity of the international NPS trade combined with the enduring demand for psychoactive drugs within the UK. If any further evidence was needed, local diversion schemes have laid the foundations for a wholesale review of the MDA 1971, making it inevitable, overdue, beyond party politics and increasingly out of step with the electorate.

Professor Fiona Measham is Chair in Criminology at the University of Liverpool and founding Director of The Loop, a non-profit harm reduction organization that introduced drug checking in the UK. She is a founding member of Drug Science and member of the Advisory Council on the Misuse of Drugs since 2008. Her co-edited collection on *Young Adult Drinking Styles* (2019, Palgrave Macmillan) won the British Medical Association award for Best Psychiatry Book 2021.

Dr Michael Pascoe is a research associate working within the field of Pharmaceutical Microbiology whose recent projects have included developing new materials for treating surfaces contaminated with bacterial biofilms and investigating the effectiveness of various control strategies to reduce Covid-19 transmission. He completed a Media Fellowship with the British Science Association in 2019 and has participated in local and international outreach activities, including the Science in Schools programme of the British Council and French Ministry of Education.

References and Extra Reading

Duke K (2020), Producing the 'Problem' of New Psychoactive Substances (NPS) in English Prisons, *International Journal of Drug Policy*, 80: 102479.

Home Office (2012), Extent and Trends in Illicit Drug Use Among Adults Aged 16 to 59 — Drug Misuse Declared 2011/12, *Statistical Bulletin*.

Home Office (2018), Annual Report on the Home Office Forensic Early Warning System (FEWS) — 2016/17. Report for the Home Office (November), London: Home Office.

House of Commons Science and Technology Committee (2006), Drug Classification: Making a Hash of It? Fifth Report of Session 2005–6, HC 1031, London: House of Commons: https://publications.parliament.uk/pa/cm200506/cmselect/cmsctech/1031/1031.pdf

Measham, F (2021), Social Issues in the Use of New Psychoactive Substances: Differentiated Demand, Displacement and Adulteration in P Dargan and D Wood (eds), *Novel Psychoactive Substances: Classification, Pharmacology and Toxicology* (Edn. 2): 157–180, London: Elsevier.

Measham, F and Turnbull, G (2021), Intentions, Actions and Outcomes: A Follow up Survey on Harm Reduction Practices After Using an English Festival Drug Checking Service, *International Journal of Drug Policy*, 95: 1–10. 103270. DOI: 10.1016/j.drugpo.2021.103270

Measham, F, Aldridge J and Parker, H (2001), *Dancing On Drugs: Risk, Health and Hedonism in the British Club Scene*, London: Free Association Books.

Measham, F, Moore, K, Newcombe, R and Welch, Z (2010), Tweaking, Bombing, Dabbing and Stockpiling: The Emergence of Mephedrone and the Perversity of Prohibition, *Drugs and Alcohol Today*, 10(1): 14–21.

Moore, K, Dargan, P, Wood, D and Measham, F (2013), Do Novel Psychoactive Substances (NPS) Displace Established Street Drugs, Supplement Them or Act as Drugs of Initiation? The Relationship Between Mephedrone, Ecstasy and Cocaine, *European Addiction Research*, 19: 276–282.

Nutt D, King L and Phillips L (2010), Drug Harms in the UK: A Multicriteria Decision Analysis, *The Lancet*, 376(9751): 1558–1565.

Office for National Statistics (ONS) (2020), Drug Misuse in England and Wales: Year Ending March 2020, *Statistical Bulletin*, ONS.

ONS (2021), Deaths Related to Drug Poisoning in England and Wales: 2020 Registrations, *Statistical Bulletin*, ONS.

Oomen, P, Schori, D, Tögel-Lins, K, Acreman, D, Chenorhokian, S, Luf, A, Paulos, C, Fornero, E, Koning, R, Galindo, L, Measham, F and Ventura, M (2022), Cannabis Adulterated with the Synthetic Cannabinoid Receptor Agonist MDMB-4en-PINACA and the Role of European Drug Checking Services, *International Journal of Drug Policy*, 100. DOI: 10.1016/j.drugpo.2021.103493

Pascoe, M, Radley, S, Simmons, H and Measham, F (2022), The Cathinone Hydra: Increased Cathinone and Caffeine Adulteration in the English MDMA Market After Brexit and COVID-19 Lockdowns, *Drug Science, Policy and Law*. DOI: 10.1177/20503245221099209

Sample, I (2015), 'Superman' Pill Deaths Spark Calls for Dangerous-drugs Alert System, *The Guardian*, 16 January: www.theguardian.com/society/2015/jan/16/superman-pill-deaths-dangerous-drugs-alert-system

Welsh Emerging Detection and Identification of Novel Psychoactive Substances (WEDINOS) (2012), PHILTRE Annual Report 2020–2021 (for Public Health Wales).

Wood, D, Measham, F and Dargan, P (2012), 'Our Favourite Drug': Prevalence of Use and Preference for Mephedrone in the London Night Time Economy One Year After Control, *Journal of Substance Use*, 17(2): 91–97.

CHAPTER 5

Cannabis: Past, Present and Future

Anne Katrin Schlag and David Nutt

'The controversy that has arisen in the United Kingdom about the proper evaluation of cannabis in the list of psycho-active drugs, should be resolved as quickly as possible, so that both the law and its enforcement as well as programmes of health education, may be relevant to what is known about the dangers of cannabis-smoking in this country, and may receive full public support.' (Wootton Report, 1968, paragraph 68)

Despite the conclusions of the Wootton Report the dispute surrounding the accurate evaluation of cannabis in the UK continues unabated over half a century later. Today, cannabis is controlled under Class B of the MDA 1971. It is also listed in Schedule 1 of the Misuse of Drugs Regulations 2001 (MDR), although cannabis-based medicinal products (CBMPs) are in Schedule 2.

But this was not always the case. This chapter discusses the socio-political landscape of cannabis in the UK over the past 50 years, outlining its past and present scheduling and the controversies associated with it, before offering some future prospects. For the scientific evidence on the harms and benefits of cannabis we refer the reader to other chapters in this book and the extensive existing and constantly evolving literature (e.g. National Academies of Sciences and Medicine, 2017; House of Lords Report, 1998).

A Summary of the Past 50 years

Today, UK cannabis classification remains controversial despite attempts by successive past Governments to develop more open-minded cannabis policies. Between 1968 and 1972 Government-appointed committees in Britain (as well as in Canada and the US) already noted the stigmatisation of cannabis, casting doubt on the medical justification for its legal status. The Wootton Report (1968) concluded that:

> 'Once the myths were cleared, it became obvious that the case for and against was not evenly balanced. By any ordinary standards of objectivity, it is clear that cannabis is not a very harmful drug.'

Hence the classification of cannabis as a Class B substance under the MDA, 1971 has been particularly contentious as the basis of this categorisation remains unclear. Nearly 30 years after the establishment of the MDA 1971, in 2000, the Police Foundation convened the Independent Inquiry into the Misuse of Drugs Act to consider whether the law should be revised to make it more effective and responsive (Police Foundation, 2000). Chaired by Viscountess Runciman (hence also known as the 'Runciman Report'), the inquiry team was not subject to the demands of re-election as the political decision makers were, and so could properly focus on the scientific evidence. As such, they were able to propose more realistic and sensible drug policy—which did not fit well with the political agenda. Politically, their suggested measures were controversial (Shiner, 2015).

Reviewing the MDA 1971 for the first time in its then 30-year history, the inquiry recommended a degree of depenalisation of cannabis: cannabis should be reclassified as a Class C drug, normal sanctions for possession and cultivation of cannabis for personal use would be out-of-court disposals, including formal warnings, statutory cautions, or a fixed fine. Prosecutions would be the exception, and only then would a conviction result in a criminal record. However, it recommended increased penalties for trafficking. The inquiry also recommended the removal of the ban on therapeutic uses of cannabis for specified medical purposes.

Concluding that the law on cannabis caused more harm than it prevents, criminalising large numbers of otherwise law-abiding young people, and bearing down heavily on minority ethnic communities, the inquiry advised to downgrade all forms of cannabis to Class C, which would have removed the power of arrest for most cannabis possession offences. Initially, the then Labour Government was reluctant to make any changes leading Viscountess Runciman to note that the law is out of touch with reality.

Shortly after publication of the Wotton Report, the Advisory Council on the Misuse of Drugs (ACMD) confirmed the Runciman analysis. Despite initial reluctance, after the proposed reclassification had been endorsed by the ACMD (2002) and the Parliamentary Select Committee on Home Affairs (2002), in 2004, in one of the most significant liberalisations in British drug laws, cannabis was downgraded to Class C. The decision to reclassify was only done once there had been a relatively positive media response, even from the *Daily Mail*, regarded as Britain's most right-wing newspaper. At the time cannabis products were in Class A (oil) or Class B (resin and hash). Moving cannabis from these classes to Class C was only the second time a controlled substance had been downgraded since the three-tiered classification system was introduced more than 30 years earlier (Police Foundation, 2000).

Yet despite this progressive approach, an intensification of policing followed, as outlined by Rudi Fortson in *Chapter 17*. Cannabis remained a highly politicised substance and the Class C scheduling continued to be criticised, leading the then Home Secretary, Charles Clarke to ask the ACMD to review the status of cannabis again. Although the vast majority of the committee argued cannabis should remain in Class C, the Government and anti-cannabis media fought this decision. As a promising response to resolve this impasse, Clarke suggested to look at the issues of drug classification itself and asked the ACMD to review the MDA 1971 which had not yet been reviewed in its history. Alas, Clarke was sacked before this review could take place, and his replacement, John Reid, scrapped the review process without consulting the ACMD (Nutt, 2020). Please see Figure 1 for a timeline of the key events of this reclassification — and subsequent reversal.

Key Events Timeline

1968 — (Dec) Wootton Report stresses cannabis needs to be properly evaluated as it is not as harmful as myths suppose.

1971 — (May) MDA 1971 receives Royal Assent and cannabis is removed from UK pharmacopeia of medicines.

1997 — (Nov) British Medical Association (BMA) publishes report on the therapeutic uses of cannabis medicines, stressing need for clinical trials and possible changes in the MDA 1971 to allow for these.

1998 — (Nov) House of Lords report on medical cannabis recommends that cannabis should be made available for medicinal purposes and moved to Schedule 2.

(Nov) BMA opposes recommendation to transfer cannabis and cannabis resin from Schedule 1 to Schedule 2.

2004 — (Jan) Cannabis is classified under Class C under the MDA 1971.

2005 — (March) Home Secretary again asks the ACMD to review classification of cannabis, in light of new evidence of mental health effects.

(Dec) ACMD advises cannabis should remain in Class C. Home Secretary announces it will do so.

2006 — (July) Science and Technology Select Committee of the House of Commons criticises approach to cannabis scheduling as unscientific.

2007 — (July) Home Secretary asks ACMD again to review classification of cannabis in light of public concerns about mental health and skunk (a 'strong' form of the drug due to its relatively high THC:CBD ratio: see elsewhere in this chapter).

2018 — (Feb) Hannah Deacon discusses the need for medicinal cannabis on BBC Breakfast TV. Home Office issues statement that there is no medical value to cannabis.

(June) Charlotte Caldwell arrives at UK airport with illicit cannabis for her son Billy and is issued temporary licence.

(June) Alfie Dingley makes history by receiving the first NHS prescription for full-spectrum CBMPs.

(Nov) Cannabis is rescheduled from Schedule 1 into 2 of the MDA 1971, allowing medical use again.

2000

(March) Independent Inquiry into the Misuse of Drugs Act calls for cannabis to be downgraded from Class B to C as part of broader drug policy reforms.

(Aug) Second House of Lords report again reviews the potential of medical cannabis, criticising the slow progress for patients, arguing in favour for a relaxation of the current regulations to allow for more research

2001

(Feb) Home Office rejects Lords' Aug 2000 recommendations.

(Oct) Home Secretary asks the Advisory Council on the Misuse of Drugs (ACMD) to review classifications in light of the scientific evidence.

2002

(March) ACMD recommends that cannabis should be moved to Class C.

Figure 1. Timeline of key events of UK cannabis classification. (Adapted from Shiner, 2015)

2008

(May) MORI poll of public opinion shows majority of the public support scheduling of cannabis in Class C.

(May) ACMD continues to recommend that cannabis remains in Class C, but Home Secretary announces cannabis will return to Class B.

2009

(Jan) Reclassification of cannabis to Class B takes effect.

2012

(Dec) Home Affairs Select Committee expresses regret that cannabis did not remain in Class C.

2017

(Jan) Hannah Deacon sets up 'Alfie's Hope' campaign to allow her son Alfie NHS access to whole plant cannabis-based medicinal products (CBMPs).

2020

(Aug) Drug Science launches Project TWENTY21 (T21), the first UK real world data registry on medical cannabis.

(Nov) ACMD publishes report on medical use of cannabis and recommends setting up a real world registry.

(Dec) World Health Organization's Expert Committee on Drug Dependence reviews the scheduling of cannabis under the United Nations 1961 convention and makes cannabis a medicine again.

2021

(July) Less than a handful of new NHS prescriptions have been written for CBMPs; cannabis remains the most widely cultivated, trafficked, and abused illicit drug in Britain.

In 2006, the UK Science and Technology Select Committee of the House of Commons published their report on drug classification. The report argued that the current classification of UK drug regulation is arbitrary and unscientific, highlighting the need for using scientific evidence to classify drugs. The committee strongly criticised the Government's approach to cannabis scheduling and cited the widespread confusion over the legal status of cannabis as evidence of a failure by previous Governments to adequately educate the public on drugs policy changes. Furthermore, the report debunked the myth of the 'gateway theory', i.e. that a softer drug, such as cannabis, leads to the abuse of harder drugs, such as heroin. Using the example of The Netherlands, with a more liberal attitude towards cannabis than the UK, Colin Blakemore, then head of the Medical Research Council (MRC), pointed out that cannabis use in that country is a little less than in the UK, and hard drug use in The Netherlands is about one third of the use in the UK, showing the lack of empirical evidence for the theory.

Unfortunately, the politicisation of cannabis became further evident when then Prime Minister Gordon Brown — as part of his political dealing and bargaining — stated that skunk was lethal, and initiated, in 2008, the third ACMD cannabis review in a decade. This focused on three main issues: the harms of skunk which had begun to dominate the market; cannabis and schizophrenia; and cannabis and driving.

It became clear that the prohibitionist policy of the UK — designed to reduce cannabis use and harms — had the opposite effect, contributing to the rise of skunk, with its higher THC concentrations and associated risks of psychosis and addiction than the traditional forms, as well as the use of 'spice', i.e. synthetic cannabis receptor agonists (SCRAs) as a potent and often toxic alternative to cannabis, which has proved a real problem amongst prisoners and the homeless (Ralphs et al, 2021). (Note: this is not the only time that drug laws have made things worse, rather than better — trying to stop the use of one drug often leads to the use of a more potent, and more harmful, alternative (Ralphs et al, 2017)).

The ACMD experts concluded that whilst skunk may be more harmful than traditional cannabis, due to its relatively high THC: CBD ratio, it is not lethal. Rather, cannabis, including skunk, has a remarkable safety profile. In relation to cannabis and driving, cannabis intoxication can impair driving performance, but it is still unclear at which THC levels impairment occurs. More research in this area is required, especially in light of the increasing number of medical users. The question of whether cannabis causes schizophrenia remains unanswered, despite decades of research to date. Overall, any association appears to be correlative rather than causative. Some of the chemicals in cannabis, particularly CBD, may actually reduce psychosis, and today some cannabis products are being trialled to treat various psychiatric conditions.

Despite the ACMD voting to maintain its recommendation of Class C status, cannabis was removed from Class C and again placed into Class B of the MDA 1971 in 2009. This upgrading occurred in opposition to public opinion. As indicated in the Timeline (Figure 1) in 2008 the ACMD commissioned a representative MORI poll on cannabis regulation. The largest group of respondents (44%) wanted cannabis to remain in the same class (Class C), with a significant minority (27%) wanting cannabis to be legal, than either in Class B (13%) or Class A (11%), with the remainder voicing no opinion.

Nevertheless, cannabis was reclassified against the advice of the ACMD, which brought Ministers and their scientific advisors into conflict. The law on cannabis had been reversed for political reasons — the scientific evidence had not changed. Professor David Nutt, then chairman of the ACMD, was later sacked, having been perceived as going too far in lobbying for policy change. Rather than influencing policymaking, science was supposed to merely support the status quo. As a response, in 2010, Professor Nutt set up the Independent Scientific Committee on Drugs (now Drug Science), where he was joined by numerous ACMD experts, who were similarly dismayed by the Government's attitude.

Medical Cannabis

The impact of the MDA 1971 and associated controversies around cannabis scheduling was also felt in the medical cannabis space. The anti-cannabis rhetoric and stigma associated with recreational use, also affected medical cannabis users, many of whom were unduly criminalised. Whilst the science of medical cannabis has been developing rapidly during the past decades, leading to cannabis being prescribed as a treatment for a broad variety of conditions in other countries, patient access to medical cannabis continues to be challenging in the

UK. Cannabis had been a medicine in the UK until 1971, when it was removed from the pharmacopeia under the 1971 Act. This is believed to be the result of continuous pressure from the US Government, who wrongly believed that banning medical cannabis would reduce recreational use. This ban had no impact on recreational use — cannabis remained the most popular illicit drug — but instead contributed to the stigmatisation of medical cannabis users in the UK.

Already in 1998, the House of Lords Science and Technology Committee carried out an enquiry into the medical effects of cannabis, taking evidence on the scientific case for and against continuing to prohibit the medicinal and recreational uses of cannabis, recommending that it should be made available for medicinal purposes, and moved to Schedule 2 (House of Lords Report, 1998). But the Government rejected any immediate changes to legislation, and indicated that, before this could be considered, safety and efficacy of a medicinal form of cannabis should be demonstrated.

A couple of years later, a second House of Lords Report (2000) again reviewed the potential of medical cannabis, criticising the slow progress for patients in need and arguing for a relaxation of the current regulations to allow for more research. The Police Foundation (2000) agreed that cannabis and cannabis resin should be moved from Schedule 1 to Schedule 2 of the regulations.

In 1997, the British Medical Association (BMA) suggested that properly controlled trials with pure cannabinoids are required and called for changes in the licensing of cannabinoids under the MDA 1971 to allow for this. However, the BMA (1998) did oppose the recommendation to transfer cannabis and cannabis resin from Schedule 1 to Schedule 2, recommending instead that certain cannabinoids should be rescheduled, and that the regulations should be made sufficiently flexible to allow clinical trials to proceed urgently. It was not until November 2018 that the UK Government again accepted the medical value of cannabis and legalised it as a medicine in the UK. Several high-profile media campaigns focusing on children with severe epilepsy only responsive to medical cannabis led to a public outcry against the legal regulations denying these children the treatment they needed. This was followed with a review by the then Chief Medical Officer (CMO) to the UK Government, Dame Sally Davies, which recommended that CBMPs be moved out of the Schedule 1 MDR 2001. As the result, CBMPs were removed from Schedule 1 and put into Schedule 2 so that they could once again be prescribed. But re-scheduling did not lead to the expected patient access. Since re-scheduling, only a very small number of NHS prescriptions have been written—and not even for the children suffering from refractory epilepsy for whom medical cannabis has proved to be effective. Reasons for this include the strict guidelines by the National Institute for Health and Care Excellence (NICE) (which were clarified in March 2021), a lack of education by physicians, as well as the lingering stigma of cannabis (Schlag et al, 2020).

This led Drug Science—together with expert clinicians, patient representatives, policy experts and industry partners—to set up the Medical Cannabis Working Group, to improve access to medical cannabis. Amongst other research efforts, in 2020, Drug Science launched Project TWENTY21 (T21), the UK's first medical cannabis registry. Offering a longitudinal real world evidence database (incidentally, the establishment of such a registry was recommended both by the BMA in 1997 and the ACMD in 2020). It is hoped that the project's findings will contribute to the scientific evidence base and further demonstrate the value of medical cannabis to the medical profession and the NHS.

Present Progress

At the time of writing, T21 has over 2,000 registered patients, who are presenting with a wide array of conditions to be treated with a range of CBMPs. In line with other international databases, the most common conditions for which CBMPs are prescribed are pain, and anxiety, followed by post-traumatic stress disorder (PTSD) and multiple sclerosis (MS: a disease of the central nervous system). Initial findings published in the peer-reviewed literature are promising, evidencing the medicinal benefits of CBMPs for patients, not only in relation to their key condition(s), but also in relation to their quality of life, which improved significantly at patients' three-month follow-ups (Sakal et al, 2021).

Although the evidence on the benefits of medical cannabis to treat a broad range of conditions continues to develop rapidly, more work remains to be done to ease prescribing and patient access. An increasing number of patient-led initiatives have sprung up in the past few years, for example to campaign for improved patient access to CBMPs (PLEA: see www.plea.org), to help patients with particular conditions (End Our Pain; see https://endourpain.org), to educate patients and potential prescribers (MCCS; MedCan: see https://medcansupport.co.uk), and to improve on the current legal framework for medical cannabis patients (Cancard: see https://cancard.co.uk).

Continuing Controversies

In contrast to the—slow but continual—improvements of medical uses of cannabis, less progress has been made in relation to recreational use. Cannabis use in the UK is the highest in Europe. Cannabis remains the most widely cultivated, trafficked and used illicit drug in Britain (ONS, 2020). After having fallen for the past four years, the number of people dealt with for drugs offences involving cannabis possession rose by over 23.1% between 2019 and 2020 (from 89,446 to 110,085), making-up 62.9% of all drug offenses (House of Commons, 2020).

Despite increases in the number and quantity of seizures, there is no evidence that cannabis has become harder to obtain or more expensive. Since the 1970s there have been increasing numbers of prosecutions under the MDA 1971, accelerating in the 1980s and 1990s. Although they have fallen in recent years, cannabis possession continues to dominate offences against the 1971 Act. According to its purpose—to prevent the misuse of controlled drugs—in relation to cannabis, the MDA 1971 has undoubtedly failed. UK policies regarding the possession and use of cannabis are not working, and it is imperative to find a more progressive way forward. The list of British politicians across the spectrum who are publicly admitting cannabis use is constantly expanding. Public petitions to the UK Government and Parliament on the re-scheduling and legalisation of cannabis are now in their hundreds. Conflicting policies abound—particularly in relation to cannabis, the chasm between science and policy remains wide. Clearly, it is time for a policy rethink.

The political argument that to downgrade (or decriminalise/legalise) cannabis would send a confusing message to the young is counterintuitive. Rather, current laws are bewildering, contributing to lack of trust in Government and policymakers. By treating cannabis the same as other, more harmful drugs, drugs education messages are undermined. The current classification of cannabis is the result of political and value judgements, rather than scientific evidence. The harms of cannabis (to the individual and to society) consistently rank lower than those of several legal drugs, including alcohol and tobacco (see, e.g. Nutt et al, 2010; and Lawrence Phillips in *Chapter 16* of this volume), and it is inequitable to criminalise cannabis users while allowing the use of tobacco and alcohol.

Conclusions and Future Avenues

With the advances of medical cannabis since 2018, public perceptions of cannabis — vital for political decision-making — are becoming increasingly positive. A recent poll by the Conservative Drug Policy Reform Group (CDPRG, 2019) found that the vast majority of the British public is in favour of the recent legalisation of CBMPs and would use these medicines themselves if in need. Moreover, an increasing number support legalisation of cannabis (48%), with 24% opposing legalisation and the remainder undecided.

Appreciating that the UK is on the (long and winding) road to reform, the issue now is not if, but rather how, the law ought to be changed. This is further discussed in Part V: see *Chapter 19*, A Modest Proposal to Decriminalise the Simple Possession of Drugs by Kirstie Douse, Niamh Eastwood and Alex Stevens; and *Chapter 20*, The Legal Regulation of Drugs in the UK by James Nicholls and Steve Rolles.

Dr Anne Katrin Schlag is a Chartered Psychologist and Head of Research at Drug Science, where she leads the research for the Medical Cannabis Working Group, and the Medical Psychedelics Working Group. She holds Honorary Senior Fellowships at both Imperial College London and King's College London, and currently is Chair of the Cannabis Industry Council Research Group.

Professor David Nutt DM, FRCP, FRCPsych, FMedSci, DLaws is Professor of Neuropsychopharmacology at Imperial College London. He is the Founding Chair of the charity Drug Science, and Chair of PAREA Europe.[1] From 2000–2009 he served on the Advisory Council on the Misuse of Drugs. He

---

1. Psychedelic Access and Research European Alliance: see https://parea.eu/

has published extensively with over 500 research papers and 36 books including *Drugs Without the Hot Air* (2021, UIT Cambridge) and his autobiography *Nutt Uncut* (2021, Waterside Press).

References and Extra Reading

Advisory Council on the Misuse of Drugs (2002), The Classification of Cannabis Under the Misuse of Drugs Act 1971, London: Home Office: https://assets.publishing.service.gov.uk/government/uploads/system/uploads/attachment_data/file/119126/cannabis-class-misuse-drugs-act.pdf (accessed July 15, 2021).

Advisory Council on the Misuse of Drugs (ACMD) (2005), Further Consideration of the Classification of Cannabis Under the Misuse of Drugs Act 1971, London: Home Office: https://assets.publishing.service.gov.uk/government/uploads/system/uploads/attachment_data/file/119124/cannabis-reclass-2005.pdf (accessed July 15, 2021).

ACMD (2008), Cannabis: Classification and Public Health, London: Home Office: https://assets.publishing.service.gov.uk/government/uploads/system/uploads/attachment_data/file/119174/acmd-cannabis-report-2008.pdf (accessed July 15, 2021).

ACMD (2020), Cannabis-based Products for Medicinal Use (CBPMs) In Humans (November): https://assets.publishing.service.gov.uk/government/uploads/system/uploads/attachment_data/file/939090/OFFICIAL__Published_version_-_ACMD_CBPMs_report_27_November_2020_FINAL.pdf (accessed July 15, 2021).

British Medical Association (1998), BMA calls for active research effort to produce new cannabis-based drugs but says crude cannabis is unsuitable for medical use, Press release: November 11.

Conservative Drug Policy Reform Group (2019), Public Attitudes to Drugs in the UK: https://static1.squarespace.com/static/5bbb29273560c345fccofade/t/5d6d287bf37f2400019d35fd/1567434878163/Attitudinal+Survey+Report+FINAL.pdf (accessed July 15, 2021).

Home Affairs Select Committee (2012), Drugs: Breaking the Cycle, Home Affairs Committee Formal Minutes, December 3, House of Commons, December 10: https://publications.parliament.uk/pa/cm201213/cmselect/cmhaff/184/18414.htm (accessed July 15, 2021).

House of Commons (2020), Drug Crime: Statistics for England and Wales, Briefing Paper 1929, October 26: https://researchbriefings.files.parliament.uk/documents/CBP-9039/CBP-9039.pdf (accessed July 15, 2021).

House of Lords Science and Technology Select Committee (1998), Ninth Report. Cannabis: The Scientific and Medical Evidence, London: The Stationery Office: https://publications.parliament.uk/pa/ld199798/ldselect/ldsctech/151/15101.htm (accessed July 15, 2021).

House of Lords Science and Technology Select Committee (2001), Second Report: https://publications.parliament.uk/pa/ld200001/ldselect/ldsctech/50/5003.htm (accessed July 15, 2021).

House of Lords Select Committee on Science and Technology (2006), Fifth Report: Incorporation of Advice into Policy: https://publications.parliament.uk/pa/cm200506/cmselect/cmsctech/1031/103107.htm (accessed July 15, 2021).

National Academies of Sciences and Medicine (2017), *The Health Effects of Cannabis and Cannabinoids: The Current State of Evidence and Recommendations for Research*, Washington, DC: The National Academies Press.

Nutt D J, King L A and Phillips L D (2010), Drug Harms in the UK: A Multicriteria Decision Analysis, *The Lancet*, 376(9752): 1558–1565. DOI: 10.1016/S0140-6736(10)61462-6

Office for National Statistics (2020), Drug Misuse in England and Wales: Year ending March 2020, ONS: www.ons.gov.uk/peoplepopulationandcommunity/crimeandjustice/articles/drugmisuseinenglandandwales/yearendingmarch2020 (accessed July 15, 2021).

Police Foundation (2000), *Drugs and the Law: Report of the Independent Inquiry into the Misuse of Drugs Act 1971:* www.police-foundation.org.uk/2017/wp-content/uploads/2017/06/drugs_and_the_law.pdf (accessed July 15, 2021).

Ralphs R, Gray P and Sutcliffe O B (2021), The Impact of the 2016 Psychoactive Substances Act on Synthetic Cannabinoid Use Within the Homeless Population: Markets, Content and User Harms, *International Journal of Drug Policy*, 97: 103305. DOI: 10.1016/j.drugpo.2021.103305

Ralphs R, Williams L, Askew R et al (2017), Adding Spice to the Porridge, *International Journal of Drug Policy*, 40: 57–69. DOI: 10.1016/j.drugpo.2016.10.003

Sakal C, Lynskey M, Schlag A K et al (2021), 'Developing a Real-World Evidence Base for Prescribed Cannabis in the United Kingdom: Preliminary Findings from Project Twenty21, *Psychopharmacology*, Online First. DOI: 10.1007/s00213-021-05855-2

Schlag A K, Baldwin D S, Barnes M, et al (2020), Medical Cannabis in the UK: From Principle to Practice, *Journal of Psychopharmacology*, 34(9): 931–937. DOI: 10.1177/0269881120926677

Shiner M (2015), Drug Policy Reform and the Reclassification of Cannabis in England and Wales: A Cautionary Tale, *International Journal of Drug Policy*, 26(7): 696–704. DOI: 10.1016/j.drugpo.2015.03.009

Wootton Report (1968), Cannabis: Report by the Advisory Committee on Drug Dependence. London: HMSO.

CHAPTER 6

Narratives of Drug-related Harm

Anna Ross and Anne Katrin Schlag

Stories in Policy: The Personal is Political

Social science is concerned with meaning making, and modern-day developments have seen narrative analysis as an important way of understanding meanings (Fischer, 2003). Narratives are a way to communicate with each other using stories, giving us an understanding of not just individual lives but the cultural or community narrative (Bruner, 1991; Reissman 1993): 'The power of narrative is not so much that it is about life but that it interacts in life' (Daiute, 2014: 2). It can be argued that policy development consists of a series of competing narratives and ideas (Roe, 1994; Smith, 2012) and these stories become master narratives that are developed to provide surety and coherence in an often complex and unstable policy environment.

When competing narratives do not have a coherent structure to them and are a series of critiques, policymakers will fall on ambiguity and harden the master narrative line, because this provides security and strength to an issue which is complex and full of risk (Roe, 1993; Stone, 2002). Therefore, policy analysts should focus on the structure of the narratives, both master and counter, and explore the similarities and differences in order to craft an alternative story that deals with the uncertainty and risk inherent in all complex policymaking (Roe, 1994, Chapter 2). Using personal stories to highlight policy narratives (both master and counter) allows the researcher to craft *meta* narratives that speak to both the policy making community, and the wider stakeholder community. In doing so the counter and meta narratives can attempt to provide the security, coherence and structure needed to create understanding of these complex 'problems' and provide viable alternatives by offering insight into the different competing narratives.

The narratives presented here are an amalgamation of multiple stories that show the representation of the 'problem' (in this case drug use), responses to that 'problem', and counter narratives. These stories come from engagement with the different policy groups, interview data, field notes, documentary analysis, informal conversations, and the researchers' backgrounds (or situated) knowledge of the field (Ross, 2020). Further, the characters in the stories are fictional characters developed from data in order to provide the frame for the kinds of drug use considered legitimate (or illegitimate) in policy participation: the sick, the recovered, the professional and the happy drug user (see Ross, ibid for a discussion on this typology). None of the actions carried out by the characters are representative of any one person, but are reflective of the different situations the various stakeholders find themselves in depending on their context. We present the master narrative, and then provide counter and meta-narratives for both historical legacies and participation.

The Master Narrative — The 'Problem' Drug User

The representation of the 'problem' of drug use is a result of historical legacies, such as the MDA 1971 that has resulted in a focus on drug-related harm. From this a master narrative was developed encompassing the kind of drug user, and drug use, policy is focused on. The following stories explore this focus.

Master narrative: the representation of the problem

> Barry turned the corner and pulled up his collar against the biting November wind. He walked slowly, not really knowing where he was going, just walking, hoping that it may provide some answers. Yesterday was his last shift at the yard, and now him, and most of his pals were unemployed. It was 1986, his dad had lost his job a year ago, and was now drinking himself

Narratives of Drug-related Harm

into an early grave while his mum watched on helplessly. Barry was finding it very difficult to get his head around what his life opportunities were now that he was unemployed, in fact he did not have the capacity to think about it at all. His life had not been easy: being a small boy he was a target for the bullies, and his older brother had vented a lot of anger on him. Growing up in a poor industrial estate had taken its toll on him, and he was not a happy young man. As he was walking his pal Neil came up to him, asked him if he wanted to stop by his and try this new stuff a pal had sold him — like hash but better. "Aye, may as well come up now, just walking around here wearing ma shoes out." The first smoke of the brown sticky stuff that smelt like burnt vanilla made him violently sick, and then horrendously itchy. His pal Neil told him to give it another go. "It takes time to get used to it but when you do…"

The second time Barry got it. He well and truly got it. You know when you have found your drug of choice, and Barry had found his. When he sank back after his hit he could feel the years of tension slip from his shoulders, his body slowly forgetting the memory of bruises, pain, shame. Wrapped in a warm fuzzy loving embrace, Barry felt safe for the first time in his life. Unfortunately, this feeling cost money, and Barry had no work, and no prospect of work in the near future. The more he took, the more he wanted, and gradually he forgot about "career choices" and spent his days finding ways to get his fix for the night. Fast forward 30 years and Barry has been dependent on heroin for three decades, most of which has been spent in and out of jail for small crimes, staying in various homeless shelters, temporary accommodation. The periods of sobriety or permanent housing never lasted long.

Now, this story has two endings, depending on what is being depicted: recovery or a drug-related death. The recovery ending:

Barry was tired: tired of being homeless, tired of the street life, tired of needing to intoxicate himself to just stay alive. At the urgings of his support worker Barry started to attend his local NA [Narcotics Anonymous] sessions. In this he heard about the concept of recovery, and began to think about his life, all the trauma he had experienced both in his childhood, and as a result of his addiction. His GP was encouraging him to reduce his methadone script and she had offered to put him in contact with his local recovery community. One day Barry made contact with the community, and since then it has been a journey of discovering a new support system that has helped him become drug free, and able to hold down a tenancy. Barry is very happy in fact he is "better than well."[1]

The drug death ending:

One cold November morning Lucy was walking to work past Waverley train station in Edinburgh and she noticed a homeless man asleep on the side of the bridge. She felt sad: nobody should be out begging in this weather, put a coin in his hat and went to work. On her way back from work she noticed that the homeless man had not moved. She made a note in her head to check the next day. The next morning, she passed him again, and he was in the same position as yesterday. She decided to call the police to ask them to check up on the man. One hour later she received a phone call from the police to update her: The man had been a homeless man named Barry McGowan, age 53, and he had died from what looked like a heroin overdose. He was given a pauper's burial and his funeral was attended by his support worker, and no one else.

Problem drug use began to be a policy 'problem' around the mid 1980s as a result of an increase in HIV/AIDS that brought heroin use to the attention of policymakers, particularly in Scotland. The narrative that is being presented in 2021 is: as a result of neo-liberal policies by the UK Government which saw the closure of many factories and industries, Scotland suffered a long-term decline resulting in high unemployment, poverty, and an ageing drug using population (MacGregor, 2017; Minton et al, 2017; Scottish Affairs Committee, 2019). This led to a community of drug users that are either 'sick' or in recovery, and the focus has been on how to encourage these drug users to access recovery based

---

1. A phrase recently coined by the recovery movement to describe how those who have been drug free for a certain period of time begin to feel better than people who have never had a drug 'problem': See further: www.scottishrecoveryconsortium.org/index.php?id=1235

treatment. This story has helped to focus responses to perceived drug 'problems' by providing a stable grounding on where the 'problem' has come from, and how to respond to it: by increasing access to treatment and addressing the social aspects such as housing, employment, therapy, etc. While these are laudable responses, and will have a positive impact on many 'problematic' drug users who are seeking such treatment, as discussed in this book, this focus hides a much deeper complex relationship with drugs, and drugs policy in society.

Counter narrative: the hidden harm of criminal justice policy

As seen above, the problem has historically been represented as a response to an increase in drug use, particularly opiate based drug use. However, there are counter narratives to this representation, namely the role the UK Criminal Justice System has in creating and/or sustaining drug-related harm. This narrative introduces new characters and scenarios to highlight this policy harm.

> Jamie was getting ready for the weekend. Shaz had phoned and her crew were wanting about 20 pills and some hash, Gerry was wanting another 20 pills, and his own crew probably wanted the same. All in all he reckoned if he got 100 pills that would sort everyone out for the weekend and leave some spare in case anyone else wanted any. He called his guy Mark—a dude he'd become friends with from buying pills, and was now effectively working for. "Mark, I'm gonnea need 100 pills and probably an ounce of your solid if you got it." "No worries pal, Come down in an hour and I'll have it sorted." John started to get ready. He stuck on his thumping house music, poured a vodka and coke, and started to wind up for the weekend. It was gonnea be a belter! Shaz was having her 21st and had hired a massive venue in Ayreshire, DJs an all, and the promise of plenty dancing, chatting hugging and all round madness was on the cards. He called a taxi to take him to Mark's.
>
> The taxi pulled up at the high rise in Easterhouse, god he hated this place. Bleak, empty, and nerve wracking. How many busts, stabbings, beatings had taken place down here? He wished Mark was up for meeting at his place in the West End, at least he wouldn't feel he was walking into a warzone just to buy some bloody drugs for the weekend. In and out in 20 minutes,

done and dusted. As he was walking down the road trying to hail a taxi (no bloody taxis in this place) a police car pulled over. "What you doing pal" said the policeman in the driver's seat. "Just walking, on my way out for the weekend." The policeman stepped out the car. "We've been informed that drug dealing has been taking place, and man fitting your description was seen leaving the suspected premises, we are now cautioning you under section 23 of the MDA 1971, for the purpose of a search."

Jamie was found with 100 ecstasy tablets and 1 ounce of low grade hashish. He was sentenced to 4 years in prison, out in 2.5 years for good behaviour. He was 18 years old, with no dependent drug use or recorded mental health problems, when he entered Barlinnie Prison.

Jamie squinted in the late afternoon sun. His mum and dad had come to pick him up from the prison but he had deliberately told them the wrong time so he could leave without them. He was broken. His body ached from the violations of prison, both from inmates and the different drugs he consumed just to survive the pain. But he also had a craving. He craved the sweet feeling of heroin as it hit his veins, the blind intoxication as the Valium mixed with heroin dissipated all the memories of the last 3 years. He needed more, but he knew his parents would not understand.

He always maintained, to anyone who would listen, that he learnt his lesson at 6 months. The following two years were spent undoing this lesson, and his life. John spent the next 15 years in and out of prison for petty crimes and drug dealing. His mental health deteriorated and he was found dead in his flat from an overdose of Valium, heroin and alcohol. He was 33 years old.

The impact that criminal justice interventions, and in particular prison sentences, have on drug users is not part of the master narrative, yet criminal justice interventions are a key aspect of the legislative framework, and governed by the MDA 1971.

The main reason that the master narrative of problem drug use persists is that it clearly illustrates the risk of harm that can result from drug use. The counter

Narratives of Drug-related Harm

narrative provided here shows the risk of harm resulting from criminal justice interventions. By using personalised stories to focus attention on the silenced or ignored aspects of drug policy, we can inspire empathy and compassion towards those experiencing this silencing, and thus effect change.

The following narrative is a meta-narrative: a fictional story that seeks a middle ground incorporating enough of the main stories to provide consistency, credibility and coherence allowing for an alternative viewpoint. It combines John and Barry's story to explore what may have happened if our legal and social relationship to drug use was different: i.e. if we implemented drug policy reform as advocated by many drug policy researchers, activists and workers.

Meta narrative: reducing the harm of drug policy

Barry and Jamie had known each other for years. They had been pals in primary school but in high school they had drifted apart. Barry was a small shy boy, and the target of bullies. He often came into school with bruises and dirty clothes: no-one really knew who his family were except to steer clear from his uncle. Jamie on the other hand sailed through high school. He had a supportive family, a good circle of friends, and despite the poverty surrounding him, he had aspirations of leaving school and getting a good job. It was 1986 and the factories were closing down around them. Barry had left school early a year ago to take up employment, but had just lost his job at the yard. The last year had been hard as he watched his dad sink deeper into an alcoholic depression, and the black dog of depression was hanging on his own shoulders most days. One day, as he was walking the streets aimlessly, he bumped into his pal Neil who asked whether he wanted to come up to his and try some smack. They'd had drug education in school, and he'd heard that smack (heroin) was a good painkiller but that it was potentially very addictive. He knew he felt shit, he knew he'd like to take something to stop himself from feeling like shit, but he didn't want to get into something he would have to rely on for the rest of his life. Knowing all this he said "Nah, you're alright. How come you into that stuff man?" "Ah pal," said Neil, "ken, ah knew it was habit forming but aye, it's just so good, once you try it, it makes you forget absolutely fuckin everything, and I mean everything." Barry nodded, there was a lot he wanted to forget, but he knew

Neil had more he needed to forget. "Heard you can get a script—pure stuff—from the doc, have you thought about that?" "Aye," said Neil, "I'm gonnae start Monday, that and some therapy. They say I've got childhood trauma shite I need to deal wi." "Good luck then pal," and Barry was off.

A little while later Barry bumped into Jamie, his old pal. "Hi Barry man, how you doing?" "Och, no so bad, no so good either to be honest," Barry replied. "Fancy coming to rave with me, Shaz and the gang," said Jamie, "It's her 21st birthday and it's gonnea be a belter! Just off to get the weekend stash sorted." In his drug education Barry had also learnt that ecstasy was not very dependent forming, and the main problem was related to quality and quantity. He was curious and needed a boost. "Aye alright," said Barry, "could do wi a bit of a blow out." "Nice one," said Jamie, "meet at mine the back 'o 8, I'm just heading to Easterhouse to pick up."

As Jamie left the high rise in Easterhouse he noticed a police car driving past. He hunkered down, didn't want to get noticed. Although technically folk weren't getting done for possession of drugs anymore, he had 100 pills and an ounce oh hash, and he wasn't sure he could swing it with that much on him. The police drove past. They recognised him as a regular at the flat. "No doubt see him out at the rave tonight eh," said one of the police. The other laughed, "Aye, giving a huge hug and snog to any polis in the vicinity most likely." The police knew that Mark was dealing ecstasy from his flat. They also knew he imported the ecstasy from Holland on a monthly basis. But they also knew that the harm caused from this activity was nothing compared to what they were dealing with in and around the local pubs, and they would rather have the local teenagers munching on ecstasy in a field, than beating up their neighbour down the pub.

Barry had a fantastic night. He danced and danced and hugged and loved and came away with 20 new best pals. Jamie and him started seeing each other as friends, and gradually they moved from clubbing and working in bars, to other more "professional jobs." Thirty years later they have 3 kids between them, and still hook up for the odd pint or smoke. Occasionally they enjoy a line of coke together but nothing on the scale of the old days.

We have tempered this story to include only policies that are possible within the current structures. It is possible, under the MDA 1971 and other legislation, to give comprehensive drugs education that tells young people about the enjoyable and negative effects of drug use. It is possible to prescribe heroin to people who have become dependent on heroin,[2] and it is possible for the police to implement a non-arrest policy for low-level drug possession and dealing.

One reading of this meta narrative is that our own personal bias towards psychoactive drug use (as opposed to opiate drug use) is being used to illustrate how different drug using choices can impact future life chances, but that was not our intention. While there is a discussion to be had on whether involvement with psychoactive drugs instead of opiates does indeed impact life chances, the intention here is to present multiple potential outcomes to the master narrative, in order to show how policy could be implemented, with different results. What we can see with these three narratives (master, counter and meta) is that they all speak to different developments of policy, and in particular how policy has, or could be, enacted. In this way these stories provide evidence for the development of a critical drug theory, by highlighting the concepts underpinning drug policy, and how these concepts could be different if the underlying premises were challenged and changed.

Fictional meets real life

Yet we do not have to remain in a fictional space to see how progressive changes in drug policies can impact lives and societies as a whole. Portugal offers a real life example. In the 1980s, as it was coming out of 40 years of authoritarian rule, with limited outside influence and low levels of education, Portugal became the 'drug capital' of Europe. The rate of heroin overdose deaths was ever-increasing, together with drug-related crime and hepatitis C. The country's HIV rate became the highest in Europe. In this desperate climate, in 2000, Portugal decided to decriminalise the possession and consumption of all illicit substances, making public health rather than public order a priority. As in our narratives, individuals caught in possession of a personal supply of drugs are no longer arrested but given a warning, or a small fine and required to attend

---

2. In Scotland, section 19 of the Scotland Act 2012 devolves power to Scottish Ministers to issue prescription licences for heroin and cocaine.

drug counselling to address any problematic drug use. Distinctions between 'hard' and 'soft' drugs were abolished (Rego et al, 2021).

These policy changes resulted in the stabilisation of the country's opioid crisis, stark decreases in problematic drug use, overdose deaths, HIV and hepatitis C infection rates, as well as a reduction in levels of drug-related crime. During the past 20 years, the country's drug use prevalence stayed relatively low, compared to other European countries, many of which have much stricter criminal sanctions, such as the UK (EMCDDA, 2019). Hence the success of the Portuguese approach is in line with the many scientific studies showing that criminalisation is not an effective deterrent to drug use.

Yet despite its successes, the Portuguese drug policy approach has been criticised, for example in relation to its ambiguity and the growing diversity of drug use patterns in the country, as well as for its failure to remove the stigma associated with drug use (Rego et al, 2021), highlighting the need for further improvements to its legal framework.

Conclusion

As this chapter shows, the use of stories and narratives in policy can help highlight hidden harms and unintended outcomes of policy. Here we saw the impact the master narrative of drug harm has on the way Governments address 'problem' drug use, depending on whether they view it as a criminal justice matter or public health matter, or a mixture of both. The counter narrative—the hidden harm of policy—shows how the legislation, in particular the MDA 1971, can have devastating consequences on an individual's life, and create the very harm it is seeking to prevent. These fictional stories interweave with real life examples in places such as Portugal, where health intervention measures have been used instead of punitive criminal justice interventions, to great success. By combining both the harm narratives, and the pleasure (hidden) narratives driving drug use, we can start to develop a policy that reflects the different kinds of drug use in society, instead of the blanket prohibitive environment encouraged by outdated legislation such as the MDA 1971.

Dr Anna Ross is a lecturer in Health at the University of Edinburgh. She has occupied a range of drug policy advisory positions for the Scottish and UK Governments, is the co-founder of the Scottish Psychedelic Research Group, and Secretary to the Scottish Cross-party Group on Medicinal Cannabis.

Dr Anne Katrin Schlag is a Chartered Psychologist and Head of Research at Drug Science, where she leads the research for the Medical Cannabis Working Group, and the Medical Psychedelics Working Group. She holds Honorary Senior Fellowships at both Imperial College London and King's College London, and currently is Chair of the Cannabis Industry Council Research Group.

References and Extra Reading

Bruner, J (1992), The Narrative Construction of Reality, *Critical Inquiry*, 18(1): 1–21.

Daiute, C (2014), *Narrative Enquiry: A Dynamic Approach*, Thousand Oaks, CA: Sage.

European Monitoring Centre for Drugs and Drug Addiction (EMCDDA) (2019), Portugal — Country Drug Report 2019, Lisbon: EMCDDA.

Fischer, F (2003), *Reframing Public Policy: Discursive Politics and Deliberative Practices*, Oxford University Press.

MacGregor, S (2017), *The Politics of Drugs: Perceptions, Power and Policies*, Basinsgtoke: Palgrave MacMillan.

Minton, J, Shaw, R, Green, M, Vanderbloemen, L, Popham, F, McCartney, G (2017), Visualising and Quantifying 'Excess Deaths' in Scotland Compared with the Rest of the UK and the Rest of Western Europe, *Journal of Epidemiology and Community Health*, 71(5): 461–467.

Reissman, C K (1993), *Narrative Analysis*, London. Sage.

Roe, E M (1994), *Narrative Policy Analysis: Theory and Practice*, Duke University Press.

Ross, A (2020), Drug Users as Stakeholders in Drug Policy in J Buxton, L Burger and G Margo (eds), *The Impact of Global Drug Policy on Women: Shifting the Needle*.

Scottish Affairs Select Committee (2019), Problem Drug Use in Scotland.

Smith, K (2013), *Beyond Evidence-based Policy in Public Health: The Interplay of Ideas*, Palgrave Publishing.

Stone, D (2002), *Policy Paradox: The Art of Political Decision Making*, New York, London: W W Norton and Company.

Rego X, Oliveira M J, Lameira C, et al (2021), 20 Years of Portuguese Drug Policy: Developments, Challenges and the Quest for Human Rights, *Substance Abuse Treatment, Prevention, and Policy*, 16(1): 59.

PART II
IMPACT ON THE MEDICAL, PHARMACY AND VETERINARY PROFESSIONS

CHAPTER 7

Chronic Pain

Brigitta Brandner and Maximilian Dewhurst

This chapter focuses on chronic pain, drug harms, drug laws, UK and international drug policy, together with practical proposals for future directions.

Section 1: Chronic Pain and the Epidemic of Opioids

There is a substantial burden of chronic pain in the UK population and this is associated with a multitude of negative health and social outcomes including mental wellbeing, anxiety, physical function, and social and physical activities. Chronic pain affects between a third to a half of the UK population, corresponding to approximately under 28 million adults, based on data from the best available published studies. This figure is likely to increase further in line with an ageing population. In Western Europe, chronic pain prevalence is estimated at 1:5, with 10% to 30% of people reported to have significant chronic pain with profound effects on quality of life.

The International Association for the Study of Pain (IASP) defines chronic pain as pain that persists beyond normal tissue healing time and is taken to be pain that persists for more than three months. The treatment of chronic pain has been a challenge as there is a limited availability of effective drug treatment. Most cancer and non-cancer chronic pain is treated in the primary care setting. Pharmacological approaches are often overused due to lack of multidisciplinary/interdisciplinary approaches to pain management. Using pharmacological therapies is supposed to be a part of an integrated plan for rehabilitation and to improve function. However, medication has often become the main approach in treating pain leading to drug overuse and polypharmacy. Long-term opioid prescribing is increasing despite poor efficacy for non-cancer pain, its potential harm, and incompatibility with best practice. Questions of equality of care arise from higher prescription rates in the North of England and in areas of greater social deprivation. A national registry of patients with high opioid use would improve patient safety for this high-risk demographic, as well as providing more focused epidemiological data regarding patterns of prescribing.

Different analgesic drugs such as weak and strong opioids are often associated with the increased risk of dependency. All parts of the UK have seen a substantial increase in prescribing opioids over recent years although there is only limited data to support the use of opioids for longer than six months.

Opioid medication has limited efficacy in chronic pain with the risk of harm increasing substantially at dose above an oral morphine equivalent of 120mg per day as with the National Institute for Health and Care Excellence (NICE) guidelines (2007). It is found that a small proportion of patients obtain effective pain relief with doses above that. The main objective of opioid therapy should be balanced on the improvement in quality of life and effective functional recovery, against the increasing problem of iatrogenic dependency.

Section 2: The Role of Legislation for Controlled Drugs

There are strict legal requirements for medical management and prescribing of controlled drugs, including opioids and gabapentinoids. This is governed by two key sets of legislations, the MDA 1971, supporting regulations, and the Controlled Drugs (Supervision of Management and Use) Regulations 2013. The main purpose of the MDA 1971 is to prevent the misuse of controlled drugs by imposing restrictions on their possession, supply, manufacture, import and export. Department of Health regulations set out strengthened governance arrangements for controlled drugs used as medicines. Drugs controlled under the MDA 1971 are those that have the potential to be misused and they are classified according to their assessed harmfulness. Many controlled drugs are also essential to modern clinical care and their legitimate, clinical use is governed by the Misuse of Drugs Regulations 2001 (MDR 2001), which categorises them into five schedules based on their therapeutic usefulness and potential harms when misused;

1. Drugs not used medicinally such as hallucinogenic drugs (e.g. LSD), ecstasy-type substances, raw opium, and cannabis.[1] A Home Office licence is required for production, possession, or supply.

2. Includes opiates (e.g heroin, morphine, methadone, oxycodone). Full controlled drugs requirements relating to prescriptions, safe custody and the need to keep a controlled drug register.

3. Barbiturates, gabapentin, midazolam. Special prescription requirements; safe custody requirements.

4. Part I: drugs that are subject to minimal control (e.g. benzodiazepines, non-benzodiazepine hypnotics). Part II includes androgenic and anabolic steroids, clenbuterol, chorionic gonadotrophin (HCG), non-human chorionic gonadotrophin, somatotropin and somatropin. Schedule 4 controlled drug prescription requirements do not apply and are not subject to safe custody requirements; no requirement for records to be kept in a register.

5. Preparations of certain controlled drugs (e.g. codeine, oramorph). Exempt from virtually all controlled drug requirements other than retention of invoices for two years.

The Shipman Inquiry was an independent public inquiry set up in 2000 to examine the issues arising from the case of Dr Harold Shipman a general practitioner convicted of serial murder using drugs, who also took controlled drugs that he had falsely obtained. The inquiry's fourth report 'The Regulation of Controlled Drugs in the Community' was published in July 2004 and focused on the methods Shipman used to divert large quantities of controlled

---

1. From 2018 medicinal cannabis is in Schedule 2.

drugs for his own purposes, and considered how he was able to do it for so long without being detected. It concluded that there were serious shortcomings in the systems for regulating the governance of controlled drugs.

In response, the Controlled Drugs (Supervision of Management and Use) Regulations 2006 were introduced and came into force in England on 1 January 2007. These have now been superseded by the Controlled Drugs (Supervision of Management and Use) Regulations 2013, which came into force on 1 April 2013 to reflect changes in the NHS. The Shipman Inquiry aimed to improve safe prescribing and reduce controlled drug manipulation. This was achieved in a variety of ways:

- new governance arrangements — such as requiring health organizations to appoint staff to monitor safe use and management of controlled drugs;

- restrictions on prescribing controlled drugs — placing clear professional requirements for prescribing controlled drugs;

- strengthening the audit trail aiming to capture and analyse information around prescribing controlled drugs, particularly in the private sector.

These changes have improved earlier detection of abuse of controlled drugs and over-prescribing of them. It has reduced the ability of diverting large quantities of controlled drugs, due to tighter rules and regulations.

Section 3: Drugs Used in Practice

The common opioid drugs used in chronic pain in a clinical setting that fall under the MDA 1971 are described in this section. The 1971 Act sets out four separate categories for drug classification: Class A, Class B, Class C and temporary class drugs (TCDs), with Class A drugs being the most regulated and controlled. Substances may be removed and added to different parts of the schedule by statutory instrument.

Commonly used opioid drugs, other analgesics and medications in clinical practice that fall under the MDA 1971 include:

- Class A: Diamorphine, morphine, pethidine, oxycodone, fentanyl, methadone.

- Class B: Tramadol, codeine, buprenorphine,

- Class C: Benzodiazepines.

- Unlicensed drugs: Cannabis, psilocybin, nitrous oxide.

All other drugs and supplements except alcohol, caffeine and tobacco are controlled under the Psychoactive Substances Act 2016 (PSA 2016). As outlined above, the MDR 2001 divide drugs into five schedules, each specifying the requirements governing supply and possession.

Opioids have been used for medical purposes for thousands of years throughout the world. Their benefits towards treatment of acute pain, chronic pain and cancer pain have been well-documented and researched for many years; however, the general public and the medical community are becoming more aware of the negative consequences of opioids including addiction, abuse and misuse. The 'Prophet of Opium', Thomas De Quincey, first took opium for pain when he was a student at Oxford. In 1822, his account, *The Confessions of an English Opium Eater*, captured in a popular form the excitement and esoterica of opium use with the result that he was often criticised for making the drug seem desirable to the uninitiated.

Samuel Taylor Coleridge similarly took opium for pain while a student at Cambridge, then later for relief from grief and even later in life for decaying teeth. One might speculate on the quantity of opiates consumed for dental complaints in the 19th century or for the commonplace results of poor sanitation, such as diarrhoea, or for cough suppression in the century of tuberculosis.

Opioids are produced from the poppy plant *papaver somniferum*. In 1973, it was found that opioids work by acting on opioid receptors. There are three main opioid receptor types in the body: Mu, Delta and Kappa. These are present throughout the nervous system. Exogenous opioids bind to these receptors in varying affinities and degrees. This difference in binding is what allows for the difference in side-effects experienced by using different opioids. Activation of these receptors leads to a cascade of effects resulting in the prevention of neurotransmitter release in order to aid in the reduction of pain. Opioids were found to play a central role in nociception (the process by which noxious stimulation is communicated through the peripheral and central nervous system). Endogenous opioids aid in modulating the experience of pain.

Opioids use in palliative pain and acute pain is well-documented and studied, but recently controversy has occurred surrounding the use of opioids in a chronic pain setting. The use of strong opioids for chronic non-cancer pain has few well-conducted clinical trials in determining the long-term effects of opioids. The main aim of opioid treatment should be to improve the patient's quality of life and ability to optimise their functions by reducing pain. These factors need to be considered and monitored if opioids are prescribed for management of chronic pain in the long-term. Safe management and monitoring of side-effects and risks should be a key component of long-term opioids prescription. The partnership between prescriber and patient should be considered with a clear treatment plan developed and agreed between the team. Factors such as previous alcohol abuse or an addictive history should be considered as primary risk factors for development of problematic opioid drug misuse.

Opioids can be prescribed and given in a variety of forms:

- orally: long-term opioids wherever possible should generally be aimed to be given in oral form, however there are marked differences in the bioavailability for oral opioids;

- rectal route: if the oral route is unavailable the rectal route can be considered, however the absorption can be slow and bioavailability can be low due to first pass metabolism;

- transdermal route: lipophilic opioids (fentanyl, buprenorphine) are suited for delivery through the transdermal route. The absorption is slow, taking up to 24 hours. This route is becoming more common for long-term opioid use in chronic pain;

- parenteral opioids: the subcutaneous route is becoming increasingly popular in treatment of chronic pain. Intramuscular injection is often too painful, and the intravenous use has increased side-effects and generally requires monitoring in a clinical setting to avoid respiratory depression.

Most common side-effects are predictable consequences of opioid pharmacological actions and include nausea, vomiting, constipation, pruritus, dizziness, dry mouth, and sedation.

- Respiratory depression is a much-feared harm associated with the use of opioids. It is mostly a concern in acute pain management where patients have not developed tolerance. For persistent pain it is most likely to be a potential problem if there has been a large, often unintended dose increase, or changes in formulation or route of administration.

- Opioids can cause irregular respiratory pauses and gasping may lead to erratic breathing and significant variability in respiratory rate. The respiratory effects of opioids are more pronounced during sleep. Fatalities have been reported in patients with obstructive sleep apnoea who are prescribed opioids and sleep apnoea may be a relative contraindication to opioid therapy. This is particularly important if patients are taking other central respiratory depressants such as benzodiazepines. If opioids are prescribed to patients with obstructive sleep apnoea, they will need up to date assessment of nocturnal respiratory function and should be compliant with therapy for this, for example continuous positive airway pressure. Patients with sleep apnoea being prescribed opioids will need regular and detailed assessment of treatment.

- There is little evidence that, in equi-analgesic doses, commonly used opioids differ markedly in the incidence of their side-effects.

- Patients using intermittent opioid dosing regimens might not become tolerant to side-effects.

- Increased absorption may occur from transdermal opioid formulations with a fever or other intercurrent illness, and if the patient is exposed to external heat, for example a hot bath or sauna. If concerns arise, closer patient monitoring will be required.

- Inadequate management of side-effects (intractable constipation, faecal impaction, bowel obstruction) and consequences of opioid treatment (falls, fractures and acute confusional state) may contribute to unplanned hospital admissions and the overall costs associated with opioid treatment.

- Patients can also develop acute opioid tolerance with opioid induced hyperalgesia. This can develop in a short time particularly with short acting opioids such as remifentanil. This is explained with pronociceptive mechanisms in the central nervous system such as glial activation, glutaminergic activation of the NMDA receptors. These mechanisms can reduce the pain threshold and lead to hyperalgesia. This is a situation where reducing the opioids can improve analgesia and pain management.

Opioid medications

The following two sub-headings describe 'strong' and 'weak' opioids prescribed in a clinical setting for pain management.

Strong opioids

Morphine
Morphine is one of the most well-known opioids used in a clinical setting. It is a strong opioid receptor agonist, and it is the gold standard to which other opioids are compared.

- The half-life is — 2 hours.

- Analgesic effects — 4 hours.

Morphine has a wide range of formulations for administration, such as oral, subcutaneous, intravenous or suppositories. In the UK, morphine is often the first line opioid to use, although it has addiction potential side-effects such as dysphoria and nightmares which have limited its use. There are however reports that the practice of discharging patients after surgery with strong opioids has led to an increased and prolonged unnecessary use of opioids.

Diamorphine
Diamorphine, more commonly known as heroin, is only used in a small number of countries in a medical setting. Its usage has significantly reduced in the UK due to supply issues, and its increased use as an abusive drug. However, the pharmacodynamics of diamorphine give excellent pain relief particularly for its epidural use.

Fentanyl
Fentanyl is a highly potent opioid receptor agonist; it has a higher potency than morphine. It is commonly given in patches due its high first pass metabolism leaving little medication to be absorbed orally. Fentanyl is becoming more common as a drug of abuse and due to its higher potency than morphine and diamorphine; it has led to an increase in accidental drug overdoses and effects in the generally community.

Oxycodone
Oxycodone is a semi-synthetic opioid with an agonist activity on mu, kappa and delta receptors. Equivalence to morphine is 1:2. Oxycodone is well tolerated and causes less central side-effects than morphine such as nightmares. This plays a part in the onset of dependence and tolerance and the intensity of these side-effects tends to decrease over the course of time. Oxycodone has contributed to a sharp increase in opioid over-use in the US and UK.

Pethidine
Pethidine is a synthetic opioid of the phenylpiperidine class. It has been widely used with a short onset of action. This led it to be mainly used in trauma, and labour. It also was thought to be advantageous in pancreatitis as it has less action on the sphincter of oddi. Additionally, in sickle cell anaemias it was deemed to

be safer than morphine. However, the nature of the short onset and offset of the drug led to some patients with 'pseudo-addiction' (see Section 4 below) as the action of the drug did not cover severe prolonged pain. High doses of pethidine can cause seizures. Now pethidine is almost never used in practice in the UK.

Methadone
Methadone is used in addiction dependency medicine as a substitute for opioids such as heroin. It can be used as an adjunct in chronic pain medicine particularly in patients with high opioid use, due to its NMDA receptor antagonist action.

Weak opioids

Codeine
Codeine is a weak opioid receptor agonist and is part of step two of the World Health Organization (WHO) pain ladder, it has around 10% of morphine analgesic effect. Codeine has a higher incidence of nausea and constipation than other opioids therefore it is often used in conjunction with other analgesics, such as paracetamol. Globally, codeine is the most used opiate, and its dependency can lead to serious morbidity therefore it is important to identify codeine dependency early for effective treatment.

Buprenorphine
Buprenorphine is a partial agonist and therefore thought to cause less addiction, so that it is used in addiction medicine but also as a pain patch in patients with chronic pain.

Tramadol
Tramadol has a complex mechanism of action and works on the serotonergic/adrenergic reuptake inhibition and opioid activity. It is used in cancer pain and neuropathic pain. In high doses, seizures can occur and its dose is limited to 400mg per kg.

Section 4: The Burden of Opioid Prescribing in Chronic Pain: Does Addiction in Chronic Pain Patients Really Exist?

In addition to numbing pain, opioid-based prescription medications can also cause the user to experience a sense of relaxed euphoria. This pleasurable sensation, combined with the addictive nature of opioid medication can lead to a cycle of continued abuse and addiction. In this context, it is helpful to understand the definitions to prevent misconceptions and mis-labelling of patients. It is a common habit to talk of addiction when it is a normal physiological consequence of the use of long-term opioids. This may lead to an unhelpful and potentially harmful doctor-patient relationship.

There is broad consensus concerning the following definitions:

- tolerance: a predictable physiological decrease in the effect of the drug over time so that a progressive increase is required;

- physical dependence: a physiological adaptation to a drug whereby abrupt discontinuation or reversal of that drug, or a sudden reduction in the dose, leads to a withdrawal syndrome;

- addiction: a disease that is characterised by aberrant drug-seeking behaviour and maladaptive drug-taking behaviours that may include cravings, compulsive drug use and loss of control over drug use, despite the risk of physical, social and psychological harm. Unlike tolerance and physical dependence, addiction is not a predictable effect of the drug;

- pseudo-addiction: behaviours that may seem inappropriately drug-seeking but are the result of under treatment and resolve when pain relief is adequate.

Section 5: When Does Opioid Prescribing in Chronic Pain Become a Problem?

The MDA 1971 represents legislative action by the UK Parliament in line with treaty commitments under the Single Convention on Narcotic Drugs, the Convention on Psychotropic Substances, and the UN Convention Against Illicit Traffic in Narcotic Drugs and Psychotropic Substances. Offences under the 1971 Act include:

- possession of a controlled drug unlawfully;

- possession of a controlled drug with intent to supply it;

- supplying or offering to supply a controlled drug (even where no charge is made for the drug);

- allowing premises a person occupies or manages to be used unlawfully for the purpose of producing or supplying controlled drugs.

In this context, it is important to understand the legalities within prescribing for chronic pain patients and red flags have to be identified early, with examples of opioid prescribing problems given below.

Example 1: Diversion
On the palliative care ward an 84-year-old patient was admitted in order to optimise her pain medication. Her MST (morphine sulphate) prescription is 120mg BD and with breakthrough medication of morphine 30–40mg four hourly. Her relatives were reporting that she was still in severe pain and not coping at home. After she received the first dose of MST, her respiratory rate dropped to two and she had to be reversed with naloxone. This then raised the suspicion that the drugs were diverted by the relatives.

Example 2: Prescribing safely
A 57-year-old patient with severe back pain claims that he has been prescribed fentanyl patches by his GP with morphine for breakthrough pain. This however

cannot be confirmed as the patient was not registered with a GP. The patient also states that he has originally been treated in the US and had received oxycodone 80mg BD whilst there. This also could not be confirmed as there were no available medical records. This can be a dangerous situation as the exact drug and dose are difficult to determine therefore leading to unwanted side-effects. It is strongly recommended to have only one prescriber for opioids with an agreed treatment plan.

Example 3: Using opioids despite ill effects

A 61-year-old patient with severe Crohn's disease has been on high dose opioids for many years. Despite numerous attempts to curtail and reduce the dose it has failed despite the patient suffering from hypoaldosteronism and impotence most likely due to the side-effects of medication. Chronic opioid use can cause hypogonadism, but its frequency, as well as the effects of opioids on other hypothalamic-pituitary-end organ hormonal axes remains unclear (de Vries et al, 2020). The prescribing physician needs to be aware that at any stage the patient may develop a dependency on medication and regular follow-ups are necessary to evaluate the risk versus benefits. The reduction and discontinuation of opioids should be questioned at each visit.

Example 4: Opioid dependency versus greater need for pain relief

A 28-year-old man with chronic back pain is having increasing flare-ups of acute back pain. He was started on codeine initially for management in the community and has now been up titrated (his dose gradually increased) to morphine. The patient has increasing episodes of accessing healthcare via A & E or general practice, requesting further opioids due to severe acute back pain. The question arises does this patient have undertreated and poorly managed pain or has he now developed an iatrogenic opioid dependency. This is a difficult question to answer as it is challenging to separate these two conditions. This may require careful monitoring with a skilled, specialist clinician. The prolonged use of opioids without strict monitoring has potentially led to opioid dependency as opioids are not a long-term strategy for management of chronic pain as per NICE guidelines.

Example 5: Schedule 5 prescription only medication

This example comes from a coroner investigation showing that a patient passed away due to an unintentional overdose of oramorph prescribed for chronic pain due to taking a 'swig out of the bottle' unaware of the possible consequences of exceeding the correct dose. The prescriber, on questioning, was unable to recall advising how to correctly take the medication. Oramorph is classified under Schedule 5 (i.e. 0.2% strength). This highlights the danger on classifying opioid drugs depending on their strength, rather than the total amount of medication prescribed. The liquid form of morphine may give the impression that the medication is less harmful.

Section 6: Is there Room for Improvement in the MDA 1971 in the Context of Pain Management?

The MDA 1971 (and the subsequent regulations put in place) has led to a more safe approach to opioid prescribing. The Shipman Inquiry and the overuse of prescription opioids has led to more stringency in the way that controlled drugs have to be prescribed, administered, and audited. Fundamentally, this has led to a safer and more rigorous approach to the prescribing and management of controlled medication for chronic pain. It can be argued that the increasing regulations have caused a reduction in the prescription of controlled medication for chronic pain potentially leading to undertreated pain. However, this needs to be balanced against the safer prescribing and management of controlled drugs in the wider social setting and the detrimental effects of opioids on the individual and society in the long-term.

The MDA 1971 provides safety for prescribers. The focus now has moved to effectively managing these patients using a focused multidisciplinary approach, utilising pain specialists, community workers and the patients themselves. The reduction of inappropriate opioid prescription in the community and acute hospital setting for chronic pain places emphasis on the focus of multidisciplinary teams to both achieve management of chronic pain and reduce misuse of controlled drugs. The treatment of chronic pain creates an ethical dilemma between relieving pain (benevolence), being stated as a human right, versus non-maleficence (the principle 'do no harm'). Pain as such is seen as a subjective measure and the treatment of it is still an enormous challenge with limited effective treatments available. This has led to an excessive use of medication that not only causes harm to the individual but also places a heavy burden on society.

Since the 1980s doctrine of 'pain free' hospitals the pendulum has swung to a liberal use of opioids. However, with the increase in iatrogenic addiction, healthcare professionals have started a much more restrictive reaction and the pendulum is now swinging back. But this challenges the clinician as to how best to fulfil the need for adequate pain relief. The quest for new ways of looking at new drugs is on. Cannabis and psilocybin, for example, might offer some new alternatives, especially in chronic pain management. The balance is between efficacy and harm in the long-term.

In Summary

Opioids are effective analgesics for acute pain and for pain at the end of life but there is little evidence that they are helpful for long-term chronic pain. A small proportion of people may obtain good pain relief with opioids in the long-term if the dose can be kept low and especially if the use of opioids is intermittent, however it is difficult to identify these people at the point of opioid initiation. If a patient has pain that remains severe despite opioid treatment it means opiods are not working and should be stopped, even if no other treatment is available. Chronic pain is very complex and if patients have refractory and disabling symptoms, particularly if they are on high opioid doses, a very detailed assessment of the many emotional and other, for example social, psychological, etc. influences on their pain experience is essential.

The MDA 1971 has led to safer prescribing for medical practitioners in the context of pain management and to more appropriate treatment for chronic pain. It has become clear that the overuse of opioids for chronic pain due to inappropriate prescribing and lack of regulation has led to harm. However due to the strict regulation of restricted drugs under the MDA 1971 it has been more difficult to undergo clinical trials to explore effective pain treatment, especially concerning drugs such as psilocybin and cannabis.

Dr Brigitta Brandner FRCA, FFPMRCA, MD is Consultant Anaesthetist at University College London and Modular Lead for the MSc in pain management. She is also the Research Lead in Acute Pain with a focus on opioids and ketamine in pain and addiction; and a NICE guidance committee member for sickle cell pain, neuropathic pain, and medical cannabis.

Dr Maximilian J Dewhurst, MB, ChB is a Senior House Officer at Barnet Hospital, Royal Free London NHS Foundation Trust.

References and Extra Reading

NICE Guidelines (2007) (January), Medicines Optimisation in Chronic Pain, Key Therapeutic Topic (KTT21).

American Academy of Pain Medicine, the American Pain Society and the American Society of Addition Medicine (2001), Definitions Related to the Use of Opioids for the Treatment of Pain, *Wisconsin Medical Journal,* 100(5): 28–9.

Breivik, H et al (2006), May Survey of Chronic Pain in Europe: Prevalence, Impact on Daily Life, and Treatment, *European Journal of Pain,* 10(4): 287–333.

Bridges, S (2011), Health Survey England 2011, Vol 1, Ch 9, Chronic Pain.

Bromley, L and Brandner, B (2010), *Acute Pain,* Oxford: Oxford University Press.

Busse, J W et al (2018), Opioids for Chronic Non-cancer Pain: A Systematic Review and Meta-analysis, *Journal of the American Medical Association,* 18 (December), 320(23): 2448–2460.

Chou, R et al (2015), The Effectiveness and Risks of Long-Term Opioids Therapy for Chronic Pain: A Systematic Review for a National Institutes of Health Pathways to Prevention Workshop, Ann Intern Med, 162(4) (February): 276–286.

de Quincey, T (1821), Confessions of an English Opium-Eater, *London Magazine.*

de Vries, F, Bruin, M, Lobatto, D J, Dekkers, O M, Schoones, J W, van Furth, W R, Pereira, A M, Karavitaki, N, Biermasz, N R and Zamanipoor Najafabadi, A H (2020), Opioids and Their Endocrine Effects: A Systematic Review and Meta-analysis, *Journal of Clinical Endocrinology & Metabolism,* 105, 4 (June): 1020–1029.

Faculty of Pain Medicine (2021), Controlled Drugs and the Law: www.fpm.ac.uk/opioids-aware-best-professional-practice/controlled-drugs-and-law (accessed October 9, 2021).

Fayaz, A et al (2016), Prevalence of Chronic Pain in the UK: A Systematic Review and Meta-analysis of Population Studies, *British Medical Journal* Open, 201 (June), 6(6):e010364; PMID: 27324708.

Harrop-Griffiths, W, Griffiths, R and Plaat, F (2015), AAGBI Core Topics in Anaesthesia in *Acute Pain Management of Opioid-Tolerant Patients,* M Jackson (2015), AAGBI: 28–38.

HM Government (2007) (February), Learning From Tragedy, Keeping Patients Safe, Overview of the Government's Action Programme in Response to the Recommendations of the Shipman Inquiry, London: The Stationery Office.

Jani, M et al (2020), Time Trends and Prescribing Patterns of Opioid Drugs in UK Primary Care Patients With Non-cancer Pain: A Retrospective Cohort Study, PLOS Med, 15, 17(10): e1003270.

Katz, N et al (2009), The Impact of Opioids on the Endocrine System, *Clinical Journal of Pain,* 25 (February): 170–175.

Marvizon, J C, Ma, Y-Y, Charles, A C, Walwyn, W and Evans, C J (2010), Pharmacology of the Opioid System in *Pharmacology of Pain*, P Beaulieu, D Lussier, F H Porreca and A Dickenson, IASP (International Association for the Study of Pain) Press: 87–110.

Mordecai, L, et al (2018), Patterns of Regional Variation of Opioid Prescribing in Primary Care in England: A Retrospective Observational Study, *British Journal of General Practice,* 68(668) (March): e225-e233.

Nielsen, S, MacDonald, T and Johnson, J L (2018), Identifying and Treating Codeine Dependence: A Systemic Review (June), *Medical Image Analysis:* 208(10).

Simonnet, G and Le Moal, M (2010), Vulnerability to Opioid Tolerance, Dependence, and Addiction: An Individual-Centered Versus Drug-Centered Paradigm Analysis in *Pharmacology of Pain,* P Beaulieu, D Lussier, F H Porreca and A Dickenson, IASP Press: 405–430.

Yu, E H et al (2016), Remifentanil Tolerance and Hyperanalgesia: Short-term Gain, Long-term Pain? *Anaesthesia,* 71(11) (November): 1347–1362.

CHAPTER 8

The Impact of the MDA 1971 on the Veterinary Profession

Polly Taylor

Clinical veterinary treatments have similarities to medical and surgical procedures in human beings and there are numerous drugs employed by both professions. Many of the drugs controlled under the MDA 1971 are therapeutic. It is this attribute that concerns the veterinary profession; harms such as addiction resulting from self administration are not a feature of sub-human animals. However, the MDA 1971 in its entirety still applies to veterinary use. This chapter explains how drugs controlled under the 1971 Act are used in animals and illustrates how, by default, it inevitably affects the veterinary profession. The main impact is from the regulations concerning purchase, handling, prescription and storage of those controlled drugs (CDs) that apply in the medical world and are equally enforced for veterinary use.

Restrictions on access to and use of therapeutic CDs has affected the medical and veterinary professions alike in their ability to provide necessary clinical treatment. This is particularly pertinent to animal welfare as many of the respective drugs are anaesthetics and analgesics. This is particularly apparent in low- and middle-income countries where finance and bureaucracy may restrict access even to essential painkilling drugs (Vijayan, 2011). Equally, although the 'opioid crisis' applies to humans, the backlash from adverse publicity for these drugs restricts their use in animals for *bone fide* clinical treatment just as much as this effect is a concern for medical use where prescribing barriers may adversely affect patients with a legitimate need for pain relief (www.aafp.org/family-physician/patient-care/care-resources/pain-management.html).

Although unrelated to the MDA 1971, it is important to note that further restrictions are imposed on the drugs a veterinarian may prescribe. Veterinary medicines require marketing authorisation (MA) from the Veterinary Medicines Directorate (VMD) to be sold and supplied in the UK. Numerous recognised veterinary treatments do not hold MA, largely because there is no financial incentive to obtain MA for products with limited indication, particularly in less common species. To enable clinical treatment in such cases, the 'prescribing Cascade' (under the Veterinary Medicines Regulations, administered by the VMD) allows prescription of medicines that would not otherwise be allowed. If there is no suitable veterinary medicine authorised in the UK to treat a condition, to avoid causing unacceptable suffering the Cascade permits treatment of the animal concerned in the following order: (1) a medicine authorised in the UK for human use; (2) a medicine authorised in another European country for use in any animal species (food animals may only be treated with drugs licensed for use in any food animal); or (3) a medicine prepared especially for the case in question. The CDs commonly used in veterinary medicine are set out in Table 1 at the end of this chapter.

Background

Most of the indications for using CDs in animals are akin to their medical use and, depending on their pharmacological effects, they are used for sedation, anaesthesia, analgesia or all of these. However, some indications for CD use are unique to animals. Anaesthesia is often required simply for restraint, or even as a means of capture of wild, unhandled individuals. Hence there may be a greater need for anaesthesia in animals than in people, simply to enable both painful and non-painful procedures to be carried out.

Most general anaesthesia for surgical and diagnostic procedures in companion animals (primarily dogs, cats and horses) is now carried out in veterinary clinics or hospitals where storage and access to CDs are similar to those in a medical hospital. However, veterinary treatment requiring CDs may also be required far from the clinic and in less-than-ideal conditions such as on a farm, at equine sporting venues and at road traffic accidents. When used to capture wild exotic species CDs are needed 'in the bush' often many miles from civilisation across inhospitable terrain. In these circumstances strict adherence to regulations for possession and storage is difficult. It is also of note that the doses of each drug may be many times that producing an equivalent effect in people: a domestic horse of 500 kilogram requires at least one gram of ketamine to induce anaesthesia; a 3,000 kilogram African elephant would require some ten mg etorphine, an opioid with more than 1,000 times the potency of morphine.

Pain relief is a fundamental service provided by the veterinary profession. In becoming a member of the Royal College of Veterinary Surgeons, in order to practice in the UK each veterinarian swears that:

> 'I promise and solemnly declare.........and, above all, my constant endeavour will be to ensure the health and welfare of animals committed to my care.'

The therapeutic CDs used to treat animals are primarily analgesics and anaesthetics and are therefore of supreme importance to the profession. Their use is not related to specific disease or animal type and therefore may be needed in a wide range of conditions and species. The veterinary profession is also privileged to be able to apply euthanasia to prevent unnecessary suffering in any animal. Many of the drugs used for this process are controlled under the MDA.

Therapeutic CDs Used in Veterinary Medicine

Opioids
Most of the opioids used in clinical veterinary practice are CDs. The opioids have two distinct roles in veterinary use. Clearly they are used as analgesics but they are also widely used to enhance sedation, resulting in profound 'chemical restraint'; large animals generally remain standing, avoiding some of the problems which may be associated with lying down (Figure 1). For analgesia, opioids are used in premedication for perioperative analgesia before surgery and in repeated doses after anaesthesia to provide post-operative pain relief. They are also used in treating trauma pain and during otherwise painful interventional

procedures in conscious animals. For sedation and chemical restraint, the opioids are used in conjunction with one or more of a number of sedatives, most commonly an alpha2 adrenoceptor agonist (alpha2) or acepromazine where the sedation produced is markedly enhanced over the original effect of the sedative alone.

Morphine has been used for many years in a wide range of species, both for analgesia and for chemical restraint. Although often still regarded as the gold standard, it carries no MA for any animal species. However, morphine is still often regarded as the best for perioperative analgesia and standing sedation in horses (Clutton, 2010). Methadone has been used in companion animals for many years, particularly in continental Europe, for both analgesia and enhanced sedation. Methadone has relatively recently gained its UK MA for perioperative analgesia in dogs and cats. It is also commonly combined with alpha2s for premedication and to produce profound sedation. Fentanyl, and less frequently alfentanil, sufentanil and remifentanil, are given by infusion to provide antinociception and decrease anaesthetic requirements during general anesthesia in dogs, for whom fentanyl has recently gained UK MA. Fentanyl is also quite commonly used during general anaesthesia in pigs undergoing surgery for research purposes under the Animals (Scientific Procedures) Act 1986.

Fentanyl is commonly administered for longer duration pain relief by transdermal patch. The variable rates of absorption in different species have been well documented, particularly in horses and cats (Figure 2). A transdermal fentanyl solution for dogs was available recently, but withdrawn a few years after its launch due to technical difficulties experienced with the precise method of administration. Human misuse was not implicated.

Combinations of fentanyl with neuroleptic sedative agents have been variously available commercially as a fixed ratio injection for chemical restraint, particularly in rabbits (Figure 3). Pethidine was used for many years in horses to treat abdominal pain 'colic' but has now largely been superseded for this indication by butorphanol, a non-CD kappa-agonist opioid, and the alpha2s.

Buprenorphine, a mu opioid receptor partial agonist (mixed agonist-antagonist) opioid was originally developed for managing pain, then opiate addiction, in humans. However it is now probably the most commonly used opioid in small animal veterinary care for routine surgery and interventional procedures, particularly neutering of dogs and cats (Capner et al, 1999). Although believed to be a less effective analgesic than the full mu-agonist opiates such as morphine it is longer acting and for less complex surgery provides ideal premedication and post-operative analgesia, particularly in cats (Steagall et al, 2014).

A number of other opioids such as hydromorphone are employed for instance in the US but are not available for clinical use in the UK. The remaining Schedule 2 opioids used on a regular basis in animals are the highly potent etorphine, thiafentanil and carfentanil. These are used either alone or more commonly combined with a sedative to anaesthetise large wild exotic ungulates where high potency is essential in order for the appropriate dose to be contained in a small volume which can be administered from a substantial distance by dart injection (Figure 4).

Codeine is used for pain relief and occasionally diarrhoea control in a manner similar to that for humans. The only codeine product with veterinary MA is a paracetamol and codeine combination licensed for dogs.

Ketamine

Ketamine has a role to play in almost every aspect of veterinary care. It was first synthesised at Parke Davis Laboratories (US) in 1962 then developed as an alternative to phencyclidine, a short acting injectable anaesthetic used in both animals and humans. Ketamine produced fewer side-effects, had a shorter duration of action and retained the benefits of limited cardio-respiratory depression in contrast with the available anaesthetics of the time.

Ketamine has been in use for veterinary anaesthesia since the 1970s and is now probably the most widely used veterinary anaesthetic. This is most likely a result of its remarkable safety, as it does not depress respiration and cardiac function which is a feature of all other general anaesthetics. Further characteristics which underlie ketamine's widespread use include excellent analgesic properties, wide therapeutic window (the difference between a lethal dose and an effective dose) and its ability to be administered by virtually any route. In the UK ketamine was a prescription only medicine (POM), not a CD, until 2006 when it was labelled a Class C Drug; in 2015 it was placed in Schedule 2.

Ketamine is now the anaesthetic induction agent of choice in horses (Wohlfender et al, 2015). Used after suitable premedication with alpha2s and benzodiazepines it produces a smooth transition into lateral recumbency and a duration of anaesthesia sufficient for a short procedure or a smooth transition to inhalation maintenance (Figure 5). The relative lack of cardiorespiratory depression is of considerable benefit in this species whose circulation is markedly depressed by volatile anaesthetics used for maintenance. It is well-known that anaesthesia in horses carries a much higher risk of death or serious complication than in people or small animals and some of this relates to devastating injury occurring during induction or particularly during recovery to standing up. Although ketamine induction does not guarantee a smooth recovery after a period of volatile anaesthetic maintenance, it does not produce prolonged hangover leading to excessive ataxia.

Ketamine's safety profile as an anaesthetic leads to its extensive use where technical support is limited, such as mass neutering programmes to control feral cat and dog populations (Figure 6). It is also of considerable value for all settings outwith controlled hospital conditions. Ketamine is used for anaesthesia and analgesia in natural disasters, sporting injuries and road traffic accidents. It is often the only anaesthetic available for all types of surgery in low- and middle-income countries. The World Small Animal Veterinary Association collected data worldwide in 2015 when there was threat of ketamine becoming unavailable due to global restrictions on use and supply. This demonstrated that ketamine was the only anaesthetic used in thousands of dogs and cats throughout the world; not dissimilar to its use for humans in low- and middle-income countries with limited hospital facilities.

Ketamine is effective by almost any route of administration. This is of considerable value in a veterinary setting where very small animals may have inaccessible veins or their co-operation for intravenous injection is unlikely. Effect by intramuscular injection makes ketamine indispensable for capturing wild exotics via dart injection. Ketamine is considerably less risky for both patient and handler than the potent opioids and is the best option for many species if the dose can be contained in an appropriately sized syringe for dart administration. Ketamine is even absorbed through mucous membranes and can be squirted into the mouth of a hissing cat to enable its capture and safe handling (Figure 7).

Ketamine's wide therapeutic index is of considerable value in the context of its use in the field. Bodyweight must be estimated for animals that cannot be caught which may lead to considerable error in dose. Failed anaesthesia is to be avoided as the animal may not become fully anaesthetised, not be caught and be left vulnerable to predators. Hence overdose is the preferred option which ketamine's high therapeutic index makes an acceptable option.

Ketamine also has a considerable role in pain management. Infusions given during anaesthesia and surgery can act pre-emptively and improve post-operative pain control. Ketamine infusions are also used after surgery or trauma to control pain in a range of conditions in several animal species (Wagner et al, 2002).

The general public still has a misconception of ketamine to the detriment of both veterinary and medical use. It is a remarkably safe drug with numerous beneficial indications, huge global benefit, comparably small cost and is essential for veterinary (and medical) care.

Benzodiazepines

The benzodiazepines have been used in veterinary medicine for many years. Diazepam has fairly recently received MA in the UK for dogs and midazolam for horses. The benzodiazepines are relatively benign in terms of their cardiorespiratory effects and are primarily used in conjunction with other sedatives and anaesthetics to promote sedation and so reduce the requirement for the more cardio depressant drugs. The benzodiazepines are also effective muscle relaxants and often used with ketamine to counteract the increased muscle tone that may be seen when ketamine is used alone. Although diazepam and midazolam are the most commonly used benzodiazepines in veterinary work, zolazepam is also used for anaesthesia in a fixed combination with tiletamine, a ketamine-like anaesthetic. This fixed combination (not CD) is potent and commonly used for wild and zoo animals, administered by dart.

Benzodiazepines are not used alone in conscious adult horses as they produce undesirable ataxia with little sedation. However, induction of anaesthesia in horses using ketamine is almost universally carried out with either diazepam or midazolam given intravenously at the same time as the ketamine injection in order to produce a slow and gentle descent from standing into recumbency (Figure 1). Benzodiazepines are used alone in very young foals where ideal anxiolysis and sedation allows a range of non-painful procedures such as imaging to be carried out without either stressing the neonate or causing cardiorespiratory depression (Figure 8).

In many species, particularly dogs and cats, alpha2s are commonly given with ketamine to improve muscle relaxation during anaesthesia for surgery. The alpha2s are cardio depressant at the required doses and using a benzodiazepine to replace part of the alpha2 dose retains the relaxant effect but makes the process safer by reducing the quantity of alpha2 administered. In sick animals the combination of benzodiazepines and opioids often provides sufficient sedation to enable at least diagnostic procedures to be carried out without producing the cardiorespiratory depression that is likely with alpha2 combinations. In healthy adult animals of most species, benzodiazepines alone produce very limited sedation; indeed, in dogs bizarre behaviour, sometimes with ataxia, may occur. In such animals the benzodiazepines are only useful in combination with other sedatives. Diazepam may be given to cats to stimulate appetite. In neonates of most species however, both diazepam and midazolam produce excellent sedation without life threatening cardiopulmonary depression.

Benzodiazepines, particularly midazolam, have been used for many years for surgery or other interventions in small laboratory animals in combinations with ketamine, opioids, alpha2s and volatile anaesthetics. As with other species, except in neonates, the benzodiazepines do not produce obvious sedation when used alone; their merit is in enhancing sedation from reduced doses of other sedatives.

Barbiturates
Pentobarbital (pentobarbitone) is now very rarely used for anaesthesia as shorter acting intravenous agents have been available for many years. Hence it is now used primarily as a concentrated solution for euthanasia of multiple animal species. The volume required for larger species is difficult to handle, and a solution containing secobarbital sodium (quinalbarbitone sodium) and cinchocaine hydrochloride is available with MA for euthanasia of horses and cattle as well as dogs and cats.

Phenobarbital (phenobarbitone) is used for oral treatment of epilepsy in dogs and has MA for both tablets and a solution for administration of oral drops.

Tramadol
Tramadol has recently gained popularity for treatment of pain in animals, particularly chronic pain in dogs in cases where non-steroidal anti-inflammatory drugs (NSAIDs) are unsuitable for any reason (https://willows.uk.net/specialist-services/pet-health-information/anaesthesia/treating-pain-in-your-pet/).

Tramadol's value as an analgesic is somewhat controversial as it is well recognised that it has variable efficacy in certain breeds of dogs and perhaps even individuals. Tramadol requires metabolism to O-desmethyl tramadol (M1) for at least some of its analgesic action; the reported variable efficacy may relate to individual differences in production of the M1 metabolite (Schutter et al, 2017). In spite of the variable activity both tramadol injection and tablets have MA for use in dogs for acute and chronic mild soft tissue and musculoskeletal pain.

Cannabis

A number of cannabinoids have been evaluated in dogs for alleviation of chronic arthritic pain, most containing cannabidiol (CBD) only, but the pharmacokinetics and limited safety data have been collected using products also containing THC (Vaughn et al, 2020). Chronic arthritic pain is common in older dogs and two studies indicate that CBD alleviates such pain in dogs (Gamble et al, 2018; Verrico et al, 2020). A single case study involving a horse reported that CBD alleviated marked allodynia (Ellis and Contino, 2021).

In 2018 the VMD stated that veterinary products containing CBD are veterinary medicines. Products containing CBD for use in animals therefore require MA for sale or supply in the UK. There are no CBD products with MA for animal use so veterinarians may prescribe licensed human CBD products via the Cascade.

There is considerable anecdotal evidence that many pet owners purchase over-the-counter CBD oil classed as a food supplement. These contain low concentrations of CBD and <0.05% THC and there is little evidence as yet to indicate efficacy or otherwise, but they appear not to cause significant harm.

Veterinary interest in the efficacy of CBD for a range of chronic pain conditions in dogs, cats and horses is growing (Mercer and Davis, 2021) and a range of investigations to elucidate the role of the various cannabinoids in veterinary treatments is underway.

Clenbuterol

Clenbuterol, a beta adrenergic agonist, is not used for analgesia or anaesthesia but is controlled under Schedule 4. It has MA for use to manage parturition in cattle and as a bronchodilator in horses.

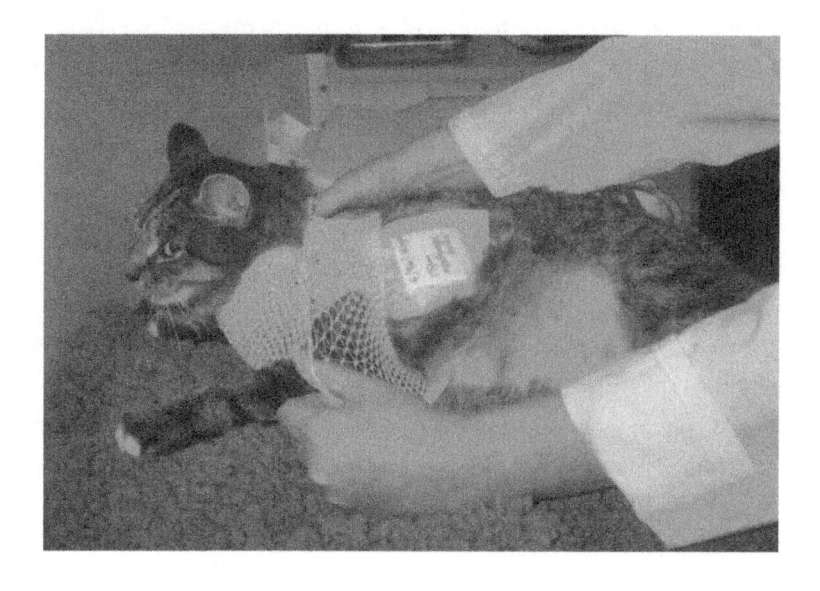

Figure 1: A horse sedated with a combination of a sedative and an opioid remains standing whilst allowing surgery in the groin.

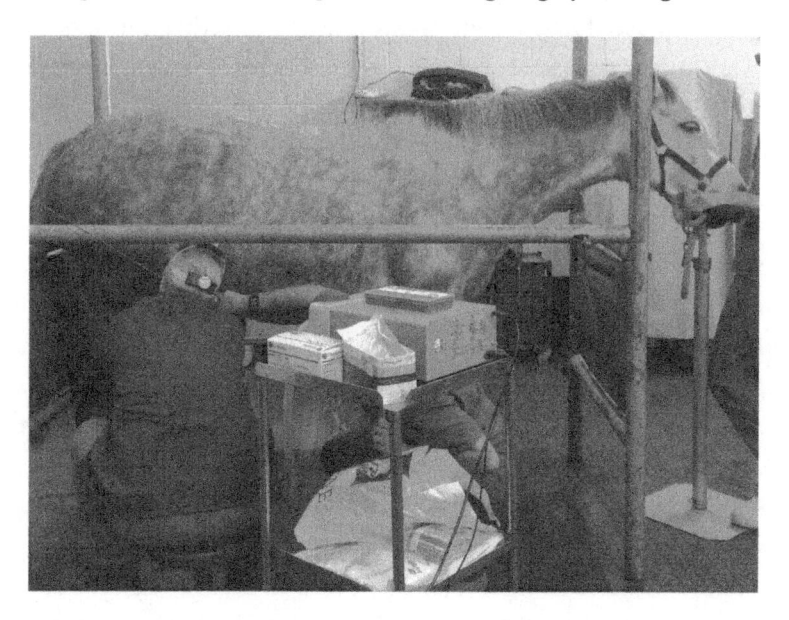

Figure 2: A fentanyl patch provides analgesia in a cat following a road traffic accident.

The Impact of the MDA 1971 on the Veterinary Profession

Figure 3: A rabbit is deeply sedated with a combination of fentanyl and a sedative.

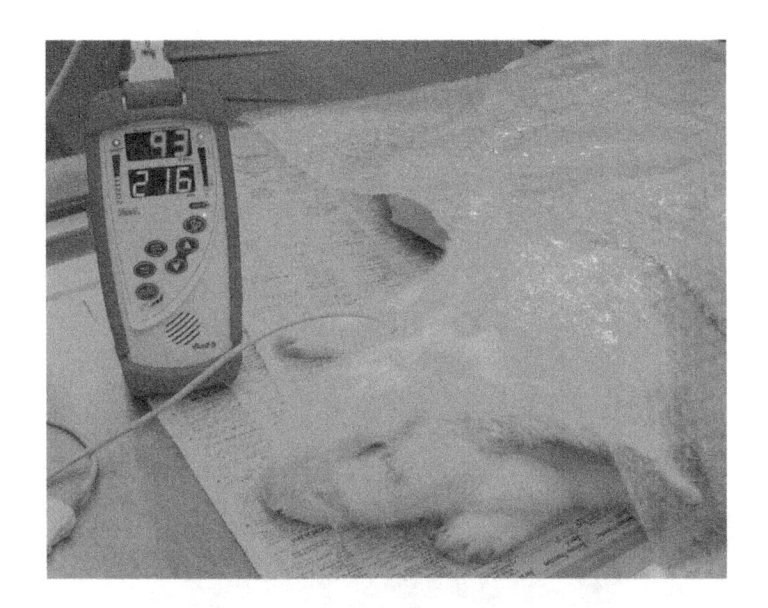

Figure 4: The anaesthetic is administered by dart to a white rhinoceros before tooth surgery.

Figure 5: A combination of ketamine and midazolam produces smooth anaesthetic induction and the horse lies down gently.

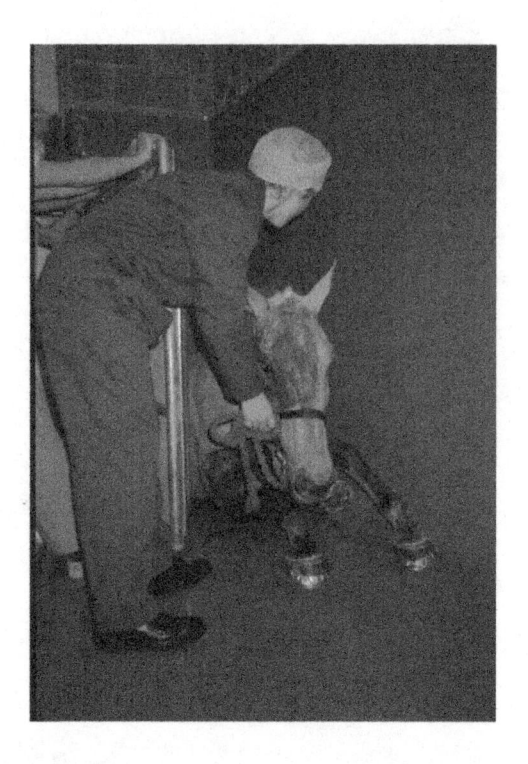

Figure 6: Ketamine forms the basis of the injectable anaesthetic used to anaesthetise many hundreds of feral cats for neutering surgery.

Figure 7: Ketamine sprayed into the mouth of an uncooperative cat induces sedation and allows it to be handled for further treatment.

Figure 8: A neonatal foal is sedated with diazepam to allow positioning for radiographic imaging.

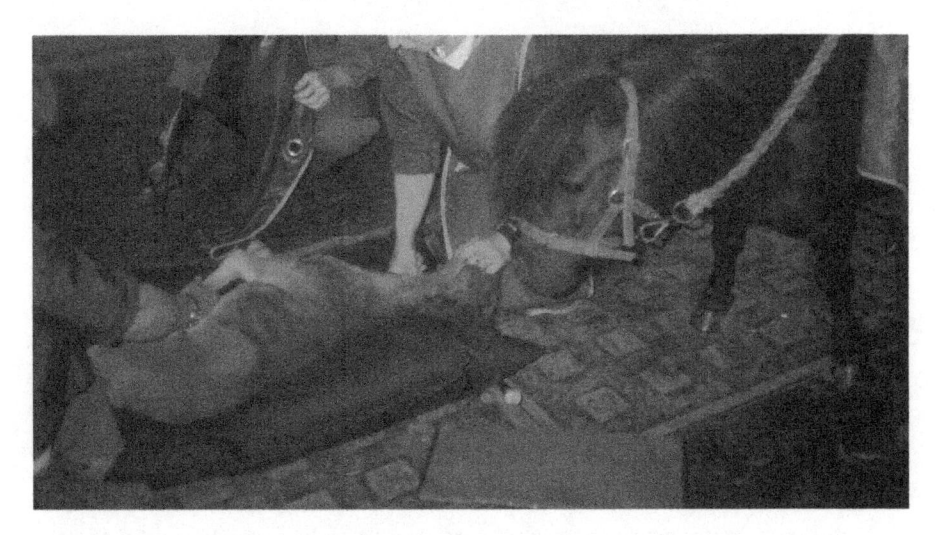

Veterinary Surgeons and Suicide

Veterinary surgeons are known to be at a higher risk of suicide compared with the general population and have a proportional mortality ratio for suicide approximately four times that of the general population and around twice that of other healthcare professionals (Bartram and Baldwin, 2010). The reasons for this divergence are not fully understood, but ready access to the relevant drugs as well as familiarity with euthanasia of companion animals and slaughter of farm animals seem likely to contribute. Alcohol as well as other substance misuse enabled by easy access may contribute to the suicide risk (Bartram and Baldwin, 2010).

Regulation of access to controlled drugs should aim to prevent or at least reduce the harm from inappropriate use. However, veterinarians must have access to these drugs in order to carry out their work. Appropriate action based on the premise that addiction and suicide are mental health problems would appear to approach the potential harms of controlled drugs more effectively than simple punitive measures that do not address the cause.

Conclusions

The impact of the MDA 1971 on veterinary treatment of animals resides almost entirely with the regulations restricting purchase, storage and prescription. However, custody of highly potent drugs, especially in the quantities required for large animals, has always been an automatic priority of the veterinary profession and the regulations simply underscore good practice. Movement of ketamine into Schedule 2 in 2015 probably had the greatest potential to affect animal welfare. Although it had long been treated as a CD and kept under tight custody the additional recording requirements were extremely onerous for out of clinic use. Since ketamine is particularly valuable for unusual and traumatic circumstances this may have led to less than perfect management of rare species and emergencies in the field when veterinarians were less willing to use ketamine outwith the clinic.

A more subtle impact on veterinary care appears to be through public perception and media reporting. For instance, ketamine is often reported as nothing but bad (see, for example, 'New health fears surrounding ketamine': www.youtube.com/watch?v=V32Y_t_OCUM and Taylor et al (2016)) and its enormous benefit to humans and animals alike in its therapeutic role is often ignored. Legislation in the UK is noted globally, and may subtly contribute to onerous bureaucracy affecting access to essential anaesthetics and analgesics in low- and middle-income countries (Vijayan, 2011).

Table 1. Controlled drugs used in veterinary treatment.

Drug	Best known as/ original product	Veterinary MA trade name	Indication
Opioids			
Morphine	Morphine	NA	Pain relief, chemical restraint
Fentanyl	Sublimaze	Fentadon	Pain relief, anaesthesia
Methadone	Physeptone	Comfortan	Pain relief, chemical restraint
Buprenorphine	Temgesic	Vetergesic	Pain relief, chemical restraint
Etorphine	Etorphine, M99	Immobilon (with acepromazine)	Chemical restraint of large wild ungulates
Carfentanil	Carfentanil	Carfentanil	Chemical restraint of large wild ungulates
Thiafentanil	Thiafentanil	Thianil	Chemical restraint of large wild ungulates
Codeine	Codeine	Pardal-V (with paracetamol)	Pain relief
Ketamine			
Ketamine	Ketamine	Vetalar, Ketaset et al	Anaesthesia, pain relief
Barbiturates			
Pentobarbital	Pentobarbitone	Euthatal et al	Euthanasia

Drug	Best known as/ original product	Veterinary MA trade name	Indication
Phenobarbital	Phenobarbitone	Epiphen	Epilepsy treatment
Secobarbital sodium (quinalbarbitone sodium)	Quinalbarbitone sodium	Somulose (with cinchocaine hydrochloride)	Euthanasia
Benzodazepines			
Diazepam	Valium	Ziapam	Sedation, muscle relaxation
Midazolam	Hypnovel	Dormazolam	Sedation, muscle relaxation
Tramadol			
Tramadol	Tramadol	Tramvetol et al	Pain relief
Other			
Clenbuterol	Clenbuterol	Ventipulmin Planipart	Bronchodilation Control of parturition

Dr Polly Taylor DipECVAA, MRCA, FRCVS is a European Veterinary and RCVS Specialist in anaesthesia, working as an independent consultant in veterinary anaesthesia. She has been a member of Drug Science since its inception. Dr Taylor has numerous publications covering research and education on anaesthesia and analgesia and is co-author of the standard text *Handbook of Equine Anaesthesia* (Elsevier, 2007).

References and Extra Reading

Bartram D J and Baldwin D S (2010), Veterinary Surgeons and Suicide: A Structured Review of Possible Influences on Increased Risk, *Veterinary Record*, 166: 388–397.

Capner C A, Lascelles B D and Waterman-Pearson A E (1999), Current British Veterinary Attitudes to Perioperative Analgesia for Dogs, *Veterinary Record*, 145: 95–99.

Clutton R E (2010), Opioid Analgesia in Horses, *Veterinary Clinics of North America: Equine Practice*, 26: 493–514.

Ellis K L, Contino E K (2021), Treatment Using Cannabidiol in a Horse with Mechanical Allodynia, *Equine Veterinary Education*, 33: e79-e82.

Gamble L J, Boesch J M, Frye C W et al (2018), Pharmacokinetics, Safety, and Clinical Efficacy of Cannabidiol Treatment in Osteoarthritic Dogs, *Frontiers in Veterinary, Science*, 5: 165.

Mercer M A and Davis J L (2021), Cannabinoids in Veterinary Medicine: Is There Evidence to Support the Trend? *Equine Veterinary Education*, 33: 177–179.

Schutter A F, Tunsmeyer J and Kastner S B R (2017), Influence of Tramadol on Acute Thermal and Mechanical Cutaneous Nociception in Dogs, *Veterinary Anaesthesia and Analgesia*, 44: 309–316.

Steagall P V, Monteiro-Steagall B P and Taylor P M (2014), A Review of the Studies Using Buprenorphine in Cats, *Journal of Veterinary Internal Medicine*, 28: 762–770.

Taylor P, Nutt D, Curran V et al (2016), Ketamine — The Real Perspective, *The Lancet*.

Vaughn D, Kulpa J and Paulionis L (2020), Preliminary Investigation of the Safety of Escalating Cannabinoid Doses in Healthy Dogs, *Frontiers in Veterinary Science*, 7; 51.

Verrico C D, Wesson S, Konduri V et al (2020), A Randomized, Double-blind, Placebo-controlled Study of Daily Cannabidiol for the Treatment of Canine Osteoarthritis Pain, *Pain*, 161: 2191–2202.

Vijayan R (2011), Managing Acute Pain in the Developing World, *Pain Clinical Update*, 19: 1–7.

Wagner A E, Walton J A, Hellyer P W et al (2002), Use of Low Doses of Ketamine Administered by Constant Rate Infusion as an Adjunct for Postoperative Analgesia in Dogs, *Journal of the American Veterinary Medical Association*, 221: 72–75.

Wohlfender F D, Doherr M G, Driessen B, et al (2015), International Online Survey to Assess Current Practice in Equine Anaesthesia, *Equine Veterinary Journal*, 47: 65–71.

CHAPTER 9

Enabling Access to Essential Medicines and Devices

Rosalind Gittins

The Misuse of Drugs Act 1971 aimed to prevent the non-medical use of substances which it defined as 'controlled drugs.' It therefore controls substances that are thought to have no medical use, as well as drugs that are used in clinical practice and research. It divides them into three categories: Class A, Class B and Class C, where Class A carries greater penalties and Class C the least. The legislation outlines associated offences relating to supply, import, export, production and possession.

The Misuse of Drugs Regulations 2001 (MDR 2001) (and subsequent amendments) complement the MDA 1971 by outlining who can undertake specified activities in relation to controlled drugs in a professional capacity. This legislation also details record keeping and prescribing requirements, where they are permitted for medical indications. The regulations categorise controlled drugs into Schedules numbered 1 to 5, where Schedule 1 includes drugs that are considered to be of limited clinical value. For this reason, Home Office licences are required to authorise the use of Schedule 1 drugs (Home Office, 2013), which are permitted usually only for the purposes of research. Home Office licences for controlled drugs can only be issued to authorised individuals under specific circumstances (ibid): they are associated with notable costs, security and compliance checks. Furthermore, in an attempt to control novel substances that were being produced in an attempt to circumvent this legislation, in 2016 the UK's Psychoactive Substances Act was introduced (see in particular *Chapters 2, 10, 15, 17* and *19* of this work).

Harm Reduction

By controlling substances in this way, illicit drug supplies are not regulated. This means that the person who takes such products will have no way of knowing what they actually contain. Their strength is unknown and the presence of potentially toxic adulterants or bulking agents cannot be verified since it is not possible to identify the contents just by looking at them. Reports of unregulated products causing harm remain frequent: examples of recent formal drug alerts have included cannabis edibles (Medicines and Healthcare Products Regulatory Agency (MHRA), 2020a), fentanyl-contaminated heroin (MHRA, 2017) and benzodiazepines (MHRA, 2020b). This places people who take them at increased risk of drug-related harms, including accidental death. Indeed, the latest drug-related deaths in England and Wales (Office for National Statistics (ONS), 2020), are the highest since records began, with an age-standardised mortality rate of 76.7 deaths per million people. Opioids such as heroin account for almost half of these deaths (ibid) and heroin purity levels are thought to be at a ten year high (National Crime Agency (NCA), 2020).

Furthermore, the NCA (ibid) reported that since 2011, cocaine use has escalated by at least 290%. Associated deaths have also increased exponentially: rising 26.5% amongst women and 7.7% amongst men in England and Wales (ONS, 2020). The use of stimulants such as cocaine can be associated with high-risk behaviours, such as unsafe sex, acquisitive crime, polydrug use and increased risk of infections or blood borne virus (such as HIV and hepatitis) transmission if drug paraphernalia is shared. Additional negative physical and mental health consequences can include cardiovascular problems, anxiety and psychosis. Cocaine can also interact with medicines, such as some antidepressants which can cause QT prolongation (affecting how the heart beats) (Mistura, 2020a), excessively raising the levels of the neurochemical serotonin (leading to serotonin syndrome) (Mistura, 2021) and when used alongside alcohol, produces the toxic metabolite cocaethylene (Mistura, 2020b), any of which may be fatal and more likely to occur if large amounts are taken. Currently cocaine is a Class A drug, though may be used in medical practice for therapeutic reasons such as the management of more serious nose bleeds.

Legislative changes which seek to regulate supplies may assist with removing the supply chain from organized crime groups, but moreover, from a harm reduction perspective, regulating substances and supply mechanisms also creates opportunities to provide people who use substances with products that have undergone quality assurance measures. The Transform Drug Policy Foundation (2020) has outlined different ways in which this could be achieved. Since the pharmacy profession already gate keeps access to medicines (including controlled drugs), provides harm reduction interventions, has demonstrable understanding of drug regulations, safe storage, supply and expertise in the management of drug interactions, such developments may be considered to be an extension of their current role or it could be viewed as a distinct professional niche (Rolles and Gittins, 2020).

Harm reduction services do not condone the use of drugs but offer practical support and advice to people to enable them to reduce drug-related harms. This includes providing people with free supplies of take home naloxone (Public Health England, 2019) which is a life-saving medicine given by injection (Martindale Pharma, 2018) or a nasal spray (Napp, 2018), and used to reverse overdoses caused by opioids (such as fentanyl, heroin and methadone).

Providing people with enough equipment for preparing and injecting substances via needle and syringe provision schemes is essential in eliminating the need for people to reuse or share paraphernalia which is a major factor in reducing the transmission of blood borne infections and the risk of injection site infections (National Institute for Health and Care Excellence (NICE), 2014). These services began in the 1980s in response to concerns about the spread of HIV (Release, 2020). Consequent developments have included provision of water for injection, which provides people with safer alternatives than water from puddles, toilet cisterns and saliva when preparing substances for injection, especially amongst people who are street homeless (Harris, Scott et al, 2020; and see *Chapter 10* of this volume by Crick and Holland).

Stimulants such as crack cocaine, typically have a short half-life, meaning that the drug does not stay in the body for very long and therefore the effect of the substance is short-lived, and so frequent administration is often desired. This means that for someone who is using dependently they need to inject multiple times a day, with escalating risks and especially physical health harms due to the impact the drug has on constricting the blood vessels and anaesthetic action, so people may not be as aware of the damage that is being caused. Smoking may be advised from a harm reduction perspective as this route of administration may be viewed as being associated with less health harms than injecting.

In 2014, legislative changes enabled needle syringe provision services to also offer foil, which people can use to smoke/inhale substances (Home Office, 2016). Whilst this foil may be used to create makeshift crack pipes, pre-made pipes are preferable and more convenient. Crack pipes are typically home made using a range of household items such as stainless-steel scouring pads, tin cans, plastic bottles or other containers which risk producing toxic fumes, cuts and burns to the lips, hands, mouth, face and airways. They are usually re-used on multiple occasions and often shared amongst individuals, so can also be associated with communicable diseases such as blood borne virus transmission (albeit at a lower risk than injecting) and of particular concern during the Covid-19 pandemic (Harris, 2020). Unfortunately, the provision of crack pipes remains illegal under the MDA 1971, so organizations cannot supply these devices, leaving people at risk until this legislation is changed.

More complex harm reduction interventions include drug checking services; however, these require funding and specialist equipment and expertise to introduce robustly (Guirguis et al, 2020). Additional approaches such as the provision of overdose prevention centres (also referred to as drug consumption rooms, safer injecting facilities or enhanced harm reduction centres: see *Chapter 10*), especially for use by people who are street homeless, could be viewed as a natural extension of such services (European Monitoring Centre for Drugs and Drug Addiction, 2018). They offer an excellent opportunity to engage people with treatment services and provide interventions such as take home naloxone and needle syringe provision, wound care, vaccination and testing for blood borne viruses. Although the Advisory Committee on the Misuse of Drugs (ACMD, 2016) recommended them, their implementation was not supported by the UK Government (Atkins, 2018) (any fresh plans being as yet unknown following the change of administration in September 2022) and the MDA 1971 makes it an offence to allow premises to be used for the consumption of certain controlled drugs. Drug Science (2020a) has consequently established the Enhanced Harm Working Group, which includes academic and policy experts and specialist treatment providers who are collaborating to develop and promote the published evidence base and establish pilot sites.

Medical Psychedelics

Class A includes drugs known for their psychedelic effects, and many are also designated as Schedule 1 substances both under UK legislation and the 1971 UN Convention on Psychotropic Substances (United Nations Office on Drugs and Crime (UNODC), 1971). Whilst widely known for their recreational use, some of these drugs are also being increasingly recognised for their potential in clinical practice. Perhaps the most widely studied of these are psilocybin, found in 'magic mushrooms,' and 3,4-methylenedioxymethamphetamine (MDMA) (Multidisciplinary Association for Psychedelic Studies (MAPS), 2021), perhaps better known as 'ecstasy' when used as a street drug.

Medical psychedelics are typically used very differently to more established and licensed psychoactive medicines. For example, psychedelics are generally utilised therapeutically in conjunction with psychotherapy sessions, which require establishing a therapeutic alliance between the individual and their assigned therapists: they may also be used by micro-dosing, where very low doses are consumed over a period of time (Anderson et al, 2019).

The psychedelic mental state that is experienced with hallucinogens can enable a 'weakening' of psychological defences, enabling the person to process otherwise repressed thoughts and feelings. Furthermore, the empathogenic and mood-altering effects of MDMA can enable people to feel more able to relax and connect with others. This useful effect may make it a helpful accompaniment to psychotherapy for the management of mental health conditions, especially where there is underlying trauma, such as post-traumatic stress disorder (PTSD) (Mithoefer et al, 2018) and alcohol dependency (Sessa et al, 2021). There are a wide range of potential applications for medical psychedelics in psychiatry, for conditions such as obsessive compulsive disorder, anxiety and anorexia, as well as in palliative care. In the UK, Carhart-Harris et al (2021) published notable findings from a phase 2 randomised controlled trial of psilocybin compared with escitalopram for depression, though the research group concluded that larger and longer trials are needed.

The lack of large, randomised controlled trials and significant amounts of published evidence limits wider roll-out. Clinicians must prescribe within their confidence and competence and there is also a lack of clinical expertise in mainstream clinical practice: what they are able to prescribe is limited by formularies, protocols and prescribing guidelines. With a limited evidence base there is a lack of systemic health system support, compounded by stigma and lack of knowledge.

Although current legislation does not preclude scientific research with these drugs, it does make them significantly more difficult, time-consuming and costly to study because research is far more difficult to undertake when substances are in Schedule 1. This means that there is an associated additional cost, bureaucracy and logistics of obtaining the substance, Home Office licences and ensuring adequate security arrangements relating to safe and secure storage and transportation. For example, the Adam Smith Research Trust (2020) noted that psilocybin costs about ten times the amount it would without the Schedule 1 restrictions, at about £1,500 per dose. Therefore, medical research can be prohibitively expensive and it can also be more difficult to obtain research funding and attract investors.

Without research, approval cannot be given to license the products or widen their use outside of clinical trials. Despite increasing interest by clinicians being able to offer this treatment and individuals wanting to receive it, whilst it is only accessible via clinical trials, medical psychedelics will not be an accessible treatment option. Therefore, Drug Science (2020b) has established the Medical Psychedelics Working Group which includes scientific, academic and policy experts, patient advocacy and industry representatives who are collaborating to develop the published evidence base, educational resources and promote de-stigmatisation.

Medical Cannabis

Where people are found to be engaging with activity viewed as being illegal, this carries the risk of prosecution, including where the person may be cultivating, preparing and possessing controlled drugs for self-management of a medical condition. Perhaps cannabis is the most common example of this, as it was reclassified from a Class C to a Class B drug in 2009. A YouGov poll commissioned by the Centre for Medicinal Cannabis (CfMC) suggested that an estimated 1.4 million people (2.8% of the adult population) in the UK are using illicit cannabis to self-medicate for chronic health conditions including depression, anxiety, sleep disorders and chronic pain (Burns, 2020; Schlag et al, 2020).

Born in 2011, Alfie Dingley suffered from a rare form of intractable epilepsy until he was given medical cannabis which helped to manage his symptoms (Deacon, 2019). Sourcing what was at the time an illicit substance in the UK, his family went to great lengths to get him access to this life-changing medication. Lobbying with End Our Pain (endourpain.org) and an associated successful media campaign, the Government took steps to review their position. Following advice from the ACMD (2018) and the chief medical adviser to the UK (Davies, 2018), the Government agreed to reschedule cannabis-based products for medical use from Schedule 1 to Schedule 2 under the MDR 2001. This allowed cannabis-based medicinal products to be prescribed by specialist doctors from 2018 and a suite of guidance and position statements consequently followed from organizations including the General Medical Council (GMC, 2021).

In 2019, NICE (2021) first published guidelines to support cannabis-based medicinal products for intractable nausea and vomiting, chronic pain, spasticity and severe treatment-resistant epilepsy. It was viewed that the guidance from NICE was too restrictive which contributed to the staggeringly low uptake with families paying thousands of pounds a month for private prescriptions (Nutt et al, 2020). High costs and problematic timely access have been related to the logistics of importation: in March 2020 restrictions loosened which should have improved this (Schlag et al, 2020). However, the Covid-19 pandemic added extra pressures to families who continued to manage the financial burden and struggled to continue to afford the treatment.

The family of another child, Charlie Hughes, were granted permission to pursue a landmark High Court case against NICE (Dyer, 2020), to enable widening of access to medicinal products. Consequently, the case was dropped after NICE issued clarification of this guidance in 2021 (NICE, 2021), saying that there was no recommendation against the use of medicinal cannabis-based products, meaning that healthcare professionals are not prevented from using them where clinically indicated for selected individuals. In accordance with NICE guidelines, for one child, Billy Caldwell, a care plan has been used to assure the continued provision of cannabis prescriptions (CfMC, 2020).

However, despite these developments UK prescriptions for medical cannabis remain scarce and this is unlikely to notably change until prescribers gain confidence and competence. This is especially the case whilst products remain unlicensed, which places additional medico-legal liability and professional responsibility on the prescriber and supplying pharmacist (Donovan et al, 2015). There remains a paucity of formal training and education of clinicians and gaps in current national guidelines to support prescribing and supply of medical cannabis, for example, in relation to duration of use, dosage, product strength and formulation.

The ongoing lack of robust evidence to support both the short- and long-term use of medical cannabis in the UK adds to the controversy and highlights the need for further research. Consequently, NICE supports the use of a registry to record prescribing details and associated clinical outcomes and adverse effects, to build upon the existing evidence by collecting 'real world data.' Currently, the UK's largest registry is operated by Drug Science's Project TWENTY21 (2020c), which aims to enable eligible individuals to access affordable medical cannabis and collate evidence of effectiveness and tolerability. Drug Science has also established the Medical Cannabis Working Group (2020d) which includes scientific, academic and policy experts, patient advocacy and industry representatives who are collaborating to develop the published evidence base, educational resources and promote de-stigmatisation.

Access to Prescription Medication

The supportive evidence base for the use of prescribed medicines (opioid substitutes such as methadone and buprenorphine) for the management of opioid dependence are well established (DHSC, 2017; NICE, 2007). Being able to afford them however, especially when drug tariff prices change and public health spending has been notably and successively cut in previous years is an ongoing challenge. For example, when the cost of buprenorphine rocketed in 2018–2019, treatment providers and local authorities cumulatively haemorrhaged millions of pounds and the continued ability to be able to offer this essential medicine was brought into question (Gittins, 2018; Wickware, 2019). Yet, investing in treatment has been shown to be cost-effective and the latest part two of Dame Carol Black's review outlines that each £1 spent saves an estimated £4 on healthcare, law enforcement and associated costs and calls for additional, much needed and long overdue investment in the sector (DHSC, 2021).

For individuals where first line oral opioid substitutes have not been effective, injectable diamorphine ('pharmaceutical heroin') may offer a viable alternative (DHSC, 2017). However significant investment is required to offer this treatment option, due to the associated cost of the medication, and where administered under supervision (in line with best practice), also Home Office licences, equipment, competent staff, facilities to store, prepare and give the injection (in accordance with Home Office requirements) (Public Health England (PHE), 2021). Furthermore, diamorphine supply shortages have continued in recent years and the need for importation of larger multi-dose products requires special arrangements and Home Office involvement and both are consequently associated with additional costs and logistical challenges.

Current legislation also dictates that Home Office licences are required to prescribe, and can only be issued to medical doctors, not nurses or other allied healthcare professionals such as pharmacists. This does not reflect recent changes made where independent, non-medical prescribers may prescribe other controlled drugs such as methadone and buprenorphine, including for the treatment of addiction. Additionally, if the doctor is not on the Specialist Register of the GMC (usually a consultant psychiatrist), they must have a nominated supervisor who is, and who must also have a Home Office licence (ibid), made more difficult by the shortage of such specialists (Rimmer, 2020), and adds yet more governance and logistical challenges to offering this treatment option.

The logistics of ensuring timely access to a prescriber, prescriptions and associated medicines became even more notable during the Covid-19 pandemic. Changes to the MDR 2001 were made in 2020 to assist; however, the emergency measures were never actually 'activated.' Prescriptions for opioid substitution can be issued in instalments, which enables the prescriber to just write one prescription and the person can have the supply of their medication issued, for example, on a daily basis up to a maximum of 14 days. This also enables the person to come into frequent contact with the pharmacy team who can provide additional health and wellbeing interventions, and where indicated also supervise the consumption of the medication. Unfortunately, in England it is still not possible to have these prescriptions sent electronically to the pharmacy (via the Electronic Prescription Service) as is the case for other prescription types. Significant postage costs and ongoing governance concerns will continue until this is enabled.

Rosalind Gittins is the Director of Pharmacy for Humankind (a national third sector drug and alcohol treatment provider), President of the international College of Mental Health Pharmacy (CMHP) and a Drug Science Scientific Committee member.

References and Extra Reading

Adam Smith Research Trust (2020), Medicinal Use of Psilocybin: Reducing Restrictions on Research and Treatment: www.adamsmith.org/s/Medicinal-Use-of-Psilocybin-Rucker-Schnall-DHotman-King-Davis-and-Neill.pdf

Advisory Council on the Misuse of Drugs (2016), Reducing Opioid-Related Deaths in the UK: https://assets.publishing.service.gov.uk/government/uploads/system/uploads/attachment_data/file/576560/ACMD-Drug-Related-Deaths-Report-161212.pdf

ACMD (2018), Letter: Scheduling of Cannabis-derived medicinal products: https://assets.publishing.service.gov.uk/government/uploads/system/uploads/attachment_data/file/727333/ACMD_advice_on_scheduling_of_cannabis_derived_medicinal_products.pdf

Anderson T, Petranker, R, Christopher, A, Rosenbaum, D, Weissman, C, Dinh-Williams, L, Hui, K, Hapke, E (2019), Psychedelic Microdosing Benefits and Challenges: An Empirical Codebook, *Harm Reduction Journal*. DOI: 10.1186/s12954-019-0308-4

Atkins, V (2018), Reducing Opioid-related Deaths in the UK Report — Further Response Regarding Drug Consumption Rooms, Ministerial Response to the Advisory Council on the Misuse of Drugs: https://assets.publishing.service.gov.uk/government/uploads/system/uploads/attachment_data/file/699825/Letter_from_Victoria_Atkins_MP_to_OBJ.pdf

Burns, C (2020), 'Urgent review' of medical cannabis access needed to curb use of street drugs, says trade body, *Pharmaceutical Journal*: https://pharmaceutical-journal.com/article/news/urgent-review-of-medical-cannabis-access-needed-to-curb-use-of-street-drugs-says-trade-body

Centre for Medical Cannabis (2020), NHS Care Plan Confirmed for Billy Caldwell: www.belfastlive.co.uk/news/belfast-news/medicinal-cannabis-victory-billy-caldwell-19131661

Carhart-Harris, R, Giribaldi, B, Watts, R, Baker-Jones, M, Murphy-Beiner, A, Murphy, R, Martell, J, Blemings, A, Erritzoe, D, Nutt, D J (2021), Trial of Psilocybin versus

Escitalopram for Depression, *New England Journal of Medicine:* www.nejm.org/doi/full/10.1056/NEJMoa2032994

Davies, S (2018), Cannabis Scheduling Review Part 1: https://assets.publishing.service.gov.uk/government/uploads/system/uploads/attachment_data/file/722010/CMO_Report_Cannabis_Products_Web_Accessible.pdf

Deacon, H (2019), Why I campaign for children like my son Alfie Dingley to be able to get medical cannabis, *British Medical Journal:* www.bmj.com/content/365/bmj.l1921

Department of Health and Social Care (2017), Drug Misuse and Dependence: UK Guidelines on Clinical Management: www.gov.uk/government/publications/drug-misuse-and-dependence-uk-guidelines-on-clinical-management

DHSC (2021), Review of Drugs Part Two: Prevention, Treatment, and Recovery: www.gov.uk/government/publications/review-of-drugs-phase-two-report/review-of-drugs-part-two-prevention-treatment-and-recovery

Donovan, G, Parkin, L, Wilkes, S (2015), Special Unlicensed Medicines: What We Do and Do Not Know About Them, *British Journal of General Practice.* DOI: 10.3399/bjgp15X688033

Drug Science (2020a), Supervised Injection Facility Working Group: www.drugscience.org.uk/supervised-injection-facility-working-group/

Drug Science (2020b), Medical Psychedelics Working Group: www.drugscience.org.uk/medical-psychedelics-working-group/

Drug Science (2020c), Project TWENTY21: www.drugscience.org.uk/project-twenty21/

Drug Science (2020d), Medical Cannabis Working Group: www.drugscience.org.uk/medical-cannabis-working-group/

Dyer, C (2020), 'Parents Can Challenge NICE Guidance on Medicinal Cannabis in Court, *British Medical Journal:* www.bmj.com/content/370/bmj.m3304

European Monitoring Centre for Drugs and Drug Addiction (2018), Drug Consumption Rooms: an Overview of Provision and Evidence: www.emcdda.europa.eu/system/files/publications/2734/POD_Drug%20consumption%20rooms.pdf

General Medical Council (2021), Information for Doctors on Cannabis-based Products for Medicinal Use [CBMPs]: www.gmc-uk.org/ethical-guidance/learning-materials/information-for-doctors-on-cannabis-based-products-for-medicinal-use

Gittins, R (2018), Vital Heroin Withdrawal Drug's Price Increased by 700% in Two Months, *Medium*: medium.com/we-are-with-you/https-view-joomag-com-drink-and-drugs-news-ddn-november-2018-0790398001541412008-short-ac8053440b1f

Guirguis, A, Gittins, R, Schifano, F (2020), Piloting the UK's First Home-Office-Licensed Pharmacist-Led Drug Checking Service at a Community Substance Misuse Service, *Behavioral Sciences:* www.mdpi.com/2076-328X/10/8/121/htm

Harris, M (2020), An Urgent Impetus for Action: Safe Inhalation Interventions to Reduce COVID-19 Transmission and Fatality Risk Among People Who Smoke Crack Cocaine in the United Kingdom, *International Journal of Drug Policy:* www.ncbi.nlm.nih.gov/pmc/articles/PMC7306748/

Harris, M, Scott, J, Hope, V, Wright, T, McGowan, C, Ciccarone, D (2020), Navigating Environmental Constraints to Injection Preparation: The Use of Saliva and Other Alternatives to Sterile Water Among Unstably Housed PWID in London, *Harm Reduction Journal.* DOI: 10.1186/s12954-020-00369-0

Home Office (2013), Drugs Licensing: www.gov.uk/government/collections/drugs-licensing

Home Office (2016), Monitoring the Legal Provision of Foil to Heroin Users: https://assets.publishing.service.gov.uk/government/uploads/system/uploads/attachment_data/file/564151/monitoring-legal-provision-foil-heroin-users-horr92.pdf

Martindale Pharma (2018), PrenoxadTM 1mg/ml Solution for Injection in a Pre-filled Syringe: www.medicines.org.uk/emc/files/pil.3054.pdf

Medicines and Healthcare Products Regulatory Agency (2017), Evidence of Harm from Fentanyl-contaminated Heroin: www.cas.mhra.gov.uk/ViewandAcknowledgment/ViewAlert.aspx?AlertID=102588

MHRA (2020a), Cannabis Oil Disguised as Confectionary: www.cas.mhra.gov.uk/ViewandAcknowledgment/ViewAlert.aspx?AlertID=103071

MHRA (2020b), Evidence of Harm From Illicit or Fake Benzodiazepines: www.cas.mhra.gov.uk/ViewandAcknowledgment/ViewAlert.aspx?AlertID=103075

Mistura (2020a), Handy Fact Sheet Prolonged QT Interval from Medicines: www.choiceandmedication.org/humankind/generate/handyfactsheetqtc.pdf

Mistura (2020b), Cocaethylene: www.choiceandmedication.org/humankind/generate/handyfactsheetpostercocaethylene.pdf

Mistura (2021), Handy Fact Sheet Serotonin Syndrome: www.choiceandmedication.org/humankind/generate/handyfactsheetserotoninsyndrome.pdf

Misuse of Drugs Act 1971: www.legislation.gov.uk/ukpga/1971/38/contents

Misuse of Drugs (Coronavirus) (Amendments Relating to the Supply of Controlled Drugs During a Pandemic etc.) Regulations 2020: www.legislation.gov.uk/uksi/2020/468/contents/made

Misuse of Drugs Regulations 2001: www.legislation.gov.uk/uksi/2001/3998/contents/made

Mithoefer, M C, Mithoefer, A T, Feduccia, A A, Jerome, L, Wagner, M, Wymer, J, Holland, J, Hamilton, S, Yazar-Klosinski, B, Emerson, A, Doblin, R (2018), 3,4-Methylenedioxymethamphetamine (MDMA) -assisted Psychotherapy for Post-traumatic Stress Disorder in Military Veterans, Firefighters, and Police Officers: A Randomised, Double-blind, Dose-response, Phase 2 Clinical Trial, *The Lancet Psychiatry:* www.thelancet.com/journals/lanpsy/article/PIIS2215-0366(18)30135-4/fulltext

Multidisciplinary Association for Psychedelic Studies (2021), Investigator's Brochure: https://mapscontent.s3-us-west-1.amazonaws.com/research-archive/MDMA+IB+13th+Edition+Final+22MAR2021.pdf

Napp (2018), Healthcare Professional Guidance Document on Training and Support for Nyxoid® (Naloxone): www.medicines.org.uk/emc/rmm/1277/Document

National Crime Agency (2020), National Strategic Assessment of Serious and Organised Crime: www.nationalcrimeagency.gov.uk/who-we-are/publications/437-national-strategic-assessment-of-serious-and-organised-crime-2020/file

National Institute for Health and Care Excellence (2007), Methadone and Buprenorphine for the Management of Opioid Dependence: TA114: www.nice.org.uk/guidance/ta114

NICE (2014), Needle and Syringe Programmes: PH52: www.nice.org.uk/guidance/ph52

NICE (2021), Cannabis-based Medicinal Products: NG144: www.nice.org.uk/guidance/ng144

Nutt, D, Bazire, S, Phillips, L D, Schlag, A K (2020), So Near Yet So Far: Why Won't the UK Prescribe Medical Cannabis? *British Medical Journal Open:* https://bmjopen.bmj.com/content/10/9/e038687

Office for National Statistics (2020), Deaths Related to Drug Poisoning in England and Wales: 2019 Registrations: www.ons.gov.uk/peoplepopulationandcommunity/birthsdeathsandmarriages/deaths/bulletins/deathsrelatedtodrugpoisoninginenglandandwales/2019registrations

Psychoactive Substances Act 2016: www.legislation.gov.uk/ukpga/2016/2/contents

Public Health England (2019), Widening the Availability of Naloxone: www.gov.uk/government/publications/widening-the-availability-of-naloxone/widening-the-availability-of-naloxone

PHE (2021), Injectable Opioid Treatment: Commissioning and Developing a Service: www.gov.uk/government/publications/injectable-opioid-treatment-commissioning-and-providing-services/injectable-opioid-treatment-commissioning-and-developing-a-service

Release (2020), Injecting Drug Use and Needle Exchange: www.release.org.uk/injecting-drugs-needle-exchange

Rimmer, A (2020), Addiction Psychiatry Could be Wiped Out in a Decade Without Urgent Government Funding, College Warns, *British Medical Journal*. DOI: 10.1136/bmj.m635

Rolles, S, Gittins, R (2020), 'Pharmacists Can Help Put An End to Illicit Drug Deaths by Being at the Centre of a New Non-medical Use Market, *Pharmaceutical Journal*: www.pharmaceutical-journal.com/article/opinion/pharmacists-can-help-put-an-end-to-illicit-drug-deaths-by-being-at-the-centre-of-a-new-non-medical-use-market#fn_16

Schlag, A K, Baldwin, D S, Barnes, M, Bazire, S, Coathup, R, Curran, H V, McShane, R, Phillips, L D, Singh, I, Nutt, D J (2020), Medical Cannabis in the UK: From Principle to Pactice, *Journal of Psychopharmacology*. DOI: 10.1177/0269881120926677

Sessa, B, Higbed, L, O'Brien, S, Durant, C, Sakal, C, Titheradge, D, Williams, T W, Rose-Morris, A, Brew-Girard, E, Burrows, S, Wiseman, C, Wilson, S, Rickard, J, Nutt, D J (2021), First Study of Safety and Tolerability of 3,4-Methylenedioxymethamphetamine-assisted Psychotherapy in Patients with Alcohol Use Disorder, *Journal of Psychopharmacology*. DOI: 10.1177/0269881121991792

Transform Drug Policy Foundation (2020), How to Regulate Stimulants: transformdrugs.org/publications/how-to-regulate-stimulants-a-practical-guide

United Nations Office on Drugs and Crime (1971), Convention on Psychotropic Substances 1971: www.unodc.org/pdf/convention_1971_en.pdf

Wickware, C (2019), Drug Rehabilitation Charities Spent Millions on Generics Price Concessions in 2018, *Pharmaceutical Journal*: https://pharmaceutical-journal.com/article/news/drug-rehabilitation-charities-spent-millions-on-generics-price-concessions-in-2018

PART III
LEGACIES OF THE DRUG LAWS

CHAPTER 10

How States Have Adapted Their Drug Laws

Emily Crick and Adam Holland

This chapter looks at how individual States have adapted their internal (domestic) drug laws within the flexibility of United Nations (UN) drug conventions to improve the 'health and welfare' of their citizens.

The UN drug conventions cite a desire to promote 'the health and welfare of [hu]mankind' (UN, 1975; 1976a; 1990). However, as the conventions were integrated into national legislation, across the world, the emphasis tended towards controlling drugs with the threat of criminal sanctions. States adopted approaches that deleteriously impact the health and social wellbeing of people who use drugs, which are incongruent with the management of other public health issues and incompatible with human rights norms (Csete et al, 2016). Whilst punitive drug control laws still predominate in many countries, this chapter explores case studies demonstrating how some States have adapted their laws and policies within the flexibility of the conventions in response to the failures of prohibition and increasing levels of drug-related harm, with relevance for drug policy in the UK.

> **UN Drug Control Conventions**
> - **Single Convention on Narcotic Drugs of 1961 (as amended by the 1972 Protocol) (the Single Convention):** dealt with 'natural substances,' i.e. cannabis, coca-based products and opiates (UN, 1975).
> - **Convention on Psychotropic Substances of 1971 (the 1971 Convention):** dealt mostly with substances that were 'manufactured by a process of full chemical synthesis' such as lysergic acid diethylamide (LSD) and tranquillisers (UN, 1976a).
> - **Convention Against Illicit Traffic in Narcotic Drugs and Psychotropic Substances of 1988 (the 1988 Convention):** primarily concerned international trafficking but also focused on precursor substances (UN, 1990).

The UN Drug Conventions

The Single Convention was proposed by the US to limit the production, trade and use of specific drugs, including opiates, coca and cannabis, to medical and scientific purposes under international law (Crick, 2018). When it was eventually established in 1967, after the US attempted to undermine the ratification process to push for more stringent controls (ibid), four schedules of drugs were created, supposedly reflecting the harmfulness and addictiveness of substances, balanced against their medical utility (International Narcotics Control Board (INCB), 2005). The 1971 Convention then similarly scheduled other mostly synthetic drugs, including amphetamines and psychedelics (UN, 1976a). As a result, most States introduced criminal sanctions for the possession or use of drugs for non-medical and non-scientific purposes (Sanchéz-Avilés and Ditrych, 2017). This interpretation was fostered by the US (Andreas and Nadelmann, 2006), and the INCB, who began to regard themselves as the 'guardians of the treaties' (INCB, 2002). Some States however, for example The Netherlands with cannabis, pursued alternative policy approaches, not relying on criminal sanctions. Although these developments were met by UN resistance, their continued acceptance highlights the flexibility within the international treaties, which could be utilised in the UK.

> ### Key terms
> - ***De facto* decriminalisation:** the removal of criminal sanctions for something as a matter of practice or policy (United Nations Office on Drugs and Crime (UNODC), 2015a).
> - ***De jure* decriminalisation:** the removal of criminal sanctions for something as a matter of law (UNODC, 2015a).
> - **Diamorphine assisted treatment (DAT):** the prescription of diamorphine (pharmaceutically produced heroin) for the management of opioid dependence (sometimes referred to as heroin assisted treatment).
> - **Drug checking service:** a service that analyses the content of substances to monitor the illicit drug market and inform consumers of the risk of adulteration or fluctuating purity.
> - **Harm reduction:** policies, programmes and practices that aim to minimise the negative health, social and legal impacts associated with drug use, drug policies and drug laws (Harm Reduction International, 2021).
> - **Needle and syringe programme (NSP):** a service providing sterile injecting commodities to people who inject drugs.
> - **Opioid agonist treatment (OAT):** the prescription of opioids, typically methadone or buprenorphine, for the management of opioid dependence.
> - **Overdose prevention centre (OPC):** a site where people can use their own drugs under the supervision of others who are trained to intervene in the event of an overdose, additionally providing an opportunity to provide sterile injecting commodities and other interventions (sometimes referred to as drug consumption rooms, safer injecting facilities or enhanced harm reduction centres).

De Jure Decriminalisation in Portugal

In response to escalating levels of drug use, the use and trafficking of drugs was made illegal in Portugal in 1970 (European Monitoring Centre for Drugs and Drug Addiction (EMCDDA), 2011). Drug use was considered in moral terms, described as a cause of crime and social movements against the country's political regime (ibid). Heroin use and public injecting increased until the 1990s, with a 1997 survey indicating the public considered drug use to be the country's predominant social issue (Domoslawski, 2011).

The possibility of decriminalising drugs in Portugal was first mentioned in a 1976 Government document, stating that the idea of drug use as a criminal act should be revised and replaced, when appropriate, within an administrative offence framework (EMCDDA, 2011). However, plans did not progress until a committee of specialists including doctors, lawyers, social workers and academics was established in 1998 to offer policy recommendations (Domoslawski, 2011). The committee proposed that possession and use of all drugs should be decriminalised, aiming to reduce problematic drug use, whilst recognising that realising a 'drug free world' was unachievable (ibid). The debate shifted away from concern about the use of drugs *per se* towards recognising the impact that policy and social conditions have on overdoses, HIV transmission and other negative outcomes of drug use (ibid).

The law, introduced in 2001, decriminalised the possession of up to ten days' supply of drugs for personal use; instead, possession became an administrative offence, along the same lines as receiving a speeding ticket, whilst criminal sanctions were maintained for drug production and trafficking (Domoslawski, 2011). New agencies (Dissuasion Commissions) were established to oversee the administrative sanction framework comprising psychologists, addiction specialists, mental health, and social workers (ibid). Those found in possession of drugs must attend a Dissuasion Commission, where they may be issued with a warning, a fine, a suspended penalty, or a treatment referral if they are dependent on the substance (Laqueur, 2015). Simultaneously, the Portuguese Government expanded drug treatment, harm reduction and outreach services (ibid).

It is not possible to disentangle the effects of decriminalisation from concurrent health service and social investment. However, following the reform, drug-related death and HIV rates decreased (Transform, 2021a). And, rather than skyrocketing as feared (Eastwood et al, 2016), overall drug use remained below the European average, with reductions in problematic use and recent use amongst young people (Rêgo et al, 2021; Hughes and Stevens, 2010).

Although the UN conventions require that States take measures to limit drugs solely to medical and scientific purposes (Article 4, Single Convention; Article

5, 1971 Convention), and possession contrary to these measures should be a 'punishable offence' (Article 36, Single Convention; Article 22, 1971 Convention) they do not stipulate what form this punishment must take. The commentaries to both conventions explicitly state that punishments may take the form of administrative sanctions (Commentary on Article 4, Single Convention; Commentary on Article 7, 1971 Convention), in line with the Portuguese approach. Although some have argued that Article 3 of the 1988 Convention places additional requirements on States to criminalise drug possession as a driver of drug trafficking (Krajewski, 1999), this is contrary to the earlier conventions, and the position has not prevented Portugal's *de jure* decriminalisation model.

The INCB was initially critical of Portugal's approach, suggesting it did not fulfil their commitment to the UN drug conventions (INCB, 2002). However, after visiting Portugal in 2004 the INCB admitted that 'the practice of exempting small quantities of drugs from criminal prosecution is consistent with the international drug control treaties' (UNODC, 2009). Similarly, the UNODC has previously been reticent to formally endorse decriminalisation. Although a 2015 UNODC briefing paper argued, 'Decriminalising drug use and possession for personal consumption is permitted by the international drug control conventions and is a key element of the HIV response among people who use drugs' (UNODC, 2015a), this was followed by a statement that the paper was a discussion document not meant for publication (UNODC, 2015b). In 2018 however, the publication of the UN common position on drugs, ratified by the chief executives of all UN agencies, including the UNODC, established a consensus position on decriminalisation, endorsing the promotion of 'alternatives to conviction and punishment in appropriate cases, including the decriminalization of drug possession for personal use' (United Nations Chief Executives Board (UNCEB), 2018).

De Facto Decriminalisation in The Netherlands

In the 1960s, in response to concerns about the emergence of 'new' drugs such as hashish and LSD, a new drug strategy was introduced in The Netherlands promoting criminal sanctions for the use of drugs (Korf et al, 1999). This led to widespread criticism from the media, and various public and governmental bodies called for decriminalisation of drugs (Mares, 2006). The Hulsman Commission argued for a legal distinction between cannabis and other illicit drugs (Korf et al, 1999), and the Baan Commission called for a distinction between 'soft' drugs, including cannabis, and 'hard' drugs, including heroin and cocaine, which were deemed to be more harmful (Mares, 2006). In response, the revised Opium Act (1976) introduced a change in the law with less severe penalties for offences related to 'soft' drugs (De Kort and Korf, 1992).

The Dutch Opium Act (1976) maintained criminal sanctions in law, however guidelines were introduced instructing police to not prosecute for the possession of drugs for personal consumption (Eastwood et al, 2016). This approach was fostered by concerns that criminalisation is inherently harmful (Mares, 2006) and could increase the negative health impacts of drug use (Spapens et al, 2015). Alongside *de facto* decriminalisation, The Netherlands introduced a comprehensive harm reduction strategy, and were the first country to implement NSPs, and later a national drug checking service (van Santen et al, 2021). Additionally, the sale of small amounts of cannabis in private spaces was tolerated, in order to prevent violence and competition between different suppliers (Spapens et al, 2015) with Government guidelines prohibiting advertising, sales to underage persons, or the sale of large quantities (Mares, 2006). By the 1980s, the 'house dealer' system evolved into local authority licensed and regulated 'coffee shops' where cannabis can be purchased (Korf et al, 1999). Although according to recent population surveys adult drug use overall is higher in The Netherlands than in the UK, the estimated prevalence of problematic drug use is lower, as is the rate of drug-related deaths (EMCDDA, 2019).

The Netherlands Government argue their approach does not contravene the UN conventions, which do not specifically state it is necessary to enforce sanctions stipulated in law (Caulkins et al, 2016). The US and countries neighbouring The Netherlands (Marshall and Van de Bunt, 2001; Spapens et al, 2015) have criticised their approach, and the INCB have argued 'coffee shops' are 'indirect incitement [to cannabis use, and] not in accordance with the spirit or the letter of the international drug control treaties' (INCB, 1998). Others argue that the Dutch approach has been successful in reducing harms related to drug use and criminalisation, which has been worth the international censure (Grund and Breeksema, 2013). Although there have been plans to increase restrictions on coffee shops to limit their use to local residents, this faced opposition from the Dutch public, judges and prosecutors and these have mostly not been pursued or enforced (Transform Drug Policy Foundation, 2018).

Harm Reduction in Switzerland and Across Europe

Regardless of domestic laws on drug possession, harm reduction approaches to drug use proliferated across Europe in the 1980s in response to increasing HIV transmission (Cook et al, 2010). As their use has become more widespread, the evidence base in their favour has grown. Amongst other benefits, evidence has demonstrated that NSPs and OAT reduce the risk of blood borne virus transmission (MacArthur et al, 2012; Platt et al, 2017) with DAT posing additional benefits for those who did not benefit from oral OAT (Ferri et al, 2011). Observational studies have demonstrated OPCs, now in operation across nearly 200 sites in 14 countries (Transform Drug Policy Foundation, 2022), may reduce drug-related deaths in local areas, and provide wider benefits including reductions in self-reported riskier drug-taking practices (EMCDDA, 2018).

Alongside Portugal and The Netherlands, Switzerland has been at the forefront of harm reduction approaches to drug use. In the 1970s in Switzerland, drug policy focused on promoting abstinence through repressive measures, with a 1975 law prohibiting the provision of sterile injecting equipment and OAT (Csete, 2010). Heroin use escalated, public injecting became more common, and by the 1980s Switzerland had the highest prevalence of HIV amongst injecting drug users in Western Europe (ibid). This led to a shift in the national debate and professionals called for easier access to treatment and support (Killias and Aebi, 2000). The first OPC opened in Berne in Switzerland in 1986 (EMCDDA, 2018) and in 1992 the law was changed to allow the provision of NSP and OAT, including DAT (Weber, 2000). The strategy aimed to reduce public drug use, crime and drug litter and to re-engage people with drug dependence into wider society, health and social services (Csete, 2010). Between 1996 and 2018, drug-related deaths in Switzerland fell by 56% (Swiss Health Observatory, 2020).

The INCB were highly critical of the expansion of harm reduction interventions. In 2002, Philip Emafo, then INCB president, criticised proponents of harm reduction for being on 'a crusade', arguing that NSPs and OPCs would 'amount to inciting people to abuse drugs, which would be contrary to the provisions of the Conventions' (Buxton, 2006). The approach, and indeed the term, has remained internationally contentious (Jelsma, 2019). At the 2016 UN General Assembly Special Session on Drugs (UNGASS), the discussion document drafted at the preceding meeting of the Commission on Narcotic Drugs (CND) recognised the importance of harm reduction methods (International Drug Policy Consortium (IDPC), 2016). However, the Political Declaration that was agreed at UNGASS failed to explicitly mention the term (UNODC, 2016). Whereas the most recent United Nations AIDS Strategy has harm reduction as one of its key tenets (UNAIDS, 2021) the term does not feature in the 2021–2025 UNODC Strategy (ibid). And although the policies of 87 countries include a supportive reference to harm reduction, the policies of many others do not (Harm Reduction International (HRI), 2020). Despite this, at a UN level there is at least a stated consensus in the 2018 common position on drugs, which specifically endorses the promotion of 'measures aimed at minimizing the adverse public health consequences of drug abuse, sometimes referred to as harm reduction' (UNCEB, 2018).

Drug Policy in the UK

The Single Convention was ratified by the UK in 1964, leading to the Dangerous Drugs Act 1964 (DDA 1964) under which punishments for illicit drug offences were the same regardless of the drug (Home Office, 2006). The MDA 1971 then established three classes of drugs: A, B and C to reflect the UN drug conventions (Rolles and Measham, 2011) that supposedly reflected the relative harms of the substances in each category, and the penalties for offences related to them (Home Office, 2006). However, like the UN schedules, the UK classes have been criticised as having 'evolved in an unsystematic way from somewhat arbitrary foundations with seemingly little scientific basis' (Nutt et al, 2007).

Historically, the UK was an outspoken advocate of harm reduction approaches. In the 1920s the so-called 'British System' was developed as a forerunner to modern DAT, whereby diamorphine was prescribed to patients and medical professionals who had become dependent on opioids in the course of treatment or practice (Berridge, 2005). In light of its successes, the UK was one of the nations that argued against the prohibition of diamorphine for medical use during the drafting of the Single Convention (UN, 1964). When the DDA 1964 was revised in 1967, the British System was amended, so that only licensed doctors could prescribe diamorphine for opioid dependence (Mott and Bean, 1998), leading to the practice becoming uncommon, although still possible under UK law (Lart, 1998). During the late 1980s and 1990s, like in much of Europe, harm reduction approaches proliferated in the UK, and drug strategies focused on public health in contrast to links between drugs and crime (Stimson, 2000). OAT provision was expanded, and NSPs were established (Lart, 2008). The UK Advisory Council on the Misuse of Drugs (ACMD) encouraged this approach, highlighting in a 1988 report that 'the spread of HIV is a greater danger to individual and public health than drug misuse' (Raistrick, 1994).

The late 1990s saw a change in tack, with Government drug strategies ever since placing less emphasis on harm reduction and instead focusing on links between drug use and criminality (Monaghan, 2012; Stimson, 2000). Drug-related death rates in the UK have consistently increased since the early 2010s (ONS, 2021; NRS, 2021) and, in 2018, the UK accounted for a third of the drug-related deaths in Europe, with Scotland having the highest drug-related death rate (EMCDDA, 2020). In response, a 2019 House of Commons Health and Social Care Committee declared that drug-related deaths in the UK had risen to the scale of a 'public health emergency' (HSCC, 2019). They advocated for a health-based approach; a consultation on decriminalisation; the establishment of OPCs; and an expansion of evidence-based harm reduction interventions including DAT (ibid). Others recommending alternative approaches in the UK include health bodies calling for decriminalisation (Royal Society for Public Health (RSPH), 2016); the ACMD, who have endorsed OPCs (ACMD, 2016); and a coalition of Members of Parliament and non-governmental organizations calling for drug policy reform (Transform Drug Policy Foundation, 2021b).

As the previous case studies have demonstrated, some level of drug policy reform in the UK is eminently possible, in terms of the international treaties. Recent developments however have demonstrated the Government's appetite to redouble efforts to promote criminal sanctions for drug-related offences. The Psychoactive Substances Act 2016 (PSA 2016) criminalised the supply of any substance nebulously defined as 'psychoactive' above and beyond those considered in the UN conventions (Stevens et al, 2015). Despite previous reviews finding no merit in the proposal, the Home Office has commissioned a further review to criminalise the possession of nitrous oxide (Hamilton and Sumnall, 2021). And the Government response to Dame Carol Black's independent review of drugs (Black, 2020 and 2021) indicated future drug strategies will focus on ensuring there are 'clear and meaningful consequences' of use that would supposedly reduce the demand for drugs (Home Office and Department of Health and Social Care, 2021). Although there is stated Government support for existing harm reduction interventions, various requests to allow OPCs to open in the UK have been rejected, as the Home Office claims, 'there is no legal framework for the provision of DCRs in the UK' (Fortson and McCulloch, 2018), and a Government Minister recently referred to the debate as 'a distraction' (BBC, 2020).

Conclusion

The UN drug control conventions are not without issue. They have been used as a lever by proponents of prohibition (Sanchéz-Avilés and Ditrych, 2017). Administrative sanctions still promote the stigmatisation, surveillance and punishment of people who use drugs (International Network of People Who Use Drugs (INPUD), 2021). Restrictions on production and trade mean 75% of the global population live with inadequate access to opioid analgesia (Marks, 2009; Burke-Shyne et al, 2017; INCB, 2016). The controls have also prevented research to explore the use of psychedelics for therapeutic purposes (Nutt et al, 2013). And the INCB's position is that regulated markets for drugs for non-medical purposes, which may be advocated as a longer-term means of reducing drug-related harm (Global Commission, 2018), are not permissible under the existing conventions (INCB, 2013). However, there is scope to reorientate domestic drug laws and policies away from a focus on criminal sanctions, to promote 'the health and welfare of [hu]mankind' as the UN conventions supposedly intended (UN, 1975; 1976a; 1990).

The UN drug conventions allow a certain amount of flexibility to achieve maximum adherence (UN, 1964). Although opinions differ on the latitude of this flexibility, and States adopting innovative approaches have faced international censure, precedent has demonstrated that international treaties would not prevent policy reforms in the UK. Drug laws are not always, nor should they be, static; they can and should evolve according to national circumstances and emerging evidence of comparative harms. Whilst the negative impacts of criminalisation on people who use drugs are clear (Csete et al, 2016) the evidence for its effects on drug use is not (Scheim et al, 2020; Stevens, 2019). The successes of other countries demonstrate it is not necessary to criminalise drugs to reduce drug-related harm; and the failures of others, the UK among them, highlight it may exacerbate the harm its proponents aim to prevent (Holland, 2020).

Dr Emily Crick teaches Drug Policy in the School of Policy Studies at the University of Bristol and is a member of the Drug Policy Interdisciplinary Network (DPIN). Her PhD analysed how drugs became identified as threatening to humans and nation states, by the USA and United Nations, and how these discourses shaped national and international drug policy.

Dr Adam Holland MFPH is an Honorary Research Fellow at the University of Bristol and a member of the DPIN. He has published various articles on the ethical and empirical arguments for different harm reduction and drug policy approaches.

References and Extra Reading

Advisory Council on the Misuse of Drugs (2016), *Reducing Opioid-Related Deaths in the UK*, London: Home Office: https://assets.publishing.service.gov.uk/government/uploads/system/uploads/attachment_data/file/576560/ACMD-Drug-Related-Deaths-Report-161212.pdf

Andreas, P and Nadelmann, E (2006), *Policing the Globe: Criminalization and Crime Control in International Relations*, Oxford: Oxford University Press.

BBC News (2010), Drug consumption rooms are a 'distraction' says UK minister, February 27: www.bbc.co.uk/news/uk-scotland-51644786

Berridge, V (2005), The 'British System' and its History: Myth and Reality in *Heroin Addiction and the British System, Volume 1: Origins and Evolution*, J Strang and M Gossop (eds), 7–16, Abingdon: Routledge.

Black, C (2010), *Review of Drugs—Evidence Relating to Drug Use, Supply and Effects, Including Current Trends and Future Risks*, London: Home Office: www.gov.uk/government/collections/independent-review-of-drugs-by-professor-dame-carol-black

Black, C (2021), *Review of Drugs Part Two: Prevention, Treatment, and Recovery*, London: Home Office: www.gov.uk/government/collections/independent-review-of-drugs-by-professor-dame-carol-black

Burke-Shyne, N, Csete, J, Wilson, D, Dox, E, Wolfe, D and Rasanathan, J J K (2017), How Drug Control Policy and Practice Undermine Access to Controlled Medicines, *Health and Human Rights Journal*, 19(1): 237–252.

Buxton, J (2006), *The Political Economy of Narcotic Drugs: Production, Consumption and Global Markets*, London: Zed Books.

Caulkins, J P, Kilmer, B and Kleiman, M A R (2016), *Marijuana Legalization: What Everyone Needs to Know?* New York: Oxford University Press.

Cook, C, Bridge, J and Stimson G V (2010), The Diffusion of Harm Reduction in Europe and Beyond in *Harm Reduction: Evidence, Impacts and Challenges*, T Rhodes and D Hedrich (eds): 37–58, EMCDDA Monographs, Luxembourg: Publications Office of the European Union.

Crick, E (2018), *Security and the Drug Control Dispositif: Analysing the Construction of Drugs as an Existential Threat to Humankind and the Nation State*, unpublished doctoral thesis, Bristol: University of Bristol: https://research-information.bris.ac.uk/ws/portalfiles/portal/169366765/Security_and_the_Drug_Control_Dispositif_FINAL_CORRECTED.pdf

Csete, J (2010), *From the Mountaintops: What the World Can Learn from Drug Policy Change in Switzerland* (Lessons for Drug Policy Series), New York: Open Society Foundations.

Csete, J, Kamarulzaman, A, Kazatchkine, M, Altice, F, Balicki, M, Buxton, J, Cepeda, J, Comfort, M, Goosby, E, Goulão, J, Hart, C, Kerr, T, Madrazo Lajous, A, Lewis, S, Martin, N, Mejía, D, Camacho, A, Mathieson, D, Obot, I, Ogunrombi, A, Sherman, S, Stone, J, Vallath, N, Vickerman, P, Zábranský, T and Beyrer, C (2016), Public Health and International Drug Policy, *The Lancet Commissions*, 387(10026): 1427–1480.

De Kort, M and Korf, D J (1992), The Development of Drug Trade and Drug Control in The Netherlands: A Historical Perspective, *Crime, Law and Social Change*, 17: 123–144.

Domoslawski, A (2011), *Drug Policy in Portugal: The Benefits of Decriminalizing Drug Use* (Lessons for Drug Policy Series), New York: Open Society Foundations.

Eastwood, N, Fox, E and Rosmarin, A (2016), *A Quiet Revolution: Drug Decriminalisation Across the Globe*, London: Release.

European Monitoring Centre for Drugs and Drug Addiction (EMCDDA) (2011), *Drug Policy Profiles: Portugal*, Luxembourg: Publications Office of the European Union: www.emcdda. europa.eu/system/files/publications/642/PolicyProfile_Portugal_WEB_Final_289201.pdf

EMCDDA (2018), *Perspectives On Drugs: Drug Consumption Rooms: An Overview of Provision and Evidence*, Luxembourg: Publications Office of the European Union: www.emcdda. europa.eu/system/files/publications/2734/POD_Drug%20consumption%20rooms.pdf

EMCDDA (2019), *Netherlands Country Drug Report 2019*: www.emcdda.europa.eu/system/ files/publications/11347/netherlands-cdr-2019.pdf

EMCDDA (2020), *European Drug Report 2020: Trends and Developments*, Luxembourg: Publications Office of the European Union: www.emcdda.europa.eu/system/files/ publications/13236/TDAT20001ENN_web.pdf

Ferri, M, Davoli, M and Perucci, C A (2011), Heroin Maintenance for Chronic Heroin-dependent Individuals, Cochrane Database of Systematic Reviews, 12: www. cochranelibrary.com/cdsr/doi/10.1002/14651858.CD003410.pub4/full

Fortson, R and McCulloch, L (2018), Evidence and Issues Concerning Drug Consumption Rooms, Queen Mary School of Law Legal Studies Research Paper No. 279/2018: https:// papers.ssrn.com/sol3/papers.cfm?abstract_id=3182568

Global Commission on Drug Policy (2018), *Regulation: The Responsible Control of Drugs*, Geneva: Global Commission on Drug Policy: www.globalcommissionondrugs.org/ wp-content/uploads/2018/09/ENG-2018_Regulation_Report_WEB-FINAL.pdf

Grund, J and Breeksema, J (2013), *Coffee Shops and Compromise: Separated Illicit Drug Markets in The Netherlands* (Lessons for Drug Policy Series), New York: Open Society Foundation.

Hamilton, I and Sumnall, H (2021), Criminalising Nitrous Oxide Users is No Laughing Matter if it Distracts from More Serious Drug Problems, *The Conversation*, September 6: https://theconversation.com/criminalising-nitrous-oxide-users-is-no-laughing-matter-if-it-distracts-from-more-serious-drug-problems-167297

Harm Reduction International (HRI) (2020), *The Global State of Harm Reduction 2020*, London: HRI: www.hri.global/files/2021/03/04/Global_State_HRI_2020_BOOK_FA_ Web.pdf

HRI (2021), *What is Harm Reduction?* HRI: www.hri.global/what-is-harm-reduction

Holland, A (2020), An Ethical Analysis of UK Drug Policy as an Example of a Criminal Justice Approach to Drugs: A Commentary on the Short Film 'Putting UK Drug Policy into Focus,' *Harm Reduction Journal*, 17(97).

Home Office (2006), Review of the UK's Drugs Classification System — A Public Consultation, London: Home Office Crime and Drug Strategy Directorate (released under freedom of information legislation, 2010): www.drugequality.org/files/Review_of_Drugs_Classification_Consultation_Paper.pdf

Home Office and Department of Health and Social Care (2021), Government Response to the Independent Review of Drugs by Dame Carol Black, UK Government: www.gov.uk/government/publications/independent-review-of-drugs-by-dame-carol-black-government-response/government-response-to-the-independent-review-of-drugs-by-dame-carol-black

House of Commons Health and Social Care Committee (2019), Drugs Policy: First Report of Session 2019, London: House of Commons: https://publications.parliament.uk/pa/cm201919/cmselect/cmhealth/143/143.pdf

Hughes, C E and Stevens, A (2010), What Can We Learn From The Portuguese Decriminalization of Illicit Drugs? *British Journal of Criminology*, 50(6): 999–1022.

International Narcotics Control Board (INCB) (1998), Report of The International Narcotics Control Board for 1997, E/INCB/1997/1, New York: United Nations.

INCB (2002), Report for the International Narcotics Controls Board for 2001, E/INCB/2001/1, New York: United Nations.

INCB (2005), Training Material, 1961 Single Convention on Narcotic Drugs Part 1: The International Control System for Narcotic Drugs, E/INCB/2005/NAR_1, New York: United Nations.

INCB (2013), US Recreational Cannabis Use Would Violate International Laws, UN Anti-Narcotics Panel Says, United Nations News Centre, 14 March: www.un.org/apps/news/story.asp?NewsID=44376#.Vvk1qvkrLcs

INCB (2016), Availability of Internationally Controlled Drugs: Ensuring Adequate Access for Medical and Scientific Purposes Indispensable, Adequately Available and Not Unduly Restricted, New York: United Nations.

International Drug Policy Consortium (IDPC) (2016), New Approaches on Harm Reduction with a Look at UNGASS 2016: Conference Room Paper 59th Session of the Commission on Narcotic Drugs, London: IDPC.

International Network of People Who Use Drugs (INPUD) (2021), Drug Decriminalisation: Progress or Political Red Herring? Assessing the Impact of Current Models of Decriminalisation on People Who Use Drugs, London: INPUD: www.inpud.net/sites/default/files/INPUD_Decriminalisation%20report_online%20version.pdf

Jelsma, M (2019), UN Common Position on Drug Policy—Consolidating System-wide Coherence, IDPC Briefing paper, London: IDPC: http://fileserver.idpc.net/library/UN-Common-Position-Briefing-Paper.pdf

Killias, M and Aebi M F (2000), The Impact of Heroin Prescription on Heroin Markets in Switzerland, *Crime Prevention Studies*, 11: 83–99.

Korf, D J, Riper, H and Bullington, B (1999), Windmills in Their Minds? Drug Policy and Drug Research in The Netherlands, *Journal of Drug Issues*, 29(3): 451–472.

Krajewski, K (1999), How Flexible Are the United Nations Drug Conventions? *International Journal of Drug Policy*, 10: 329–338

Laqueur, H (2015), Uses and Abuses of Drug Decriminalization in Portugal, *Law and Social Inquiry*, 30(3): 746–781.

Lart, R (1998), Medical Power/Knowledge: The Treatment and Control of Drugs and Drug Users in *The Control of Drugs and Drug Users: Reason or Reaction*, R Coomber (ed.): 49–68, Boca Raton: CRC Press.

Lart, R (2008), Drugs and Health Policy in *Drugs: Policy and Politics*, R Hughes, R Lart and P Higate (eds): 92–112, New York: Open University Press.

MacArthur, G J, Minozzi, S, Martin, N, Vickerman, P, Deren, S, Bruneau, J, Degenhardt, L and Hickman, M (2012), Opiate Substitution Treatment and HIV Transmission in People Who Inject Drugs: Systematic Review and Meta-analysis, *British Medical Journal*, 345: www.bmj.com/content/345/bmj.e5945

Mares, D R (2009), *Drug Wars and Coffeehouse: The Political Economy of the International Drug Trade*, Washington DC: CQ Press.

Marks, S P (2009), Access to Essential Medicines as a Component of the Right to Health in *Realizing the Right to Health*, A Clapham and M Robinson (eds) (Swiss Human Rights Book Series), 3: 82–101, Zurich: Rüffer & Rub.

Marshall, I H and Van de Bunt, H (2001), Exporting the Drug War to The Netherlands and Dutch Alternatives in *Drug War American Style: The Internationalization of Failed Policy and Its Alternatives*, J Gerber and E L Jensen (eds): 197–218, New York: Garland Publishing.

Mott, J and Bean, P (1998), The Development of Drug Control in Britain in *The Control of Drugs and Drug Users: Reason or Reaction*, R Coomber (ed.): 31–48, Boca Raton: CRC Press.

National Records of Scotland (2021), Drug-related Deaths in Scotland in 2020, National Records for Scotland: www.nrscotland.gov.uk/statistics-and-data/statistics/statistics-by-theme/vital-events/deaths/drug-related-deaths-in-scotland/2020

Nutt, D, King, L A. Saulsbury, W and Blakemore, C (2007), Development of a Rational Scale to Assess the Harm of Drugs of Potential Misuse, *The Lancet*, 369(9566): 1047–1053.

Nutt, D, King, L and Nichols, D (2013), Effects of Schedule I Drug Laws on Neuroscience Research and Treatment Innovation, *Nature Reviews Neuroscience*, 14: 577–585.

Office for National Statistics (ONS) (2021), Deaths Related to Drug Poisoning in England and Wales: 2020 Registrations, ONS: www.ons.gov.uk/peoplepopulationandcommunity/birthsdeathsandmarriages/deaths/bulletins/deathsrelatedtodrugpoisoninginenglandandwales/2020

Platt, L, Minozzi, S, Reed, J, Vickerman, P, Hagan, H, French, C, Jordan, A, Degenhardt, L, Hope, V, Hutchinson, S, Maher, L, Palmateer, N, Taylor, A, Bruneau, J and Hickman, M (2017), Needle Syringe Programmes and Opioid Substitution Therapy for Preventing Hepatitis C Transmission in People Who Inject Drugs, *Cochrane Database Systematic Reviews*, 9: www.ncbi.nlm.nih.gov/pmc/articles/PMC5621373/pdf/CD012021.pdf

Raistrick, D (1994), Report of Advisory Council on the Misuse of Drugs: AIDS and Drug Misuse Update, *Addiction*, 89(10): 1211–1213.

Rêgo, X, Oliveira, M J, Lameira, C and Cruz, O S (2021), 20 years of Portuguese Drug Policy — Developments, Challenges and the Quest for Human Rights, *Substance Abuse Treatment, Prevention, and Policy*, 16(59): https://substanceabusepolicy.biomedcentral.com/articles/10.1186/s13011-021-00394-7

Rolles, S and Measham, F (2011), Questioning The Method and Utility of Ranking Drug Harms in Drug Policy, *International Journal of Drug Policy*, 22(4): 243–246.

Royal Society for Public Health (2016), Taking A New Line On Drugs, RSPH: www.rsph.org.uk/static/uploaded/68d93cdc-292c-4a7b-babfc0a8ee252bc0.pdf

Sanchéz-Avilés, C and Ditrych, O (2017), The Global Drug Prohibition Regime: Prospects for Stability and Change in an Increasingly Less Prohibitionist World, *International Politics*, 55: 463–481.

Scheim A I, Maghsoudi N and Marshall, Z (2020), Impact Evaluations of Drug Decriminalisation and Legal Regulation on Drug Use, Health and Social Harms: A Systematic Review, *British Medical Journal Open*, 10: https://bmjopen.bmj.com/content/10/9/e035148

Spapens, T, Muller, T and van de Bunt, H (2015), The Dutch Drug Policy from a Regulatory Perspective, *European Journal for Criminal Policy Research*, 21: 191–205.

Statistical Service Scotland (2021), Drug-related Deaths in Scotland in 2020, National Records for Scotland: www.nrscotland.gov.uk/statistics-and-data/statistics/statistics-by-theme/vital-events/deaths/drug-related-deaths-in-scotland/2020

Stevens, A (2010), Is Policy 'Liberalization' Associated with Higher Odds of Adolescent Cannabis Use? A Re-analysis of Data From 38 Countries, *International Journal of Drug Policy*, 66: 94–99.

Stevens, A, Fortson, R, Measham F and Sumnall, H (2015), Legally Flawed, Scientifically Problematic, Potentially Harmful: The UK Psychoactive Substance Bill, *International Journal of Drug Policy* 26: 1167–1170.

Stimson, G V (2000), 'Blair declares war': the unhealthy state of British drug policy, *International Journal of Drug Policy*, 11, pp. 259–264.

Swiss Health Observatory (2020), *Drug-related deaths*, Swiss Health Observatory: www.obsan. admin.ch/en/indicators/MonAM/drug-related-deaths

Transform Drug Policy Foundation (TDPF) (2018), *Cannabis Policy in the Netherlands: Moving Forwards Not Backwards*, Bristol: TDPF: https://transformdrugs.org/blog/cannabis-policy-in-the-netherlands-moving-forwards-not-backwards

TDPF (2021a), *Drug Decriminalisation In Portugal: Setting The Record Straight*, Bristol: TDPF: https://transformdrugs.org/publications/drug-decriminalisation-in-portugal-setting-the-record-straight

TDPF (2021b), *Drug Policy Fit for the 21st Century*, Bristol: TDPF: https://transformdrugs.org/mda-at-50

TDPF (2022), Overdose Prevention Centres, Bristol: TDPF: https://transformdrugs.org/drug-policy/uk-drug-policy/overdose-prevention-centres

United Nations (UN) (1964), Official Record of the United Nations Conference for the Adoption of a Single Convention on Narcotic Drugs. Volume I: Summary Records of the Plenary Meetings, E/CONF.34/24- e, New York: United Nations.

UN (1973), Commentary on the Single on Narcotic Drugs 1961, E.73.XI.1, New York: UN.

UN (1975), The Single Convention on Narcotic Drugs of 1961 as amended by the 1972 Protocol, New York: UN.

UN (1976a) Convention on Psychotropic Substances of 1971, New York: UN.

UN (1976b), Commentary on the Convention on Psychotropic Substances, E/CN.7/589, New York: UN.

UN (1990), United Nations Convention Against Illicit Traffic in Narcotic Drugs and Psychotropic Substances, 1988, New York: UN.

UN Central Executive Board (UNCEB) (2018), United Nations System Common Position Supporting the Implementation of the International Drug Control Policy Through Effective Inter-agency Collaboration: Annexe 1, CEB/2018/2, New York: UN.

United Nations Office on Drugs and Crime (ONODC) (2009), World Drug Report 2009, Vienna: UNODC: www.unodc.org/documents/wdr/WDR_2009/WDR2009_eng_web.pdf

UNODC (2015a), Briefing paper: Decriminalisation of Drug Use and Possession for Personal Consumption: http://news.bbc.co.uk/1/shared/bsp/hi/pdfs/19_10_11_unodcbriefing.pdf

UNODC (2015b), UNODC Spokesperson Statement in Response to the Briefing Paper on Decriminalisation: www.unodc.org/unodc/en/press/releases/2015/October/statement-by-the-spokesperson-for-the-un-office-on-drugs-and-crime.html

UNODC (2016), Our Joint Commitment to Effectively Addressing and Countering the World Drug Problem: Resolution Adopted by the General Assembly on 19 April 2016, A/RES/S-30/1, New York: United Nations.

UNODC (2021), UNODC Strategy 2021–2025: www.unodc.org/unodc/en/strategy/full-strategy.html

UNAIDS (2021), Global AIDS Strategy 2021–2026 — End Inequalities. End AIDS, UNAIDS: www.unaids.org/en/resources/documents/2021/2021-2026-global-AIDS-strategy

van Santen, D, Coutinho, R A, van den Hoek, A, van Brussel, G, Buster, M and Prins, M (2021), Lessons Learned from the Amsterdam Cohort Studies Among People Who Use Drugs: A Historical Perspective, *Harm Reduction Journal*, 18(2).

Weber, W (2000), Heroin Prescription for Addicts in Switzerland Improves Quality of Life, *The Lancet*, 356(9236): 1177.

CHAPTER 11

The Sixties, Barbara Wootton and the Counterculture
Revisiting the Origins of the MDA 1971

Toby Seddon

More than half a century ago, on 27 May 1971, the MDA 1971 completed its passage through the UK Parliament and gained Royal Assent. Niamh Eastwood, executive director of the drug policy non-governmental organization Release, recently declared the 1971 Act to have led to '50 years of failure' (Eastwood, 2021) and the hashtag #50YearsOfFailure has become part of a social media campaign calling for radical drug law reform. The MDA 1971 is seen by many as emblematic of the failed twentieth-century experiment with drug prohibition and as representing a particular strain of right-wing populist moralising about drugs and drug policy. For most in the field, the Act seems to have little to commend it and calls for its repeal reached a crescendo during its 50th year.

Historians, however, might offer an alternative perspective. The origins of the Act potentially tell a rather different story. Although enacted by a Conservative Government the MDA 1971 was based very closely on a Bill that had been prepared by the preceding Labour Government which had then, somewhat unexpectedly, lost the 1970 General Election before having the chance to pass it into law. This might make us pause, firstly, to reconsider its political roots. The story takes a further twist when we note that the Labour Bill had been strongly shaped by the work of a sub-committee of the Advisory Committee on Drug Dependence whose report on cannabis, known as the Wootton Report (ACDD, 1968), was viewed as radical and progressive. Indeed, Barbara

Wootton, who had chaired the sub-committee, was accused at the time in Parliament of being unduly influenced by the 'cannabis legalisation lobby' (see Oakley, 2012). This was a reference to the fact that the report had been prepared against the backdrop of the 'Summer of Love' in 1967 when drug law reform had been at the heart of the counterculture, a backdrop to which the report itself alludes in its introduction. History suggests, then, that the 1971 Act is to some degree connected to this important countercultural moment of the late 1960s. Interestingly, within the drug field perhaps the only other extant legacy of that moment is Release, which was first born in July 1967 when art student Caroline Coon met radical lawyer Rufus Harris at a demonstration and they decided to create a legal advice service for drug users (Mold, 2006: 55).

How might we make sense of this striking disjunction? On the one hand, we have a piece of legislation seen as the epitome of outdated moralising prohibitionist thinking. On the other, this same legislation has its roots in the late 1960s, a time of social change in which radical drug law reform was centre stage. This chapter explores this question by revisiting the origins of the Act in the 1960s, drawing partly on an archival research project on the countercultural origins of the Wootton Report (for a fuller account of this project and its findings, see Seddon 2020a), but primarily through an analysis of the parliamentary debates that took place as the Misuse of Drugs Bill passed through the law-making process in 1970 and 1971. Some implications of this analysis for drug law reform today are considered in conclusion.

Origins and Development of the MDA 1971

Origin stories are perennially fascinating. This is partly because of our intuition that beginnings are important and that they may sometimes provide a clue to hidden or buried truths. Origin *stories* further appeal by drawing on our deep human attachment to narratives and storytelling. For sociologists, they have proved to be central to the critical analysis of social policy because of the ways in which the framing of social problems is so often shaped by the creation of particular narratives about their origins. Deconstructing these stories is an important part of how we develop new insights on law and policy.

For the MDA 1971, clearly at one level it needs to be situated in the twentieth-century story of drug prohibition. Its origins, in that sense, lie in the first two decades of that century, when the British participated in a series of international meetings before and after the First World War, culminating in the passing of the Dangerous Drugs Act 1920 (see Berridge, 1984). This Act was superseded by a succession of new pieces of legislation over the following 50 years. The 1971 Act can therefore be understood at one level as just a further iteration or configuration within the basic template of prohibition established a century ago. Yet, even when we step back and take the long view in this way, it stands out in this timeline for its longevity. It remains the primary drug control legislation more than 50 years later and looks likely to continue to be so for some time to come, despite the best efforts of reform advocates.

It is important, then, to explore and try to understand the specific origins of the 1971 Act. A core thesis of this chapter is that these lie in the 1960s and that this perspective provides an alternative origin story with relevance for thinking about drug law reform today. Reading the parliamentary debates on the Misuse of Drugs Bill, which took place between March 1970 and May 1971, immediately makes these 1960s roots very apparent. There can be little doubt, for example, that the Wootton Report was at the forefront of parliamentarians' minds, with either the report or Wootton herself being mentioned well over 100 times (and Wootton in fact spoke in the debate when it reached the House of Lords). The Labour peer Baroness Serota referred to 'the great cannabis debate which has been going on in this country now for some three or four years', explicitly linking the Bill to the countercultural movement from 1967 onwards (HL Deb 4 February 1971, c. 1365). Another strong theme was the idea that the drug problem had changed and worsened during the 1960s and that the new Act was needed to deal with this new situation. Indeed, Home Secretary James Callaghan, in his first contribution to the debates in March 1970 (before the General Election in June), introduced his comments with the observation that 'compared with even three years ago, the pattern of misuse of drugs is much more complicated and more serious... our defences are far too inflexible against these evils... the drug scene is constantly changing' (HC Deb 25 March 1970, cc. 1446–8). Others made similar points.

Much of the debate was surprisingly reasonable and measured, although it is also clear that knowledge of the issues was fairly thin and limited for most contributors, often even for those who claimed some level of special expertise or relevant experience. Not all members were able to resist more absurd rhetoric, of course, with Tom Price (Labour MP for Westhoughton) providing a particularly choice example when linking the 'resort to drugs' to the 'decline of Western civilisation' and describing the Wootton Report's recommendations as *avant-garde* (HC Debate 25 March 1970, cc. 1517–21). From across this body of debate, spanning 14 months, three points can be drawn. The claim here is not that these are necessarily the most central to or prominent within the debates but that they have something to tell us about the Act's origins that is of relevance to thinking about drug law reform in the 2020s.

The *first* is about the place of law within strategies for drug control. Writing in the *Modern Law Review* the year after the Act was passed, legal scholar Harvey Teff (1972: 232) asserted that 'undoubtedly the new Act brings a fresh approach to problems of control', although he concluded that its impact will 'inevitably be marginal' because of the 'inherent limitations of legal control' (ibid: 241). Teff's scepticism about the capacity of prohibitive laws to regulate drug problems effectively has a distinctly contemporary ring but also in fact resonates with many of the speakers in the parliamentary debates. Callaghan, for example, stated:

> 'The law has a part to play—hence the Bill—but it is by no means the only agency, because law enforcement which attempts to control personal consumption is difficult. I emphasise at the outset that there is a need for a concerted effort in the legal, social and medical fields. The Bill on its own, although it would serve a useful purpose, would by no means deal with the problem, which is growing so fast today'. (House of Commons Debate, 25 March 1970, c.1446)

When the Bill came to the House of Lords in early 1971, Wootton herself in her contribution to the debate noted this widespread agreement about the limits of law, describing it as a 'more sober, rational, constructive and less hysterical' approach than her cannabis report had received a couple of years earlier (HL Debate 14 January 1971, c.252).

Why is this important? First of all, it rather undercuts the #50YearsOfFailure line of critique. The lawmakers at the time did *not* claim the Act on its own would significantly ameliorate the problem and repeatedly argued that by itself it would have a marginal impact. As I have argued elsewhere, the failure over the last 50 years has been more one of policy than law, and the legal structure of the Act in fact builds in considerable flexibility to allow potentially for a wide range of policy approaches (Seddon, 2021). Again, it is clear in the debates that this flexibility was both deliberate and also seen as a positive feature of the Act. For example, the Labour MP for South Shields, Arthur Blenkinsop, observed that 'it is right to keep emphasising that the situation changes rapidly [...and] one of the great merits of the Bill is that it takes account of that' (HC Debate 25 March 1970, c.1471). An understanding of the limits of law is also important as it serves as a corrective both to those who see ratcheting up law enforcement and legal punishment as key *and* those who see changing the law as the principal way forward. Ironically, this understanding seemed stronger back in 1970 and 1971 than it does today. In a fairly recent paper, I have set out a theoretical basis for this need to broaden out from a law-centric focus to a regulatory approach (Seddon, 2020b).

The *second* point follows from the first: if parliamentarians did not believe the new laws were more than marginal to efforts to control the drug problem, then what did they think they *were* doing when passing this Act. What did they say the objectives were? What was the stated purpose of the Act? There have been many assertions about lawmakers' intentions but what did they actually say during the extensive debates in 1970 and 1971?

When we examine the text of the debates, there is surprisingly little reference to the stereotypical tropes of prohibitionists—the 'evils' of drugs, the immorality of drug-taking, the need for strict law enforcement, the desirability of harsh punishment—although these are certainly there. In fact, it is possible to see a considerable consensus coalescing in the debates that the Act was intended to achieve three principal goals. First, by introducing a classification system, it would allow the strictness of controls to vary according to the degrees of harm presented by different drugs. The flexibility of that system (that is, the ability to upgrade, downgrade, add or delist substances) would enable the legal framework to adjust in the face of changes in patterns of drug-taking. The aim was that these decisions about classification would be shaped by expert advice and scientific knowledge. Second, possession offences were to be separated from supply offences, so that the latter could be targeted for harsher punishment.

Third, the new Act aimed to consolidate and 'tidy-up' drug control provisions that over time had become fragmented across multiple pieces of legislation. A good example of this consensus came in one of the many contributions to the debates from Norman St John-Stevas, Conservative MP for Chelmsford:

> 'The principles on which a good law on this subject should be based are threefold. First, drugs must be controlled; everyone is in agreement about that. They should be more or less strictly controlled according to their degree of danger; the reclassification in the Bill does that. Thirdly, a distinction should be drawn between different types of offences, and the Bill does that. Pushing is certainly one thing and possession is another. Clearly, pushing a drug should be punished much more severely than merely having possession of it. (House of Commons Debate, 16 July 1970, c.1818)

This reinforces the point that lawmakers at the time presented a relatively modest set of objectives. Assessed on their own terms, rather than against their imagined goals or intentions, it could be argued that the primary point of failure in subsequent decades has been in the use of the classification system. The mechanisms for drawing on scientific advice, particularly over the last couple of decades, have often been subverted (see Stevens, 2021) and the flexibility provided by the Act has become a 'policy ratchet' that tends to move only in a more coercive direction (Stevens and Measham, 2014). These are failures driven by policymakers rather than deriving directly from the Act itself.

The *third* interesting feature of the debates is a thread running through them in which the question is raised as to why alcohol and tobacco are excluded from the Bill. This is probably surprising to most readers. After all, this is the type of question drug law reform advocates raise and it is slightly jarring to see it appear as a recurring theme in these debates. Eric Deakins, newly elected Labour MP for Walthamstow West and making his maiden speech, put the point most sharply:

> 'The Bill is...rather hypocritical. It attacks socially unacceptable drugs but does nothing about socially acceptable drugs. It attacks the drugs of young people, but does nothing about the drugs of middle-aged and elderly people.' (House of Commons Debate, 16 July 1970, c.1766)

Before the first debate in the House of Commons in March 1970, an amendment was tabled calling for the House to decline to give a Second Reading to the Bill on the grounds that it omitted reference to 'the most dangerous drug currently available, namely tobacco' (HC 25 March 1970, c.1446). Although this amendment was not selected by the Speaker, there was nevertheless considerable discussion of tobacco (and alcohol), often making comparisons with cannabis. Liberal Life Peer Lord Foot, for example, asserted:

'It is demonstrable that the use of tobacco is more injurious to the individual than the use of cannabis, and that taking alcohol is more injurious to the individual, and to society, than the use of cannabis. I should have thought that was beyond question.' (House of Lords Debate, 14 January 1971 c.240)

Building on this theme, a recurring strand in the debate is about the 'cannabis challenge,' with a view repeatedly expressed that cannabis should be treated differently in some way. Here, we see the strongest links made with the countercultural moment of the late 1960s. Whilst only a small number of members called for the legalisation of cannabis, many others argued for the lowering of penalties for possession and even for a special classification to be made for cannabis. Others, of course, argued in favour of a more punitive approach but it is certainly clear from the debates that there was not only a wide range of views on how to deal with cannabis but also some awareness of the conceptual 'fuzziness' of distinctions between cannabis, tobacco and alcohol.

Conclusion

So what conclusions can we draw from this excursion into the history of the 1971 Act and, in particular, the parliamentary debates from 1970 and 1971 which led up to its enactment? I think we can see the outlines of an alternative origin story which may have some different insights for the drug law reform enterprise today. The historical analysis has shown that instead of the Act being just an especially prominent staging post in the post-1945 story of the ever-tightening screw of prohibition, it has a distinctly more mixed and complex genesis and character. It lies squarely in the prohibition template *but* was also shaped by the radical countercultural calls for cannabis law reform. It satisfied lawmakers who were concerned about the need not to be 'soft' on what they saw as a worrying social problem *but* was also designed to respond in a rational and flexible way to emerging new scientific evidence. It accepted the twentieth-century boundaries drawn between 'drugs' and alcohol/tobacco *but* also allowed for substances potentially to shift within, into and out of the classification system.

This origin story positions the Act not as a monolithic piece of punitive prohibitionist legislation but rather as something more protean and polymorphous. From the vantage point of the 2020s, we can draw at least two important lessons for drug law reform from this, one historical and one political. The historical lesson is that there have been previous moments where reform seemed on the verge of happening, only to fade away. In the summer of 1967, radical change to the drug laws, particularly relating to cannabis, seemed to be gathering an unstoppable momentum in the UK (see Seddon, 2020a). Yet half a century later it still has not happened. Some of the more hyperbolic commentary on recent developments in the Americas might be taken as implying we are moving along an inevitable trajectory towards reform. History tells us this may not be so. Advocacy for reform will need to continue to work hard, not only to achieve change but also to ensure that reform develops in ways that include adequate constraints on corporate power and give due regard to social and racial justice.

The political lesson is perhaps the most important. As I have tried to show in this chapter and elsewhere (Seddon, 2021) much of what is critiqued about the 1971 Act is actually more to do with how it has been implemented in a wider policy context rather than the form, structure or intent of the legislation itself. The realm of policy and politics therefore needs to be brought much more centrally within reform discourse and analysis. Drug law reformers tend to identify 'politics' as part of the problem—in the sense of politicians ignoring science and evidence in order to push more populist prohibitionist approaches—and something that therefore needs to be neutralised or avoided. In my view, this is mistaken. There needs to be a proper theoretically informed understanding of the relationships between law, policy and politics and an analytical embracing of the inherently political nature of State efforts to control citizens' psychoactive consumption practices. The drug question is deeply entangled with some of the core ideas of modern political thought—freedom, rights, justice, citizenship—and so thinking about reform needs to be approached on a much wider basis than simply as a technical matter of rewriting the drug laws.

Professor Toby Seddon is Professor of Social Science at University College London and Head of the UCL Social Research Institute. He has been researching and teaching in the area of Drug Policy for over 25 years and is currently a Trustee at Release. His latest book is *Rethinking Drug Laws: Theory, History, Politics* (2022, Oxford University Press).

References and Extra Reading

Advisory Committee on Drug Dependence (ACDD) (1968), Cannabis: Report by the ACDD, London: Home Office.

Berridge, V (1984), Drugs and Social Policy: The Establishment of Drug Control in Britain 1900–30, *British Journal of Addiction*, 79: 17–29.

Eastwood, N (2021), The Misuse of Drugs Act: 50 Years of Failure, *Socialist Lawyer*, 87: 45–47.

HC Deb (25 March 1970), Misuse of Drugs Bill, Vol 798, Col 1446.

HC Deb (16 July 1970), Misuse of Drugs Bill, Vol 803, Col 1749.

HL Deb (14 January 1971), Misuse of Drugs Bill, Vol 314, Col 221.

HL Deb (4 February 1971), Misuse of Drugs Bill, Vol 314, Col 1360.

Mold, A (2006), 'The Welfare Branch of the Alternative Society?' The Work of Drug Voluntary Organization Release, 1967–1978, *Twentieth Century British History*, 17(1): 50–73.

Oakley, A (2012), The Strange Case of the Two Wootton Reports: What Can We Learn About the Evidence-policy Relationship? *Evidence & Policy*, 8(3): 267–283.

Seddon, T (2020a), Immoral in Principle, Unworkable in Practice: Cannabis Law Reform, The Beatles and the Wootton Report, *British Journal of Criminology*, 60(6): 1567–1584.

Seddon, T (2020b), Markets, Regulation and Drug Law Reform: Towards a Constitutive Approach, *Social & Legal Studies*, 29(3): 313–333.

Seddon, T (2021), From Law to Regulation: Re-appraising the Misuse of Drugs Act 1971, *Drugs and Alcohol Today*, 21(4): 289–297.

Stevens, A (2021), The Politics of Being an 'Expert': A Critical Realist Auto-Ethnography of Drug Policy Advisory Panels in the UK, *Journal of Qualitative Criminal Justice & Criminology*, 10(2):4.

Stevens, A and Measham, F (2014), The 'Drug Policy Ratchet': Why Do Sanctions for New Psychoactive Drugs Typically Only Go Up? *Addiction*, 109(8): 1226–1232.

Teff, H (1972), Drugs and the Law: The Development of Control, *Modern Law Review*, 35(3): 225–241.

CHAPTER 12

The Ongoing Impact on the Racialised Policing of Black Communities

Bisola Akintoye, Amal Ali and Alex Stevens

In his ground breaking book on the 'social meaning of drug use' the critical criminologist Jock Young (1971) predicted that the MDA 1971 would lead to disproportionate impacts on 'bohemians' and people who are racialised as black. For him, the 1971 Act was an 'absolutist' attempt to control people who were seen as potentially dangerous 'outsiders'. This places the Act in a broader history of subjugation of the scapegoated 'other' in drug policy (Wincup and Stevens, 2021), in British colonialism abroad (Koram, 2019), but also in the control of migrant communities within the UK (Kohn, 2001; Mills, 2013).

This chapter looks at the ongoing impacts of the MDA 1971 on the policing of black communities from two mutually reinforcing perspectives. First, we look at data generated by police forces which show the accuracy of Young's prediction. The numbers of people stopped, searched, arrested, and sentenced clearly shows that the 1971 Act is a major driver of the overall ethnic disproportionality of policing in England and Wales, and especially in London. Then, we use qualitative data from an ethnographic study of the lived experiences of being subjected to this racialised policing in that city. Going beyond the usual focus on the over-policing of young black men, we also consider the experiences of women, and of the friends and families of people who are directly policed.

We bring these data together to consider how these experiences affect not only the relations between black communities and the police, but also their wider relationship with the British State. In closing, we discuss how the powers that the police have to stop, search and arrest people under the MDA 1971 could be reformed or repealed. We argue that this could both reduce the harms of criminalisation and improve the lives of people who are racialised as black.

By way of introduction, we begin by describing the powers that police have in enforcing the MDA 1971. Section 5 of the Act makes it an offence to possess the drugs listed in the Act's schedules. Section 23 authorises stop and search where an officer has 'reasonable grounds to suspect' that an individual is in possession of controlled drugs. Stops are conducted under the Police and Criminal Evidence Act 1984 (PACE) Code of Practice 2005 for the exercise of these statutory powers, which enables officers to 'allay or confirm suspicions about individuals without exercising their power of arrest'.

Officers are required to inform the individual of the reason for the stop and search, but many are conducted without explanation. As shown below, the majority of stops and searches are for suspected drug offences. 'The smell of cannabis' is frequently the pretext for unjustified and racially discriminatory stops and searches. Many stops and searches fail to meet the threshold for reasonable suspicion (Her Majesty's Inspectorate of Constabulary and Fire and Rescue Service (HMICFRS), 2021).

Quantifying Disparities

In this section, we focus on the statistics which demonstrate how the MDA 1971 drives ethnic disproportionality in the Criminal Justice System (CJS). We draw on official records from the annual Home Office collection on police powers and procedures in England and Wales statistics, in addition to the Ministry of Justice publication on statistics on the CJS. We look specifically at data from and prior to 2019 in recognition that 2020 was an exceptional year due to the Covid-19 pandemic.

Stop and search
While the use of stop and search powers is often presented as being to tackle knife crime, drugs dominate stop and search policing. In the year ending March 2019, 61% of all stop and searches in England and Wales were for drugs. This as compared to only 16% of searches being undertaken for offensive weapons

(see Chart 1). There is however significant variation in the use of stop and search between different police force areas. For example, 62% of stop-searches in Avon and Somerset were for drugs, compared to 45% in the West Midlands. The data suggest that, contrary to political rhetoric, stop and search powers are not always used to target the most serious offences.

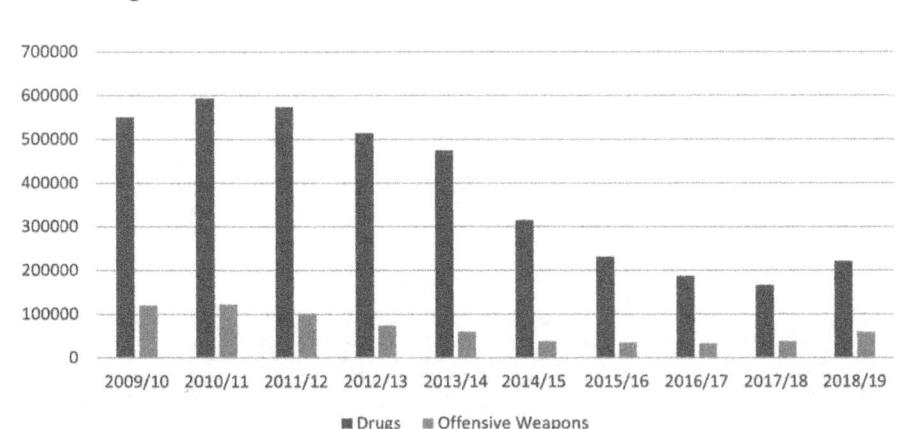

Chart 1: Number of stop-searches for drugs and offensive weapons, England and Wales, 2009/10 to 2018/9 (HM Government, 2020a).

The number of stops and searches fell after 2010, as police numbers were cut, and use of the stop and search was restricted by the 'Best Use of Stop and Search Scheme' (BUSSS). As the numbers fell, stop and search powers were increasingly concentrated on drug offences. The proportion of searches for drugs has increased over the last decade, accounting for 48% in 2009/10 and 61% in 2018/19.

Stop and search powers are disproportionately applied to ethnic minority groups, particularly young people and those identifying as black (Shiner et al, 2018). In 2019, black people were stopped at a rate nine times higher than their white counterparts. Similarly, Asian and people of mixed heritage were stopped for drugs at a rate three times higher than white people.

Arrests, sentencing and imprisonment

Drug law enforcement is a key gateway into the CJS. Offences under the MDA 1971 accounted for 46% of all arrests in 2019. Black people are arrested for drugs offences at eleven times the rate of white people. There have been reductions in the overall number of arrests for drug offences, following a reduction in the overall use of stop and search. However, these have not been evenly distributed across different ethnic groups, leading to increased racial disproportionalities. Arrests from drug searches halved for white people between 2009/10 and 2018/19. They fell by only 13% for black people (See Chart 2). This deepening inequality in the application of the 1971 Act drives ethnic disparities in later stages of the justice system.

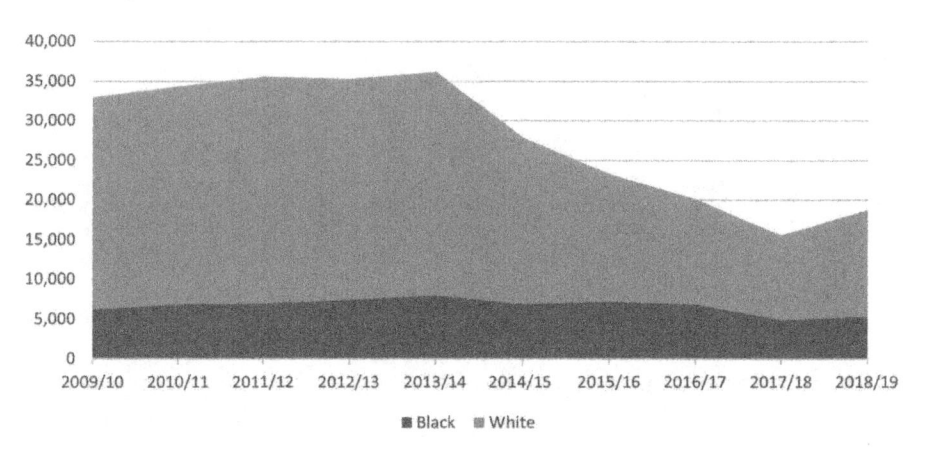

Chart 2: Number of Black and White people arrested for drugs, England and Wales, 2009/10 to 2018/19 (HM Government, 2020b).

More than 40,000 people were prosecuted for drug offences in 2019. Similarly to previous stages, black people were more likely to be proceeded against for drug offences; at 8.7 times the rate of white people (see Table 1), increasing to nine times for possession offences. Black people are more likely to be sent to prison for drug offences than other defendants. Black people are sentenced to immediate custody for drug offences at 8.2 times the rate of white people but given suspended sentences at 4.9 times the rate of white people. This reinforces findings by the Sentencing Council on the association between an offender's sex and ethnicity and the sentence imposed at the Crown Court for drug offences (Sentencing Council, 2020).

Table 1: Disproportionality in defendants proceeded against, convicted and sentenced for drug offences in 2019, England and Wales.

		Black	Asian	Mixed	Other
All drug offences	Proceeded against (charged)	8.7	2.0	3.6	2.8
	Found guilty	8.3	1.8	3.3	2.7
	Total sentenced	8.2	1.8	1.9	2.7
	Immediate custody	8.2	2.1	3.4	4.0
	Suspended sentence	4.9	1.3	2.3	1.6
	Community sentence	9.1	1.8	3.8	2.7
	Fine	8.8	2.0	3.1	2.6
	Absolute discharge	5.8	1.0	3.4	4.6
	Conditional discharge	7.6	1.5	3.4	1.9
	Otherwise dealt with	7.9	1.1	2.8	2.7

The data shown above have not been adjusted for any of the many factors that may influence these disparities, in addition to direct and indirect discrimination against black people. Other explanations that have been put forward include the younger average age of black people, their geographical concentration in higher crime and more highly policed areas, the idea that more black people are visibly 'available' to be stopped on the street, and the notion that black people use drugs or offend at different rates to white people (CRED, 2021; Waddington et al, 2004).

However, the most regular and large-scale survey of drug use consistently reports lower, rather than higher, rates of drug use among people categorised as black compared to white. Attempts to explain away racialised disparities in drug policing fail to acknowledge that young black people are more likely to be targeted by the police, even accounting for their rates of drug use or offending (Stevens, 2008; Vomfell and Stewart, 2021). And these statistical disputes have little relevance to the actual experiences of black communities, or for how these disparities affect the relationship between these communities, the police, and the State.

The Intersectional Experience of Being Policed for Drugs

The records show that people who are racialised as black are targets of drug law enforcement, but these statistics cannot tell us how this disproportionality is experienced. Here, we draw on ethnographic data focusing on the intersectional experience of policing in black communities. The research took place in London in 2020 and 2021, involving field observations and interviews with 50 young people, their families, and community workers. Participants have been anonymised in this chapter.

We find that, while black people across the spectrum remain disproportionately subject to stops, arrests and convictions for drug offences, this is mediated by age, immigration history, gender, and class. This research reveals that the harms imposed by the MDA 1971 are experienced more sharply by some black people than others. However, in the 50 years since the MDA 1971 was enacted, multiple generations have experienced its negative, racialising effects.

Experiences of drug policing generally peak in adolescence and early adulthood. Participants in the research held relatively positive perspectives of the police in childhood that eroded over time due to negative direct and reported experiences. Parents and guardians who had arrived in the UK as adults had few experiences of drug policing, but many second and third-generation participants with a Caribbean background had experienced frequent drug stops and searches in their youth.

Many stops and searches for drugs were initiated by the police for the 'smell of cannabis'. Adults described a gradual reduction in the level of threat they were perceived to pose as they transitioned from youth to adulthood. However, the long-term, intergenerational experience of drug policing remains a key driver of negative perceptions of the police in black communities. Many participants described receiving instructions from their parents to stay out of trouble and on how to interact with the police. This is sometimes referred to as 'the Talk':

'My dad had bad experiences with the police when he was young so he always told us to just stay out of their way...but if we did get stopped, we should be polite, don't be aggressive. Just try and calm the situation down, cos sometimes [officers] are on one [acting unreasonably].'

Ahmed, 15, North London

Younger participants were mindful of their rights, and many opted to record stops and searches on phones to ensure there was evidence of the incident. This provided a feeling of agency and reduced perceptions of powerlessness against drug policing. Marcus, a 38-year-old man of mixed British-Caribbean heritage, explained that in his youth he had experienced numerous stops and searches, the majority of which were for suspected drug offences. He intended to discuss his negative experiences with 'viciously racist' police officers with his daughter, echoing the intention of many parents with personal experiences of racialised drug policing in their youth. This indicates that, while black people may 'age out' of stop and search, these experiences have a lasting effect that is passed from generation to generation, creating entrenched negative perceptions of the police.

The use of 'the Talk' is influenced by immigration history. Lanre, 65, a Nigerian man who moved to the UK as an adult, had no direct experiences of drug policing. He characterised his experiences of policing in Nigeria as 'so terrible' that he had a relatively positive attitude towards the police in the UK as 'they are nothing compared to [the police in Nigeria].' Lanre did not consider it necessary to have 'the Talk' with any of his four children. This reinforces research finding that first generation immigrants tend to hold more positive attitudes towards the police than their children and grandchildren (Bradford et al, 2017). The relatively positive perspectives of first-generation immigrants may be due to both cultural expectations about British institutions that influenced the decision to migrate in the first place, alongside a lack of direct experiences of policing and negative experiences of policing in countries of origin. By contrast, Lanre's 35-year-old son Lekan described being stopped and searched frequently by aggressive police officers as a teenager for suspected drug offences. As a result, he intended to have 'the Talk' with his children in the future, displaying a different response to racialised policing than his father, despite both being male, living in the same neighbourhood and having similar socio-economic status.

Black women and girls experience disproportionately high levels of stop and search compared to their white counterparts. Increasing focus in recent years on the role of female adolescents in gangs (Young, 2009) has led to calls for expanding stop and search. Black female participants described receiving harsh treatment from the police:

'They don't even care that you're a girl. They do the same to you as if you were a man. And it's just like…would you be treating me like this if I was white?'

Portia, 23, East London

Female participants reported aggressive treatment in police interactions, being regarded as troublemakers, heavily supervised and given severe punishments. This is exacerbated by broad police failures to understand the specific cultural realities of many black women caught up in the drug trade, for example relationships of coercion, violence, abuse and exploitation, which frequently serve as the backdrop to drug couriering (Allen et al, 2003). The gendered experience of policing is also mediated by class, which consistently emerges as a key factor in managing police encounters:

'The two times I've [been stopped and searched], I was basically able to talk my way out of it. Once they heard the way I speak I guess they decided I wasn't one of "those black people".'

Cece, 25, North London.

Middle-class black women like Cece may be able to negotiate experiences of drug policing in accordance with the norms of middle-class femininity. Participants identifying as working-class were considerably more likely to have frequent experiences of drug policing than middle-class respondents. They described feeling 'powerless' in managing policing interactions and instead focused on avoiding the police entirely. However, visual indicators of professional respectability enable some working-class participants to reduce experiences of drug policing. Mohson, a 39-year-old youth worker, encouraged the young ex-offenders he employed to display the youth organization's badge to pre-empt police interactions by indicating responsibility and respect for the law.

This study confirms that drug policing represents a key driver of racially disproportionate and racially discriminatory policing of black and minority ethnic communities. These findings convey that the same practices of drug policing are experienced differently within different sectors of black communities.

The Effect of Drug Policing on Relationships Between Black Communities, Police and the State

Experiences of drug policing are the norm for many black British people and many describe feeling targeted by the police throughout their lives. The frequent and highly visible experience of stop and search not only entrenches false narratives about black predilection to drug use, but also engenders distrust of the police in black communities. The impact of drug policing extends beyond the stop and search itself, all too frequently resulting in long-term harmful consequences for black communities, hindering education, housing, and employment opportunities across generations:

> 'Criminalisation is the fulcrum of racialised social exclusion; it is where the metaphor of social exclusion is transformed into an explicit, formal social practice and into the personal experience of being literally excluded from society through imprisonment and all that flows from that.' (Bowling and Phillips, 2002)

Many participants felt unable to move freely through their neighbourhoods due to fear of police 'harassment', and describe adapting their behaviour to avoid police interactions:

> 'Half the time when you're out and about and they stop you, you just want to go back to your yard [home], 'cos you know they'll just keep stopping you so you may as well just stay at home cos then they can't get you.'
> *Corinne, 15, North London*

As Corinne describes, the lasting impact of these interactions is fear and anxiety, limiting the freedom of many young black people to move freely.

Participants also described a lack of respect, hostility, and aggression in police interactions. Many young people report unjust stop and searches for drugs escalating to caution or arrest for public order offences due to their resistance being misinterpreted as aggression by police officers (Keeling, 2017). Zane, 13, was tackled, tasered and handcuffed by plainclothes police officers after being mistaken for a suspect in a drug offence. Zane described his fear at seeing adult men chasing him and running away from them, which he felt had been misinterpreted as fleeing. After being released without charge, Zane's parents reported the incident to the Independent Office for Police Conduct. However, fear and mistrust arising from direct and reported experiences of police violence prevents many black people from seeking police assistance. Complaints are often felt to be 'pointless,' contributing to feelings of isolation and dehumanisation:

'You just feel like the police don't trust you, don't like you and of course you know why…'cause you're black or maybe because of what you're wearing or whatever. It makes you not trust them either. Why would I trust them? I know what they're thinking. I wouldn't even bother making a complaint, 'cause I know it wouldn't do anything.'

Jamal, 35, London

Low levels of trust in the police are linked to lower conviction rates and ineffectiveness of police investigations into serious violent offences (Deuchar et al, 2019), reducing both co-operation and reporting. A result is the widespread belief that the police do not take black victims of crime seriously. As one woman who witnessed a crime said,

'We called them and they didn't show up.'

Viola, 27, London

Viola drew on her previous negative victim experiences and vicarious experiences of black people more broadly as the basis for her lack of confidence in the police. Her fear of the police stemmed from negative community narratives. This aligns with research finding that black and mixed-race victims of crime are less likely to report crimes than other ethnic minority groups (Yarrow,

2005), reinforcing the harmful impact of drug policing on community experiences of policing.

Experiences of drug policing are a key factor in relations between black people and their socio-political environment. The role that the police as a core State institution play in status-conferral is acutely felt by people in black communities. As the police are a 'face' of the State, drug policing plays a central role in showing black communities that their position within British society is highly conditional. The effects of disproportionate drug policing go beyond directly empowering the State to exercise social control through coercion, containment, and surveillance:

> 'It's their way of reminding you that you don't have anything. Like, it doesn't matter what you do, how hard you work, how much money you earn...at the end of the day, you're still just a black man.'
>
> *Lekan, 35, London*

Racialised drug policing emerges from the wider context of Britain's imperial legacy, and socio-political discourse surrounding race, drugs, and policing. The so-called 'war on drugs' forms an intersection between the racialised other and the State. Decades of racially disproportionate drug policing have resulted in an entrenched lack of trust and mutual hostility between the police and some black communities, leaving many black people across different gender, age, immigration and socio-economic brackets feeling over-policed and under-protected.

Reducing Disparities, Increasing Trust

From both quantitative and qualitative analysis, the policing of drug offences emerges as a crucial mechanism of racialised policing. The disproportionate impact of policing on black communities reveals that the kind of social control Jock Young warned about still underpins drug policy. The systemic failure to address ethnic disparities in the application of the MDA 1971 perpetuates a lack of legitimacy and breeds further distrust in the police. The claim — repeated in the Government's 2021 'Beating Crime Plan' — that increased policing is the best way to protect communities is undermined by community members consistently describing feeling unprotected by the police.

In *Chapter 19* of this book, 'A Modest Proposal to Decriminalise the Simple Possession of Drugs,' Douse, Eastwood and Stevens propose that drug possession should be decriminalised in order to reduce harms and save money. The form of decriminalisation proposed is to repeal section 5(1) and (2) of the 1971 Act. This would remove the criminal offence of simple possession (without intent to supply). It would also remove the power of the police to stop and search people on suspicion of possessing controlled drugs, unless there were grounds to suspect intent to supply. Such legislative reforms would reduce opportunities for the discriminatory use of discretionary police powers.

In the absence of decriminalisation, the Government should introduce robust safeguards to mitigate the harms caused by the MDA 1971 and drug law enforcement. Past efforts to lower the overuse of stop and search for drugs have failed to address operational failings. In 2014, then Home Secretary Theresa May introduced the voluntary 'Best Use of Stop and Search Scheme' and promised that stop and search would focus on violent and serious crime. In the announcement, she stated;

> 'Nobody wins when stop and search is misapplied. It is a waste of police time. It is unfair, especially to young black men. It is bad for public confidence in the police.' (Home Office, 2014).

Seven years on, stop and search continues to be overwhelming used to detect drugs, disproportionately targeting back and ethnic minority communities, leading to the deterioration of community and police relations. The Government vowed to bring forward legislation to make BUSSS a statutory requirement if forces did not comply. It should now fulfil its promise by mandating BUSSS and introducing sanctions for non-compliance.

Stop and search should be based on intelligence and not on nebulous, unprovable grounds such as the 'smell of cannabis'. The College of Policing's (2021) Authorised Professional Practice (APP) has advised that it is not good practice for an officer to base grounds for search on a single factor, such as the smell of cannabis alone, or an indication from a drugs dog. However, HMICFRS (2021) found that police are still basing stops and searches on these grounds.

The Government should mandate the current College of Policing guidance on the smell of cannabis across all police forces.

Beyond legal and policy considerations, it is essential that the police make sustained efforts to improve the quality of engagement with black communities, who feel targeted and victimised by the police based on their ethnicity. In the long term, it eradicates trust and confidence in the police and alienates entire communities. Scrutiny and accountability are key to ensuring public confidence however community scrutiny mechanisms have been described as having insufficient representation from black and ethnic minority communities (Kalyan and Keeling, 2019). The Government should mandate the current College of Policing (2020) guidance on community scrutiny, which includes a requirement for forces to consider the extent to which the composition of scrutiny panels reflect the diversity of their local areas.

In order to effectively monitor the use of police powers on people of different ethnicities, ethnicity data should be recorded accurately and consistently. The lack of data acts as a barrier to accurately identifying levels of racial disproportionality in drug stop and searches. There are a proportion of searches in which ethnicity is recorded as 'unknown'. In the year ending March 2019, ethnic background was either not stated or not recorded in 13% of searches under the MDA 1971 in England and Wales. We echo HMICFRS's recommendation for forces to record and monitor both self-defined ethnicity and officer-defined ethnicity.

These reforms are necessary steps towards effective, targeted, evidence-informed, intelligence-based policing that does not alienate large sections of British society. Implemented correctly, reforms to drug law and policing could both reduce the harms of criminalisation and improve the lives of people who are racialised as black.

Conclusion

We have shown that the MDA 1971 drives disparities in policing. We have also explored how these disparities affect communities who experience them. Some of these harms may be reduced by changing how the police use the powers that the 1971 Act gives them. But we have seen police practices ebb and flow over recent years, changing with the political tide, but never substantially reducing the over-policing of black people that is driven by the Act. More fundamental reform will require changes to the legislation, not just to the way it is enforced.

Bisola Akintoye is a PhD candidate in Social Policy at the University of Kent. Her postgraduate research takes an ethnographic approach to the intergenerational experience of racialised policing in black communities. She is also a qualified Solicitor who obtained a masters degree in law at University College London, and has taught undergraduate Criminology at the University of Kent.

Amal Ali is a PhD candidate at the London School of Economics in the Department of Methodology. Her research examines the underlying drivers of racial/ethnic disparities in police use of force in England and Wales.

Professor Alex Stevens is Professor in Criminal Justice at the University of Kent. He was a member of the Advisory Council on the Misuse of Drugs (2014–2019) and President of the International Society for the Study of Drug Policy (2015–2019). He is currently a board member of Harm Reduction International and Chair of Drug Science's Enhanced Harm Reduction Working Group. His publications include *Drugs, Crime and Public Health* (Routledge, 2011) and *Drug Policy Constellations* (Policy Press, forthcoming).

References and Extra Reading

Allen, R, Levenson, J and Garside, R (2003), *A Bitter Pill to Swallow: The Sentencing of Foreign National Drug Couriers*, London: Rethinking Crime and Punishment.

Bowling, B and Phillips, C (2002), *Racism, Crime and Justice*, Harlow: Longman.

Bradford, B, Sargeant, E, Murphy, T and Jackson, J (2017), A Leap of Faith? Trust in the Police Among Migrants in England and Wales, *British Journal of Criminology*, 57(2).

College of Policing (2020), Stop and Search: Transparent: www.app.college.police.uk/app-content/stop-and-search/transparent#community-engagement

College of Policing, Authorised Professional Practice (2021): www.app.college.police.uk/app-content/stop-and-search/transparent#community-engagement

Commission on Race and Ethnic Disparities (2021), Report of the Commission on Race and Ethnic Disparities, Cabinet Office.

Criminal Justice System Statistics; www.gov.uk/government/statistics/criminal-justice-system-statistics-quarterly-december-2019

Deuchar, R, Miller, J and Densley, J (2019), The Lived Experience of Stop and Search in Scotland: There Are Two Sides to Every Story, *Police Quarterly*, 22(4): 416–451.

Her Majesty's Inspectorate of Constabulary and Fire and Rescue Services (2021), *Disproportionate Use of Police Powers. A Spotlight on Stop and Search and the Use of Force*, London: HMICFRS.

Home Office (2014), Stop and Search: Theresa May announces reform of police stop and search, 30 April: www.gov.uk/government/news/stop-and-search-theresa-may-announces-reform-of-police-stop-and-search

Home Office (2019), Police Powers and Procedures England and Wales ending 31 March 2019.

HM Government (2020a), Stop and Search Statistics: Data Tables: Police Powers and Procedures Year Ending 31 March 2019: www.gov.uk/government/statistics/police-powers-and-procedures-england-and-wales-year-ending-31-march-2019

HM Government (2020b), Arrest Statistics: Data Tables: Police Powers and Procedures Year Ending 31 March 2019: www.gov.uk/government/statistics/police-powers-and-procedures-england-and-wales-year-ending-31-march-2019

Kaluyan, K K and Keeling P (2019), Stop and Scrutinise: How to Improve Community Scrutiny of Stop and Search, Criminal Justice Alliance Briefing.

Keeling, P (2017), No Respect: Young BAME Men, the Police and Stop and Search, London: Criminal Justice Alliance.

Kohn, M (2001), *Dope Girls: The Birth of the British Drug Underground*, London: Granta.

Koram, K (2019), *The War on Drugs and the Global Colour Line*, London: Pluto Press.

Mills, J H (2013), *Cannabis Nation: Control and Consumption in Britain, 1928–2008*, Oxford: Oxford University Press.

Sentencing Council (2020), Investigating the Association Between an Offender's Sex and Ethnicity and the Sentence Imposed at the Crown Court for Drug Offences.

Shiner, M, Carre, Z, Delsol, R and Eastwood, N (2018), The Colour of Injustice: 'Race', Drugs and Law Enforcement in England and Wales, London: StopWatch.

Stevens, A (2008), Weighing up Crime: The Overestimation of Drug-Related Crime (United Kingdom), *Contemporary Drug Problems*, 35(23), 265.

Vomfell, L and Stewart, N (2021), Officer Bias, Over-Patrolling and Ethnic Disparities in Stop and Search, *Nature Human Behaviour*: 1–10.

Waddington, P A J, Stenson, K and Don, D (2004), In Proportion: Race, and Police Stop and Search, *British Journal of Criminology*, 44(6): 889–914: www.nature.com/articles/s41562-020-01029-w (accessed April 10, 2021).

Wincup, E and Stevens, A (2021), Scapegoating and Othering in Drug Policy: A Special Themed Section, *International Journal of Drug Policy,* 87: 103093.

Yarrow, S (2005), The Experiences of Young Black Men as Victims of Crime, London: Criminal Justice System Race Unit and Victims and Confidence Unit.

Young, J (1971), *The Drugtakers: The Social Meaning of Drug Use*, London: Paladin.

Young, T (2009), Girls and Gangs: 'Shemale' Gangsters in the UK? Youth Justice, 9(3): 224–238.

PART IV
PERSPECTIVES AND APPROACHES

CHAPTER 13

Challenging Stigma, Changing Minds

Jane Slater and Mary Ryder

'My life ended when I lost my two sons Torin and Jacques so unexpectedly in one night. I never wanted to join a group like Anyone's Child—but having lost everything, I feel that it's all I can do now—to try and stop others from having to go through what I've been through—and for me that means campaigning for the legal control and regulation of drugs.'

Ray[1]

This chapter looks at the role of families in drug policy reform. The MDA 1971 and the subsequent political rhetoric around drugs has focused on how criminalisation and the prohibition of drugs is intended to deter young people from taking drugs in order to protect them. But far from protecting our young people it has fuelled stigma and caused enormous harm to people who use drugs and their families (Barrett, 2011). This chapter unpicks a lesser voiced consequence of the MDA 1971: the stigmatisation and discrimination of drug users and their families. This stigma is so insidious that it has made sensible, rational discussion of alternative drug policies unthinkable. Those who do call for alternative drug policies risk being accused of hedonism, and not being concerned for the safety and wellbeing of young people (Rolles, 2011: 59). Such prejudice and fear is very difficult to dispel with evidence alone, which is where Anyone's Child is relevant.

---

1. All of the family members included in this chapter have given their explicit permission to be named. Their stories have been published on the Anyone's Child: Families for Safer Drug Control website: www.anyoneschild.org

Some young people will always want to use drugs. Prohibition has proved ineffective at stopping people from doing so and drug-related deaths are higher than ever before (Office for National Statistics (ONS), 2021). In 1971 when the MDA was introduced there were less than 100 drug-related deaths; in 2021 there were over 4,000 (Transform, 2022). Prohibiting drugs has created a vast illegal drug market run by organized crime groups. There is no minimum age, quality control standards, or duty of care towards users and suppliers. Young people in particular are vulnerable to exploitation and violence, including via 'county lines' drug trafficking to supply drugs across the country (ibid). In addition, a criminal record for drug possession can wreck a young person's life, ruining job prospects, their status in society, and their future. Furthermore, and of key importance for this chapter, using the Criminal Justice System (CJS) to solve a public health problem has proven not only ineffective, but also socially corrosive; promoting stigma and discrimination which is often directed most heavily towards already vulnerable and marginalised groups.

Overall, this reflective chapter tells our story of the Anyone's Child campaign and the families involved, and how lived experience is helping to ignite the reform discussion in the UK. Launched in June 2015, Anyone's Child: Families for Safer Drug Control is a campaign of the charity Transform Drug Policy Foundation. We work in a professional capacity as the campaign manager and coordinator. This involves supporting the families in their advocacy efforts for safer drug policies, connecting people with others who have had similar experiences and creating space for their stories to be heard, all the while promoting care, compassion and understanding.

Anyone's Child is an international network of families who have suffered some of the most negative consequences of drug prohibition.[2] Many have lost loved ones to accidental overdose deaths, others have been exploited by organized crime groups involved in the illegal drugs trade, and many more struggle in a CJS not designed to help those in pain or suffering from trauma. The families involved draw on their lived experience to inform the wider public of the true human cost of the 'drug war' and to put pressure on politicians to reform the UK's drug laws. Storytelling and human faces are prioritised to evoke empathy

---

2. Anyone's Child is based in the UK, but we also work with families in Canada, Kenya, Mexico and Belgium, who are running similar campaigns under the Anyone's Child brand to reform drug laws in their jurisdictions.

and support, and to make conversations about drug policy accessible and relatable. The stories are shared on the Anyone's Child website and in radio, TV, print and online media.

Throughout the chapter you will read quotes from some of the families. Collated over the course of the campaign, through first-hand stories provided by the family members, field notes and group meetings, these are honest, brave, first-hand accounts which recount the stigma and discrimination they have experienced because of the MDA 1971. Discrimination is understood here as the prejudicial treatment of a person or group based on the group, class or category to which they belong. It is inevitably linked to stigma which is defined as negative attitudes, beliefs or stereotypes of a person or group based on something considered to be socially unacceptable — in this case, problematic drug use or drug dependency. We demonstrate how the campaign seeks to accelerate public understanding of the failure of our current drug laws and the potential benefits and opportunities of legal control and regulation of the drug trade, particularly in terms of addressing the stigma attached to people who use drugs. We acknowledge the challenges the families involved face, and describe the opportunity offered by the campaign to provide a space free of judgement.

The MDA 1971: Harming Not Protecting Families

The UK has a strong history of parental narratives which have been used in campaigns for stronger prohibitionist approaches, to enforce the MDA 1971. One prominent example was launched in 1995 after 18-year-old Leah Betts tragically died after taking an MDMA pill. In response, a £1 million poster campaign erected 1,500 billboards across the country, telling the viewer to 'Just say no' (Betts et al, 1999). Such stories have been used to emphasise the dangers of drug consumption and in turn to justify following a tough prohibitionist approach to drugs. Around the time of Leah's death the then Prime Minister, John Major commented on her story in Parliament:

> 'Only in the last few days we have seen a particularly highly publicised and tragic case of how drugs can devastate a family…In an evil trade like this, no drug is soft, and no drug is safe.'
>
> John Major, Prime Minister

Public stigma towards people who use drugs occurs in popular and political discourse which emphasises the danger of drugs to reinforce the mantra that 'drugs threaten families and communities.' This 'threat' in turn justifies a tough prohibitionist approach. Speaking at the Methadone Alliance Conference in 2000, Professor Gerry Stimson, one of the UK's leading advocates of harm reduction, attributed the language employed under Tony Blair's administration, following the death of Leah Betts, to a moral panic around drugs and an 'unhealthy drug policy'. Phrases like 'a war on drugs,' 'tough new power,' 'a crackdown on the drugs industry,' have in turn served to further marginalise and stigmatise the vulnerable and their families (Stimson, 2000).

> 'The stigma, that's what the biggest problem is. It makes us feel ashamed and silences us. That's why we've got to speak up.'
>
> Sandra

Media reporting fuels the notion of drug use as a moral failure or character flaw. This can be observed through the language and imagery used across different media platforms—terms such as 'druggie,' 'junkie,' 'addict,' 'crackhead' and 'zombie' are frequently used to describe individuals which reinforce images of someone who is hopeless. Such language also serves to dehumanise people who use drugs (Sumnall et al, 2021):

> 'Never did they see a person, they only see a "junkie." As my son used to say—they treat me like a second class citizen mum.'
>
> Denise.

Under the MDA 1971, producing, supplying and possessing controlled drugs are criminal acts. Consequently, the 1971 Act has led to the mass criminalisation of people who use drugs. More than three million criminal records have been issued under the MDA 1971 since its inception (Transform, 2022). Some of the Anyone's Child families suggest that receiving a criminal record for non-violent drug offences served only to 'brand' their loved ones and ostracise them from wider society. This in turn ruins job prospects, a person's status in society and their future, and can make seeking help and long-term rehabilitation more difficult as two families involved in the group observed:

'Much of my son's life was hidden from us, a consequence of the stigma and shame created by criminalisation.'

Brian

'Little did I know laws and the system weren't designed to help, they only served to make life more difficult, you were labelled and given a criminal record, so therefore would find it harder to recover from any addiction or obtain any employment or career.'

Hilary

It is important to point out that this narrative masks the true picture of the drug market which is multifaceted and includes a wide range of substances and patterns of use. Some 90% of drug users use drugs unproblematically (although the unknown purity of substances means that some recreational use proves fatal) and drug users span all social classes and demographics (United Nations Office on Drugs and Crime (UNODC), 2021). Additionally, it is worth highlighting the arbitrary moral distinctions the MDA 1971 promotes, given the absence of alcohol and tobacco, two substances which are at least as harmful as illegal drugs. Despite successful public health education campaigns in recent years about the dangers of excessive drinking or smoking, their use remains by and large publicly acceptable and encouraged. It should also be noted that, as scholars and practitioners have documented elsewhere, while the severe form of public disapproval is reserved for users of all illegal drugs, this stigma is exacerbated by politically-manufactured moral panics around certain drugs, and experienced disproportionately by marginalised groups or populations (Transform, 2015; Koram, 2019).

The effects of this stigmatising discourse and the illegality of the problem are so far reaching that even individuals who use drugs may internalise this stigma or stigmatise other users. This can lead to a vicious circle of use and further marginalisation from wider society and this often serves as a barrier to individuals seeking help or speaking out about their drug use (Matthews, Dwyer and Snoek, 2017).

> 'Without illegality and the stigma that attends it Kevin could have sought help much earlier in his addiction.'
>
> *Pat*

Simply by having drug users or suppliers within their families, many of those involved with the campaign have been discriminated against, excluded from communities and isolated. One mum recounts how for years she went to work knowing that life was chaotic at home but unable to confide in any of her colleagues or friends due to the illegality of her son's behaviour. The fear of judgement and other repercussions of speaking out was so great.

Stigma, blame and disgust are also directed at people bereaved by drug-related deaths (Dyregrov and Selseng, 2021). These societal stereotypes in turn lead people to feel that those who use drugs deserve to experience harm due to their deviant behaviour. One mother found that she even experienced stigma at the bereavement group she had attended when she stated that her husband had died from an overdose. She was shunned by the group and nobody felt able to comment on her situation. Another mother, when visiting her son's grave, encountered a stranger who asked how her son had died. When the mother replied that it was due to a heroin overdose, the response she received was, 'That served him right.' These stories are all too common within the group.

Such moral judgements can reproduce cycles of trauma, violence and pain for those who use drugs and their families. This stigma clearly demonstrates why historically many families have been reluctant to speak out on the issue and their experiences for fear of a societal backlash and judgement.

Reframing Drug Policy to Protect Child Wellbeing: Storytelling From the Front Line of the UK's Drug War

'People will always find a way to obtain drugs. If there was some way of regulating it (the trade) it will protect the people who currently don't know what they're taking, and take control away from criminals.'

Chris

The MDA 1971 did not prevent harm to the many families who have joined Anyone's Child to campaign for drug law reform, nor has it reduced the number of young people experimenting with drugs. The name Anyone's Child is designed to reduce stigma, and suggests that, due to current drug policies, 'anyone's child' could be the next casualty of what has proved to be a futile, unsustainable, short-sighted drug war. The key message is that prohibition and criminalisation is endangering children (in the broadest sense) and that regulation would help to keep them safer from the harms of prohibition.

The family members who make up Anyone's Child recognise that there is no such thing as a 'drug-free world' and any efforts to achieve this will not succeed. Rather, they accept drug use exists and are driven to advocate for a world in which drug use is made safer with child protection placed firmly at the heart of drug policy. The families are calling for drugs to be treated through a health lens rather than through the CJS, and ultimately for drugs to be made legally available to adults from doctors, pharmacists, and licensed retailers and produced under strict controls and regulations—as we already do for other consumable products. Guided by concerns over safety and wellbeing, the more restrictive controls would be used for more risky products, and, correspondingly, less restrictive controls for lower-risk products (Transform, 2010).

As Andy, another member explains:

'That is why we are campaigning with Anyone's Child, we want to prevent the loss of any more precious young lives. Production needs to be regulated so the content of drugs can be trusted; and supply needs to be controlled, just the same as over-the-counter drugs, so that distribution is also closely governed and comes with some basic guidelines. This can only be achieved by challenging the illegal status of drugs and current drug policies. Legal control and regulation will then open the door to honest education in schools and colleges so the generations to come are correctly informed about drugs and their dangers.'

Tackling the very real emotional and moral responses that people have to drug use, much of which is wrapped up in this stigma, is clearly critical in shifting the conversation here in the UK.

Studies have suggested that activities to 're-humanise' people who use drugs including compassionate media portrayal can reduce stigma (Sumnall et al, 2021). The campaign shows that the drug war construction that all drug takers are socially problematic is not really the case. This deliberately challenges some preconceptions and assumptions around drugs, encouraging broader discussion of the policy implications helps to break down these misconceptions around people who use drugs and makes drug policy reform less of a taboo.

The campaign tries to engage new audiences by utilising street art, theatre performances, photography, town hall events, and interactive-documentaries to raise public awareness around the need for reform. Telling intimate, painful family stories time-and-again can take its toll. For this reason, Transform has co-created short videos of family members which aims to prevent individuals from being re-traumatised through retelling their story. The families involved are engaged at different levels: most share their story in written form, some have participated in filmmaking, and others regularly present the campaign to the media and at public events.

Dialogue With Policymakers: Speaking Truth to Power

Both the UK and Canada are G7 countries experiencing unprecedented levels of drug-related deaths, many of which are avoidable and preventable (ONS, 2021; SAC, 2021). The examples below demonstrate how human stories speak to power and can be a useful tool for those wishing to call for reform.

Hearing the testimonies of real families is intended to evoke empathetic reactions and is effective in changing both hearts and minds, even at the highest political level. By illustrating the human cost of the drug war, Anyone's Child creates a new space within which even the most senior of policymakers are able to talk in a personal capacity, allowing them to consider options that might otherwise seem too risky (e.g. for fear of the media backlash that might impact chances of re-election). In this way the campaign has created an environment apt for dialogue about effective policy changes to protect those impacted by the current framework. The Anyone's Child campaign has also provided cover for politicians wishing to speak out in favour of drug policy reform.

To illustrate, in 2016, families from around the world came together at the United Nations General Assembly Special Session (UNGASS) on drugs—a meeting of UN member States to discuss drug control priorities, to demonstrate that prohibition is not protecting young people or their families. The Anyone's Child campaigner, Canadian mother, Donna May, was mentioned by Jane Philpott, Canadian Health Minister, as she announced Canada's moves to change policy and legalise cannabis (UNGASS, 2016).

> '…in preparation for this event, I met with a group of NGOs in Ottawa. There were lawyers, doctors and highly articulate activists. But the most powerful voice of all belonged to a mother. She was there to tell the story of her young daughter, who lost her life due to complications of substance use. She described watching her daughter slip away, as she struggled to access the treatment and services that may have saved a beautiful, fragile life. Stories like this are far too commonplace. Today, I stand before you as Canada's Minister of Health, to acknowledge that we must do better for our citizens.'
>
> *Jane Philpott, (now) Former Canadian Minister of Health*

Similarly, British families who campaign for Anyone's Child have been quoted in every parliamentary debate on the issue since the group's formation. In the most recent such debate on the MDA 1971 in 2021, Jeff Smith MP stated:

> 'I will leave the final words to Anne-Marie Cockburn, who is a campaigner for Anyone's Child: Families for Safer Drug Control. Anne-Marie's daughter Martha, like people through the generations for thousands of years, just wanted to have a bit of fun and get high. She researched on the internet how to get high safely. She was 15 years old when she took an overdose of MDMA that killed her. Anne-Marie says: "As I stand by my

daughter's grave, what more evidence do I need that UK drug policy needs to change?"'

The families involved in Anyone's Child have described feeling empowered after meeting with politicians. Telling their stories allows them to dignify their loved ones and to regain control over the narratives of their experience, which, in some cases, have been silenced or denied for years, out of fear and stigmatisation.

'When I joined the project I wasn't sure what I had to offer the group — but I knew my boys would have wanted me to be part of it. Our family were stigmatised because my sons used drugs and I felt shunned, shut out and ashamed. Today I can claim I've given a presentation in the Houses of Parliament, appeared on GMTV and spoken to numerous journalists and media outlets. I have found my voice again having kept so much secret for so long.'

Rose

'I came to Anyone's Child and it was a big relief for me. I faced the truth I didn't want to face. People said Daniel was unlucky, that he only did it once, but that wasn't true. It was quite cathartic facing the truth. I am doing this for Daniel. I am doing it for him. I feel proud that he is helping to keep other children safe.'

Marie

As the families speak out the stigma is starting to reduce leading to more and more people getting in contact and telling their story. Wherever the families speak we find that people from all walks of life start to speak out in support often about their personal situation (many for the first time). At one event in the Houses of Parliament a police officer joined the families in speaking out about her husband's struggles and the fear she lived in because of how this might impact her professional life, sharing these stories in turn leads others to speak out and to further erode stereotypes. Through telling their stories Anyone's Child are making real strides in changing the public and political conversation around drugs, taking it from taboo to the mainstream

'By telling their powerful stories, the Anyone's Child families have genuinely helped to change the national conversation around drugs and the need for reform by putting a human face to the statistics of escalating drug-related deaths.'

Professor Fiona Measham (Manchester University),
Director of The Loop Drug Safety Checking Service

As legal regulation becomes a reality around the world, Anyone's Child is starting to tell the positive stories of change, stories of those who were not criminalised by their drug use, those who have criminal records expunged and were given a second chance and offered support rather than punishment.

Conclusion

The stories of people who have suffered some of the most devastating effects of prohibitionist drug policy demonstrate that the MDA 1971 is a root cause for many situations that endanger child wellbeing. This chapter has explored how drug prohibition and criminalisation actively promote shame, stigma and discrimination of people who use or supply drugs, the burden of which is largely carried by already marginalised or vulnerable populations (Sumnall et al, 2021).

Through the Anyone's Child campaign families are actively challenging the stigma that exists around drug use and enabling conversations to start all over the country around this subject that has been taboo for so long. The campaign has also accelerated public understanding of current drug laws and the potential benefits of a controlled and regulated drug market. This in turn is encouraging others to come forward and speak out which is starting to change hearts and minds. This change is now slowly encouraging MPs to speak out for the first time on the need for a review of the MDA 1971 and lasting reform.

Jane Slater is Deputy Chief Executive Officer at the Transform Drug Policy Foundation. She founded and now leads the Anyone's Child: Families for Safer Drug Control campaign.

Mary Ryder is a doctoral researcher in Security, Conflict and Human Rights at the University of Bristol. Her research explores the impacts of prohibitionist drug policies in Colombia. She also works at the Transform Drugs Policy Foundation on the Anyone's Child: Families for Safer Drug Control campaign.

References and Extra Reading

Barrett, D (ed.) (2011), *Children of the Drug War: Perspectives on the Impact of Drug Policies on Young People,* IDEBATE Press.

Betts, J and Betts, P and Sage I (1999), *Leah Betts: The Legacy of Ecstasy,* London: Robson Books.

Dyregrov, K and Selseng, L B (2021), 'Nothing to Mourn, He Was Just a Drug Addict' — Stigma Towards People Bereaved by Drug-related Death, *Addiction Research & Theory:* 1–11.

Essex Live (2020), Leah Betts 25 years on: The tragic photo and story of Essex girl's death that shocked a nation, November 16: www.essexlive.news/news/essex-news/leah-betts-25-years-on-4704289 (accessed January 11, 2022).

Koram, K (2019), *The War on Drugs and the Global Colour Line,* London: Pluto Press.

Matthews, S, Dwyer, R and Snoek, A (2017), Stigma and Self-Stigma in Addiction. *Journal of Bioethical Inquiry,* 14(2): 275–286.

Office for National Statistics (ONS) (2021), *Deaths Related to Drug Poisoning in England and Wales: 2020 Registrations* (accessed January 10, 2022).

Rolles, S (2011), After the War on Drugs: How Legal Regulation of Production and Trade Would Better Protect Children in D Barrett (ed.) (2011), *Children of the Drug War: Perspectives on the Impact of Drug Policies on Young People,* 59–72, IDEBATE Press.

Smith, J (2021), Misuse of Drugs Act Volume 697: debated on Thursday 17 June: https://hansard.parliament.uk/commons/2021-06-17/debates/A1B14B26-EBB7-415F-9AA8-1620726307C5/MisuseOfDrugsAct

Stimson, G (2000), 'Blair declares war,' speech delivered at the Conference Methadone and Beyond: Expanding and Exploring Drug Treatment Options, March 22, London: www.ukhra.org/stimsonspeech.html (accessed January 10, 2022).

Special Advisory Committee on the Epidemic of Opioid Overdoses (SAC) (2021), Opioid and Stimulant-related Harms in Canada, Ottawa: Public Health Agency of Canada: https://health-infobase.canada.ca/substance-related-harms/opioids-stimulants/ (accessed January 10, 2022).

Sumnall, H, Atkinson, A, Gage, S, Hamilton, I and Montgomery C (2021), Less Than Human: Dehumanisation of People Who Use Heroin, *Health Education*.

Transform (2015), The War on Drugs: Promoting Stigma and Discrimination, Count the Costs: 50 Years of the War on Drugs.

Transform (2020), Reforming Drug Policies to Reduce the Trafficking and Exploitation of Vulnerable People.

Transform (2022), *The Misuse of Drugs Act 1971: Counting the Costs*.

United Nations General Assembly Special Session (UNGASS) (2016), Plenary Statement for the Honourable Jane Philpott Minister of Health — UNGASS on the World Drug Problem: www.canada.ca/en/health-canada/news/2016/04/plenary-statement-for-the-honourable-jane-philpott-minister-of-health-ungass-on-the-world-drug-problem.html

Note: For more information of Transform's vision for a legally regulated drugs market, please see Transform Drug Policy Foundation (2010), *After the War on Drugs: Blueprint for Regulation*. The stories of the members of Anyone's Child can be found at anyoneschild.org/stories

CHAPTER 14

The MDA 1971: No Education

Patrick Hargreaves

The opening provision of the MDA 1971 concerns the formation and constitution of the Advisory Council on the Misuse of Drugs (ACMD). One of their duties is to 'advise Government on measures which ought to be taken for educating the public and in particular the young in the dangers of misusing such drugs'. This is the only instance where there is specific reference to education in the entire Act whereas it should be central to policy, sharing equal status with treatment and enforcement.

In order to set the scene a few key terms will be described and defined in order to clarify some areas of potential confusion. This is followed by an outline of the models of Personal Social and Health Education (PSHE) including 'best practice' recommendations and suggestions for a new strategy. Finally, other influences on young people's behaviour are considered and how education and a new MDA framework must go hand in hand, based on the best evidence, regularly updated.

> **Key terms**
> - **Drug** A drug is any substance that enters the human body and can change either the structure or function of the human organism. (www.nurseslearning.com)
> - **Drug prevention** Aims to prevent substance use. In other words, the implication is that the intervention should aim to stop drug use.

> - **Drug education** Informs people about facts and explores attitudes and contexts, behaviours and consequences. 'The key aim of drug education is to enable children to make healthy, informed choices' (Drug Education in Schools, Ofsted 2005). It considers all drugs including medicines, volatile substances, alcohol and tobacco.
> - **Personal Social and Health Education** 'PSHE is a planned programme of learning opportunities and experiences that help children and young people grow and develop as individuals and as members of families and of social and economic communities' (PSHE Association, 2011). This chapter concentrates mainly on school-based drug education as part of PSHE.

Measuring the effectiveness of educational interventions on health-related behaviour can be problematic. The wide range of confounding variables, together with the likelihood of incidental, unplanned or delayed factors, makes evaluation of such work extremely difficult. However, the difficulty of measuring impact does not mean it does not exist. This is an assumption that non-educationalists are sometimes rather quick to make: 'Most schools in the UK provide drug education programmes. Research indicates that these probably have little impact on future drug use. There should be a careful reassessment of the role of schools in drug misuse prevention. The emphasis should be on providing all pupils with accurate, credible and consistent information about the hazards of tobacco, alcohol and other drugs' (ACMD, 2006). The view that educational interventions have little impact on drug use together with its focus purely on hazardous use, proposed by a committee comprised of non-educationalists, ran counter to the thinking in the profession at the time. It heralded years of resource reduction, which still continues.

'The key aim of drug education is to enable children to make healthy informed choices' (Office for Standards in Education, 2005). Even if someone chooses to continue using substances, they may do so less dangerously and will have the tools to make an informed decision should they decide to change. However, it could take around ten years before any impact from interventions with teenagers become evident. Similarly, in their 2021 Annual Report, the ACMD wrote that '... initiation of substance misuse, particularly at a young age is an important predictor of adult substance related harm.' It can also delay first use and in this way can be seen as having a harm-reduction outcome. Some drugs have the potential to cure serious illness; they may also be lethal if misused. We do not seek to 'prevent' their use but educate about it. Neither do we aim to 'prevent' alcohol in our culture, much of which revolves around its consumption: we seek to reduce the harm which can result from its use. The term 'drug prevention' itself and the mindset it represents stands in the way of any real progress in alleviating the harms caused by drug misuse. For instance, the 'drug' paracetamol is potentially far more dangerous than the 'drug' cannabis and the 'drug' morphine is of great benefit in alleviating pain while it can also be lethal. This is why, in education, we must consider the use and misuse of the full range of substances.

Drug education considers all drugs, including medicines, volatile substances, alcohol and tobacco. This chapter concentrates on school-based drug education as part of PSHE education. However, drug education goes on in a wealth of settings—formal, informal and vicarious; in the family, through the media and among friends which will also be considered. Thus the first hurdle for evaluators to clear is that of trying to factor out a huge range of confounding variables whenever an assessment of the impact of an educational programme is attempted.

Personal Social and Health Education in Practice

Needs analysis and spiralling curriculum
Needs analysis means planning an intervention based on the needs of the group at the time, to inform a spiralling curriculum where key concepts are presented repeatedly but with deepening layers of complexity, responsive to the latest trends (McWhirter, 2009). PSHE is about the provision of information and the development of knowledge, skills and attitudes that enable young people to make effective choices which will help them to live happy, healthy, successful lives, now and in the future. It also provides an opportunity for them to reflect on issues which do not arise elsewhere as part of the formal curriculum, for example understanding themselves, their interests and needs, managing

challenging relationships, understanding their personal response to risk, and recognising the contribution they make to the wider community.

It is important that drug education is taught as part of PSHE as the range of issues needs to be seen in context. Risk behaviour does not happen in a vacuum but in a socio-cultural context where the substance, the people and the situation are inextricably linked and of equal importance. A bottle of illicit vodka in the park with your friends is different from a glass of beer at a meal with your family. The substance (alcohol) is the same, the people and the situation are very different. 'Pupils should have opportunities to consider how they will respond if they are in different real life situations... give them space to rehearse some of these choices' (ibid). In 2011, the Department for Education (DfE) wrote:

> 'The government recognises that children can benefit enormously from high-quality PSHE and that good PSHE supports young people to make safe and informed choices about their lifestyles, health, careers and finances both now and as they prepare for the responsibilities of adulthood. Good schools understand the connections between pupils' physical and mental health, their safety and their educational attainment. Good schools will also be active promoters of health because healthy children with high-self-esteem learn and behave better at school.' (DfE, 2011)

Incidentally this document was published when the programme supporting drug education in PSHE was being reduced and the Government discontinued its support for local authority PSHE advisors.

Models of Drug Education

Broadly, drug education programme delivery styles fall into two categories. One is based on information and rational decision making, the other is rather more complex.

Behavioural model
The most basic model of drug education is a behavioural one, the traditional but increasingly contested starting point for health promotion. Its premise is

that we respond to a stimulus to change behaviour. The model assumes that we know and understand the benefits of change (e.g. giving up smoking) then make a rational decision based on costs and benefits. Key to the model is that we have an incentive to change; feel our present behaviour is disadvantageous; believe the benefits outweigh any costs; and feel competent to realise our aim. This model is the basis of many educational approaches and informs the Government's view today. However, in practice, we know that knowledge alone is rarely enough to change our behaviour, so educational approaches based only on information will indeed be ineffective (Stead and Angus, 2004). The statutory obligations on schools around drug education are minimal, meaning that it may merely be addressed, in passing, within the science curriculum, a knowledge-based programme. Fear arousal is also ineffective and may even impact negatively, exaggeration breeding contempt for the overall health message. Health-related decision-making is very much more complex than a series of rational calculations based on factors over which the individual may have no immediate control.

Interactive learning model

Interactive learning is arguably the most important aspect of effective drug education, providing a stimulus for young people through group investigation, simulation, and role play to identify and avoid risky situations, develop skills to manage situations involving drugs, and be able to avoid particularly harmful misuse.

In interactive teaching the teacher becomes a facilitator, creating a safe and supportive environment where young people can consider new and challenging information and ideas. Risk is explored, offering the opportunity to develop 'risk competence'—the capacity to recognise, assess and manage risk in stimulating and challenging situations. Studies here have shown that young people with stronger social skills are more able to resist peer influence and abstain from misuse for longer. (Hansen, 1992; McGrath et al, 2006). The ACMD eventually accepted this view in their Prevention of Drug and Alcohol Dependence briefing (ACMD, 2015).

Investment in training teachers to deliver quality PSHE has all but vanished. There is no incentive for schools to engage professionally trained PSHE teachers to bring the standard of delivery into line with other subjects. Around a third of schools have one or more staff who have undertaken PSHE continued professional development (CPD), for which it is now increasingly difficult to be released or funded. As many as 90% of teachers teaching PSHE have no specialist qualification, unthinkable in other subject areas. There is generally scant regard paid to PSHE in initial teacher training courses. In general, PSHE enjoys higher status among leaders, staff and pupils in primary schools compared with secondary schools, largely due to the value placed on Social and Emotional Aspects of Learning (SEAL), making clear connections between PSHE and developing learning and standards. This conceals an assumption that adolescents 'do not need' SEAL.

In many secondary schools, PSHE is not on the timetable but is 'covered' in assemblies, tutor time, perhaps by a quiz squashed in between registration and announcements, or on 'drop down days' where students immerse themselves in sex, drugs, alcohol, crime and safety for a day. These sessions typically involve a range of agencies sharing information on their individual areas of expertise. The problem with such interventions is that they provide a huge overload of information which is rarely considered or debated properly. Further, after the session, the providers leave, so students cannot revisit with them questions they formulate over time. Finally, the student who is absent, possibly who needs it most, will have missed the input for the year. This leads on to the use of outside visitors in general. Because of the lack of training referred to above, many teachers assigned to PSHE delivery do not have the expertise and/or confidence to discuss sex, or drug use, with their students. The school may then decide to enlist an agency to deliver sessions on these themes. While there may be value in involving community and health organizations and the police in PSHE programmes, it is of the utmost importance that the teacher leads the programme and that these contributors are just that—contributors, not sole providers. A very clear service level agreement must be negotiated with agencies prior to their being engaged.

Negative approaches based on scaring children, often favoured by the police, should be avoided. Some observers have hoped that negative approaches—such as showing young people what it is like to be in jail or enabling them to hear from and speak with ex-prisoners or recovering addicts—can scare them into better behaviour. However, a number of rigorous evaluations have assessed such 'scared straight' approaches and found that they fail to deter juvenile crime or promote more positive behaviours (ACMD, 2015). Moreover, there are a number of evangelical organizations and sects, including Scientologists, masquerading as drug and alcohol agencies, offering glossy programmes free to schools but with a pernicious hidden agenda. As well as training teachers and supporting schools with delivery, local authority drug and alcohol advisers could quality assure what is on offer. These posts have all gone.

A New Strategy for Drug and Alcohol Education

Attitudes
If we revisit the quotation at the beginning of this chapter, we can see the progress that was made in the ACMD's understanding of these issues over the nine years since the publication of the Pathways to Problems report. This progress is exemplified by the cut and paste job done on it to inform the ACMD's (2010) response to the drug strategy consultation. This said: 'The emphasis should be on providing all pupils with accurate, credible and consistent information about the hazards of alcohol and other drugs.' It continued: 'However, the ACMD stresses that research has indicated that such programmes have little impact on drug use,' a statement which could be caricatured as: 'It's no good but it's what we know so we'll carry on anyway.' A welcome indication however of changing attitudes towards 'prevention' is shown in the ACMD's Recovery Committee Report (ACMD, 2015).

Change in the substance use landscape
As has been discussed throughout the book, it is not only attitudes that change, but the substances themselves. For example, synthetic cannabinoids (spice) and the active psychoactive ingredient in cannabis, THC, are very different drugs. Synthetic cannabinoids can lead to serious, life threatening side effects and are only linked to cannabis in that they bind to the same receptor in the brain as THC.

'New' psychoactive substances (NPS) (often misleadingly referred to as 'legal highs') pose a highly significant risk to users precisely because of their unpredictability and confusing legal status for anyone trying to equate the MDA classification system to an actual risk of harm (Nutt et al, 2010).

Substance use by young people between 1990 to the present

While not wanting to fall into the trap of mono-causal outcomes, it seems clear that local authority drug and sex education advisory posts, in place from 1999–2011, and the resultant school programmes played a significant part in a range of health improvements. National data tell us that over ten years (2001–2011) smoking, drinking and drug use among young people all fell consistently year-on-year; and the rate of conceptions among 15 to 17 year olds (at 38.2 per 1,000) was the lowest for 30 years (NHS Information Centre, 2011). This was despite the fact that this was within an environment of increased availability and decreased price, a huge illicit tobacco and alcohol market, an exponential rise in NPS available on the internet and a moral panic about the sexualisation of children. Together these issues impact disproportionately on the young. This shows not only that there is no room for complacency but also demonstrates the folly of an over-reliance on enforcement and tax hikes on alcohol and tobacco to influence behaviour without parallel input from education. Currently, it is estimated that 16% of pupils have smoked and 5% are current smokers, 10% of pupils drank alcohol in the past week (2% of 11 year olds and 23% of 15 year olds of whom 22% had been drunk in the last four weeks) and 24% of pupils reported having taken drugs (9% of 11 year olds and 38% of 15 year olds) (NHS Digital, 2019).

A Realistic Role for PSHE

As has been mentioned previously, education should not be confused with prevention. It is realistic to expect schools, adequately supported, resourced, and encouraged, to provide education programmes about drugs and other substances. It is not realistic to expect schools, by virtue of such programmes, to be prevention agencies. Education can contribute to prevention but the two are not synonymous and it is unrealistic to pretend that they are. Harm reduction — risky behaviour delayed or reflected on — is a realistic and worthy aim and outcome of school-based drug education (and other PSHE topics) but is hindered by the reluctance of Government to use the term in its strategies. Young people must be encouraged to develop their decision-making, risk analysis and life skills competences, from the nursery ages, within an appropriate spiralling curriculum throughout their educational careers. They need to discuss, debate and consider drugs and drug use in a socio-cultural context alongside health, sex, relationships, risk, bullying, offending and so on. 'Life skills training has demonstrated a positive effect on reducing indicators of drug use. Programmes based on life skills were the most consistent at reducing drug use'.

The range of issues young people are likely to face should be considered in context. We know that where young people are taking risks, they are often taking more than one. For example, 'early drunkenness is correlated with smoking, cannabis use, injuries, fights, low academic performance and unsafe or unwanted sexual intercourse'. The science curriculum alone is not an adequate vehicle for the delivery of such a programme. The 2015 Education Select Committee Report on PSHE recommended statutory status for PSHE, with funding for training—specifically, the PSHE Certificate course, introduced as part of the Healthy Schools Programme in 2005; and the resumption of regular Ofsted subject surveys. The first two recommendations were rejected in the Government's response to the Select Committee Report. At the time of writing, the most recent DfE guidance now gives statutory status only to Relationships Education (primary) and Relationships and Sex Education (secondary). If these recommendations around quality PSHE sound familiar (DfE, 2015), they are. They are very similar to those suggested by the MacDonald Report on PSHE published in 2009 (MacDonald, 2009). A change of Government in 2010 ensued and the recommendations were ignored completely. It is imperative that we continue to lobby hard for their adoption this time round.

Drug prevention is differentiated from drug education as the latter aims to provide information and advice about drugs upon which individuals can base decisions. Unlike prevention, it is not the primary objective of drug education to change behaviour, although prevention activities may include prominent educational components (ACMD, 2015).

This enlightened documentation from the ACMD is to some extent qualified by concerns about corporate learning. Within the ACMD, although there have been periods when individuals with an understanding and expertise around substance use, young people and education have been able to inform the council, this level of knowledge has not been sustained within the council once those individuals' terms of office have ended; or if Governments persistently overrule advice from their own advisory bodies. As with Governments, changes in make-up and personnel seem to necessitate a process of 'learning from scratch' rather than developmental and increased institutional knowledge and understanding. We know that preventing drug and alcohol misuse among young people is a cost-effective policy option. At the dawn of the millennium the Government invested heavily in PSHE with the appointment of drug education and sex and relationships education advisers in most local authorities. Schools valued and made use of the support and challenge they provided prior to their defunding as a result of spending cuts. This reflects the disconnect between rhetoric (ministerial statements about the importance of drug education in young people's lives) and reality—reduced resourcing, the ending of training programmes, in-service and initial, and the downplaying or disappearance of drug education in any meaningful sense as a curriculum requirement.

The Family and Other Influences

We know that poor attachment with parents and parental substance misuse are major risk factors and supportive relationships with family members and clear expectations are major protective factors for mental, emotional and behaviour disorders. We also know that most 11 to 15 year olds would go to their parents first for useful information about alcohol (77%) and drugs (72%) (NHS Digital, 2019).

Largely because of the continually changing situation around drug availability and use, parents are often reticent to address the subject, feeling unskilled and lacking in knowledge and understanding. Schools should provide accessible information events, workshops and signposting. Find good sources of advice such as that at drugscience.org.uk. One of the keys here is to start the conversation early. We need to acknowledge that as parents, we actually begin 'drug education' soon after the birth of the child when we talk to them about the medication we may be administering. As soon as they can crawl around, we warn them about dangerous substances around the house. Sadly, when they are out and about, many of our children may come across discarded drug paraphernalia in our parks and streets and we talk with them about it. This reflects the necessity, highlighted when we considered formal education, for needs analysis and a spiralling curriculum, i.e. give them sufficient knowledge, skills and understanding, appropriate for their age and situation, to keep them safe, and revisit and refine the conversation regularly as they grow and develop.

We need to consider our behaviour and rehearse our responses to their questions regarding drug and alcohol use. Role modelling is of the utmost importance. Children need to see that when they are taken to an event such as a football match or a meal out at a restaurant, the adults do not have to consume alcohol. As a result of the closure of many public playgrounds, 'family pubs' sprang up offering play facilities for children, making this link between entertainment and alcohol stronger still.

Media

All children will encounter drug use from an early age (remember our definition of 'drugs') and they will see it in films, on TV, and hear references to it in music. This has long been the case and can actually be a useful starting point for child/parent discussion. Many of us have campaigned long and hard for a ban on sponsorship by the alcohol industry of sport and music events, impacting disproportionately on young people. However, this is clearly not going to happen any time soon. 'An insidious threat to child health and wellbeing is the predatory commercial exploitation that is encouraging harmful and addictive activities that are extremely deleterious to young people's health (WHO-UNICEF-Lancet Commission, 2020).

Social media poses yet more complex issues. Parents may not be familiar with the platforms their youngsters are accessing. In their 2019 study, Volteface reported on their findings on how social media is being used as a marketplace for illicit drugs and the impact this is having on young people — social media's primary user group (Volteface, 2019). Around a quarter of young people have seen drugs advertised and/or know friends who have bought drugs on social media, mainly Snapchat and Instagram. Cannabis is by far the most common, followed by cocaine and ecstasy. This impacts on young people by normalising drugs and facilitating trade. Dealers become 'friends' and their lifestyle is advertised, while the young person's personal life is exposed. Social media companies must better monitor and regulate their sites (ibid).

Conclusion

In conclusion, we know that drug use is rising (Office for National Statistics, 2020). Children and young people face new and emerging challenges. There is an urgent need for a consistent, evidence-based education programme to help them deal with these. Politicians and policymakers must be willing to face the realities around young people and drug use and prioritise and equip them with the best tools and support available. Schools should be required to implement a health education and policy programme, co-produced with students, carers and local partners; draw from DfE recommended resources; deliver drugs education every year and do so also in post-16 settings; and cover topics that relate to real life situations and decision-making. The DfE should provide funding for schools to support the implementation of mandatory drugs education and ensure that the content of initial teacher training includes PSHE.

The DfE, Department of Health and Home Office need to fund, develop, implement and evaluate a co-ordinated education programme based on a harm-reduction approach, including quality training in teaching and learning. Such programmes should be accompanied by an ongoing evaluation process. We need Ofsted to report specifically on PSHE education and on the personal development of and support for young people. And we need consistently funded longitudinal research into the use of all substances, to show trends, prevalence and the emergence of new substances, new patterns of use and new drug using populations.

Schools and other services need to provide accessible information events and workshops for parents/carers enabling them to best support their children. The Government needs to introduce a regulatory requirement for social media companies to monitor activity on their sites and act accordingly.

The most commonly used drug in the UK is cannabis, reflected by its prevalence on social media (Volteface, ibid). Leaving it unregulated places a £2.5 billion market into the hands of criminals who have made full use of the opportunities provided by social media. Cannabis legalisation is the policy which would be most effective in alleviating these problems by tackling the illicit market, restricting access to underage use, regulating the products available and facilitating research into its positive benefits. With the majority in the UK in favour of reform and more and more countries abandoning prohibition, its legalisation should now be seen as an inevitability, so that a considered legislative and regulatory framework that is fit for purpose may be planned.

At the beginning of this chapter, I opined that *education* should be a central strand of the MDA 1971 alongside *enforcement* and *treatment*, both of which would have fewer demands on them as a result of solid educational policies around drugs and alcohol. Education and a new framework to deal with drugs must go hand in hand and be based on the best evidence regularly updated and enshrined within a new Act.

For 30 years, practitioners in PSHE have argued for the approaches outlined in this chapter but over that time there has been little real progress and politicians' actions have not matched their words. The focus continues to be on the risks, harms, dangers and criminality of drug use (DfE, 2019). Educators and policymakers thus make use of scare tactics to promote abstinence. Not only does this approach fail to prevent use, it also fails to keep those who use drugs safe. When young people try drugs and see that it doesn't lead to the consequences they've been warned about, they mistrust authority altogether. Within Relationships and Sex Education, rather than simply promoting abstinence, we have educated young people about contraception, consent and the advantages of delaying sexual relationships, acknowledging that they may choose to have sex. We need to treat drugs and alcohol in the same way. Illicit drug use is becoming increasingly normalised. Sixty-two per cent of higher education students are relaxed about drug use, while 30% of 15 year olds think it's 'OK to try cannabis' and 17% think it's 'OK to use it once a week' (NHS Digital, 2019).

The illegal status of drugs does not prevent use either. On the contrary, it allows illegal drugs to be more accessible for anyone. Fifty-three per cent of young people aged 16-to-24 report that obtaining illicit drugs within 24 hours would be easy (Home Office, 2019). As has been argued, drug dealing on social media platforms needs to be addressed in the Act.

Most illicit drug use by young people is experimental. Young people take risks; the majority of young people who took illicit drugs for the first time did so to 'see what it was like' (NHS Digital, 2019, op cit). We must help young people navigate this risk-taking period safely. Anyone looking to the MDA 1971 for an indication of relative harms of different substances would be sadly misled. The classification of drugs within the Act bears little or no relation to actual drug harms. Further, it creates a misconception that legal drugs are less harmful than illegal ones (See Nutt, et al, 2010, op cit).

Finally, we need a Misuse of Drugs Act that considers drugs from a scientific perspective, which can be enshrined and reflected within an educational programme comprised of unbiased, evidence-based information together with the skills to process it and examine the attitudes around it. The time is right for a new Act that can instil practices that reduce harm and save lives and can inform policy not only in *enforcement* and *treatment* but in *education* as well.

Patrick Hargreaves is a retired Headteacher and Inspector in all phases of education, specialising in PSHE, both in the UK and abroad. His work on child centred education has been widely published and won the MentorUK Champ Award in 2010.

References and Extra Reading

Advisory Council on the Misuse of Drugs (ACMD) (2006), Pathways to Problems, London: Home Office.

ACMD (2010), Drug Strategy Consultation, London: Home Office.

ACMD (2015), Recovery Committee Prevention Briefing, London: Home Office.

ACMD (2021), Annual Report, London: Home Office.

Allen, L M (2014), Why Schools Should Promote Pupils' Health and Well-being, *British Medical Journal*, Vol. 348: 3078.

Anderson, P, Møller, L and Galea, G (2013), Alcohol in the European Union: Consumption, Harm and Policy Approaches, World Health Organization.

Canning, U, Millward, L, Raj, T and Warm, D (2004), Drug Use Prevention: A Review of Reviews, Health Development Agency.

Coggans, N, Cheyne, B and McKellar, S (2003), The Life-skills Training Drug Education Programme: A Review of Research, University of Strathclyde/Scottish Executive.

Department for Education (DfE) (2011), Review of PSHE Education.

DfE (2015), Government Response: Life Lessons, PSHE and SRE in Schools.

DfE (2019), Statutory Guidance: Physical Health and Mental Wellbeing.

DfE/Association of Chief Police Officers (2012), Drug Advice for Schools.

Department for Education and Skills/Department of Health (2005), National Healthy School Status: A Guide for Schools.

Hansen, W (1992), School-based Substance Abuse Prevention: A Review of the State of the Art in Curriculum, 1980–1990, *Health Education Research*, Vol. 7, No. 3: 403–30.

Hargreaves, P and Watts, L (2010), *Just for a Laugh,* Durham County Council.

Home Office (2019), 2018/19 Crime Survey England and Wales.

McGrath, Y, Sumnall, H, McVeigh, J and Bellis, M (2006), *Review of Grey Literature on Drug Prevention Among Young People,* National Institute for Health and Clinical Excellence.

McWhirter, J (2009), *The Theory of PSHE Education,* PSHE Association.

MacDonald, A (2009), Independent Review of the Proposal to make PSHE Education Statutory, Department for Families, Schools and Children.

Misuse of Drugs Act 1971: www.legislation.gov.uk/ukpga/1971/38/contents

NHS Digital (2019), Statistics on Smoking Drinking and Drug Use Among Young People in England.

NHS Information Centre (2001–2011), Smoking Drinking and Drug Use.

Nutt, D J, King, L A and Phillips L D (2010), Drug Harms in the UK: A Multi Criteria Decision Analysis, *The Lancet*, 376: 9752.

Office for National Statistics (2020), Drug Use Alcohol and Smoking: www.gov.uk/government/publications/united-kingdom-drug-situation-focal-point-annual-report/uk-drug-situation-2019-summary

Office for Standards in Education (Ofsted)(2005), *Drug Education in Schools.*

Ofsted (2013), *Not Yet Good Enough — PSHE in Schools.*

Ofsted (2015), *School Inspection Handbook.*

PSHE Association (2011), *PSHE Definitions.*

Public Health England (2014), Public Health England's Key Priorities for Keeping People Well.

Stead, M and Angus, K (2004), Literature Review Into the Effectiveness of School Drug Education, Scottish Executive: https://lx.iriss.org.uk/content/literature-review-effectiveness-school-drug-education

United Nations Office on Drugs and Crime (2010), World Drug Report 2010: Understanding the Extent and Nature of Drug Use.

UN Office on Drugs and Crime (2014), World Drug Report 2014: Extent of Drug Use: Global Overview.

Volteface (2019), DM for Details: Selling Drugs in the Age of Social Media: https://volteface.me/publications/dm-details-selling-drugs-age-social-media/ DM for Details.

WHO-UNICEF-Lancet Commission (2020), A Future for the World's Children.

CHAPTER 15

The Impact of Drug Legislation on Climate Change

Rosalind Gittins, Steve Rolles and Katherine Watkinson

As previous chapters of this book have highlighted, current UK legislation does not permit regulation of the supply of 'illicit substances' such as heroin or crack cocaine. Whilst there are consequent notable harms to the people who use them, their loved ones and wider society (including the Criminal Justice System, health and social care services), the impact on the environment is often overlooked.

Drug Use Paraphernalia

Given the notable ongoing increase in the use of cocaine (National Crime Agency, 2020) and associated harms, interventions to reduce risk are becoming increasingly important and people are typically advised to smoke or snort rather than inject. Unfortunately, providing people with professionally made reusable pipes as a harm reduction measure is not permissible under current legislation (National Archives, 1971). This results in people using homemade devices constructed from household items such as metal scouring pads, cans and plastic containers which can cause burns injuries and the release of toxic chemicals when heated. If legislation enabled pre-made, glass pipes to be issued by treatment services (perhaps as an extension to needle syringe provision), this would not only reduce harms but also facilitate their recycling. This would improve sustainability and, with greater access to safe disposal facilities, reduce drug-related litter too.

Ensuring adequate coverage of paraphernalia is essential to reduce the need for people to share or re-use equipment which increases the risks of communicable disease transmission, such as blood borne viruses and Covid-19 (Harris, 2020; Vickerman et al, 2012). However, this requires the increased use of single use plastics; therefore, procurement processes should prioritise the use of paraphernalia made with minimal and reprocessed plastics, where manufacturers are required to meet ISO 14001: 2015 standards which relate to environmental management systems (International Organization for Standards (ISO), 2021) and which utilises approaches such as Operation Clean Sweep® which focuses on limiting plastic pellet loss to the environment (Operation Clean Sweep, 2021).

Drug litter where paraphernalia is inappropriately discarded is not only unsightly, but also creates environmental and sharps injury risk. It is perhaps more likely to occur where inappropriate equipment is supplied, or where there is a lack of access to safe disposal facilities. There can be challenges with getting such facilities installed in public places and, because the use of illicit substances is associated with notable stigma and has legal implications, people can be concerned about being seen to access them too. Additionally, once filled, their contents are unlikely to be separated for recycling and the bins are typically incinerated making them single use. Enabling waste bins to be reused may therefore improve sustainability: this could be applied to all waste types, to include sharps, pharmaceutical and clinical waste.

Prescribed Interventions

The issue of single use plastics is perpetuated where prescribed interventions for the use of substances are offered too. For example, oral opioid substitute medication is often administered under supervision using single use plastics and liquids dispensed in daily dose containers using plastic bottles rather than glass to reduce costs, the risk of accidental breakage and dosing errors which can occur when supplied in larger containers. Currently there are no incentives, national guidance or systems in place to support the return and sterilisation of containers to enable their reuse or recycling. Additionally, as the medicines used are controlled drugs, the potential for this is complicated by the risk of diversion, as well as confidentiality breaches if dispensing labels are not removed and concerns about bottles being rinsed and the medication entering the sewage system.

The production of prescriptions also has an environmental impact: in the UK instalment prescriptions that allow people to have their opioid substitute treatment (such as methadone and buprenorphine) issued to them where needed daily or where they have their consumption supervised, cannot be sent electronically to the pharmacy, unlike with other prescription types. Due to them being controlled drugs, the actual prescription (not, e.g. a photocopy or email) must be received by the pharmacy prior to them being able to make a supply, which adds to the cost of postage, the need for envelopes, carbon footprint associated with transportation and can delay peoples' access to their medication. Ongoing governance concerns regarding the number of lost, stolen and misplaced prescriptions will also remain until this is changed.

Nitrous Oxide

The substances that people use may themselves also have a direct impact upon the environment, such as the medical gas nitrous oxide, which is used to manage short acting pain. Although useful clinically, it is a well-known greenhouse gas, and steps are being taken to eliminate its medical use (Association of Anaesthetists, 2021). Nitrous oxide is also used recreationally, producing feelings of calmness and fits of giggles when inhaled (hence the name 'laughing gas'). It is thought to be relatively safe when misused, though if taken without care or if used heavily for prolonged periods, problems such as conditions associated with vitamin B12 depletion can occur. Whilst the quantity associated with recreational use is likely to be minor in comparison to other sources, the containers that the nitrous oxide is typically released from are associated with littering. The problem with the small canisters, sometimes referred to as 'whippets' being inappropriately discarded in public places has contributed to the Government considering the need to review the legal status of nitrous oxide (Advisory Council on the Misuse of Drugs (ACMD), 2021). Perhaps approaching the littering problem by instead incentivising the recycling of the canisters rather than rescheduling nitrous oxide could be a more suitable alternative approach (Drug Science, 2020).

Safe Spaces for Using Substances

Drug littering (with the environmental harms and public health risk issues outlined above) frequently occurs because people resort to using substances in public places when they have no alternative places to go. As well as acting as an assertive engagement strategy, these facilities can minimise waste by ensuring that only the required paraphernalia is issued to individuals. Such 'safe spaces' have been implemented elsewhere in the world with success: they are supported by the European Monitoring Centre for Drugs and Drug Addiction and in the UK by the Faculty of Public Health and numerous other organizations (FPH, 2021; EMCDDA, 2018). However, creating safe spaces for people who use substances is not currently supported by the Government (Atkins, 2018), though their ACMD has recommended them (ACMD, 2016). Currently, Drug Science (2020) has a working group with various collaborators who are working together to develop a research-based approach to implementing safe consumptions sites.

Safe spaces for people who choose to use substances also need to be considered in the context of music festivals. In these settings, due to stigma and concerns about the legal implications of being caught with illicit substances, people may decide to dispose of their unwanted drugs into the local environment. Such festivals are typically held in rural areas and often on land used for farming. Providing people with improved access to anonymised safe disposal facilities for unwanted substances and ensuring adequate sewerage systems could help to avoid the contamination of the local environment (Aberg et al, 2022).

Illicit Production and Supply

Due to the international distances travelled, drug trafficking has a notable carbon footprint, further exacerbated by deforestation whilst creating cattle ranches and plantations to facilitate money laundering, for coca growing and the creation of roads and aircraft landing strips for illicit transportation (Transform, 2020; United Nations Development Programme (UNDP), 2015). Contamination of waterways and soil and the release of greenhouse gases also occurs due to the use of large volumes of toxic chemicals needed for production and associated by-products, for example when MDMA is produced illicitly (Transform, 2020).

As outlined in Transform's 'Alternative World Drug Report' (2016) herbicides (especially when aerial sprays are used in an attempt to reduce illicit cultivation levels of coca leaf) cause significant and indiscriminate damage to flora and fauna and contaminate waterways. This creates an increased threat to already endangered and protected species in areas such as the Andes and Amazon basin which are of ecological importance, and the herbicides used include glyphosate which is thought to be carcinogenic (Guyton et al, 2015). These approaches have a negligible impact upon production levels since farmers simply choose to relocate and adapt their cultivation techniques and the problems they cause have also been highlighted by the UN Office on Drugs and Crime (UNODC, 2016).

Regulated production would not be associated with the same degree of environmental harms. For example, in comparison to outdoor growing, indoor cultivation for illegal cannabis farms has a notable carbon footprint and requires significant amounts of electricity. However, if changes to legislation supported regulated production, this could mandate the growers to make use of renewable energy sources. Additionally, fully synthetic cocaine whilst technically feasible is not economically viable: new (or novel) psychoactive substances which are designed to mimic its effects remain illegal under the Psychoactive Substances Act 2016. Indeed, the use of other substances associated with a notable carbon footprint such as alcohol (Hallström et al, 2018) would be subject to these issues if alternative products were developed. Furthermore, at an international level, the continued drug war conflicts and corruption impacts upon the implementation of environmental strategies. The need to consider sustainability and the impact of the MDA 1971 on the illicit drugs trade is too often forgotten and needs to be brought to the fore.

Rosalind Gittins is the Director of Pharmacy for Humankind (a national third sector drug and alcohol treatment provider), President of the international College of Mental Health Pharmacy (CMHP) and a Drug Science Scientific Committee member.

Steve Rolles is a Senior Policy Analyst for the Transform Drug Policy Foundation, a UK-based charity, operating internationally, advocating for more just and effective drug policy and law. He is the author of a number of books on alternative approaches to the war on drugs.

Katherine Watkinson is the Head of Medicines Optimisation and Pharmacy Services at Turning Point (a national third sector health and social care provider).

References and Extra Reading

Aberg, et al (2022), The Environmental Release and Ecosystem Risks of Illicit Drugs During Glastonbury Festival, *Environmental Research:* www.sciencedirect.com/science/article/abs/pii/S0013935121013566

Advisory Council on the Misuse of Drugs (ACMD) (2016), Reducing Opioid-related Deaths in the UK: www.assets.publishing.service.gov.uk/government/uploads/system/uploads/attachment_data/file/576560/ACMD-Drug-Related-Deaths-Report-161212.pdf

ACMD (2021), Nitrous Oxide: Home Secretary's Letter to the ACMD: www.gov.uk/government/publications/nitrous-oxide-home-secretarys-letter-to-the-acmd/nitrous-oxide-home-secretarys-letter-to-the-acmd-accessible-version

Association of Anaesthetists (2021), Nitrous Oxide Project: www.anaesthetists.org/Home/Resources-publications/Environment/Nitrous-oxide-project

Atkins, V (2018), Reducing Opioid-related Deaths in the UK Report—Further Response Regarding Drug Consumption Rooms, Ministerial Response to the Advisory Council on the Misuse of Drugs: www.assets.publishing.service.gov.uk/government/uploads/system/uploads/attachment_data/file/699825/Letter_from_Victoria_Atkins_MP_to_OBJ.pdf

Drug Science (2020), Enhanced Harm Reduction Working Group: www.drugscience.org.uk/supervised-injection-facility-working-group/

Drug Science (2020), Parliamentary Briefing on Tackling the Misuse of Nitrous Oxide: www.drugscience.org.uk/parliamentary-briefing-on-tackling-the-misuse-of-nitrous-oxide/

European Monitoring Centre on Drugs and Drug Addiction (EMCDDA)(2018), Drug Consumption Rooms: An Overview of Provision and Evidence: www.emcdda.europa.eu/system/files/publications/2734/POD_Drug%20consumption%20rooms.pdf

Faculty of Public Health (FPH) (2021), A Call to Pilot Overdose Prevention Centres (Supervised Injecting Facilities) in the UK: www.fph.org.uk/media/3412/fph_opc_statement-04-01-2022.pdf

Guyton K Z, Loomis D, Grosse Y, El Ghissassi F, Benbrahim-Tallaa L, Guha N, Scoccianti C, Mattock H and Straif K (2015), Carcinogenicity of Tetrachlorvinphos, Parathion, Malathion, Diazinon, and Glyphosate, *The Lancet Oncology:* www.thelancet.com/journals/lanonc/article/PIIS1470-2045(15)70134-8/fulltext

Hallström, E, Håkansson, N, Åkesson, A, Wolk, A and Sonesson, U (2018), Climate Impact of Alcohol Consumption in Sweden, *Journal of Cleaner Production*, 201, 287–294.

Harris, M (2020), An Urgent Impetus for Action: Safe Inhalation Interventions to Reduce COVID-19 Transmission and Fatality Risk Among People Who Smoke Crack Cocaine in the United Kingdom, *International Journal of Drug Policy:* www.ncbi.nlm.nih.gov/pmc/articles/PMC7306748/

International Organization for Standards (ISO) (2021), ISO 14001:2015 Environmental Management Systems—Requirements With Guidance for Use: www.iso.org/standard/60857.html

Misuse of Drugs Act 1971: www.legislation.gov.uk/ukpga/1971/38/contents

National Crime Agency (2020), National Strategic Assessment of Serious and Organised Crime: www.nationalcrimeagency.gov.uk/who-we-are/publications/437-national-strategic-assessment-of-serious-and-organised-crime-2020/file

Operation Clean Sweep (2021), Operation Clean Sweep: www.opcleansweep.org/

Transform Drug Policy Foundation (2016), Alternative World Drug Report: www.transformdrugs.org/publications/the-alternative-world-drug-report-2nd-edition

Transform Drug Policy Foundation (2020), How to Regulate Stimulants: www.transformdrugs.org/publications/how-to-regulate-stimulants-a-practical-guide

United Nations Development Programme (UNDP) (2015), Addressing the Development Dimensions of Drug Policy: www.undp.org/publications/addressing-development-dimensions-drug-policy

United Nations Office on Drugs and Crime (UNDOC) (2016), The Impact of Drug Policy on the Environment: www.unodc.org/documents/ungass2016//Contributions/Civil/OpenSociety/The_Impact_of_Drug_Policy_on_the_Environment.pdf

Vickerman P, Martin N, Turner K and Hickman M (2012), Can Needle and Syringe Programmes and Opiate Substitution Therapy Achieve Substantial Reductions in Hepatitis C Virus Prevalence? Model Projections for Different Epidemic Settings, *Addiction*: www.onlinelibrary.wiley.com/doi/10.1111/j.1360-0443.2012.03932.x

CHAPTER 16

An Application of Decision Conferencing and Multi-criteria Decision Analysis

Lawrence D Phillips

This chapter shows how decision conferencing and multi-criteria decision analysis (MCDA) support the work of Drug Science. First, I explain how MCDA came to be used in the UK for modelling the harm of drugs, and how by 2021 it had migrated to nicotine, opioids, and drug harm policy. Along the way, I'll explain what MCDA is and report on what was learned from these applications.

The Beginnings

In August 2006 media coverage about research on the harm from misusing drugs showed that alcohol and tobacco are more harmful than Class A drugs such as ecstasy and cannabis. When I read that the research relied on experts' ranking of harms, which were averaged across the experts and the harm criteria, I became concerned that this approach to creating a single harm figure for each drug could lead to incorrect results. So, I wrote a letter to Professor Colin Blakemore,[1] who the media had named as a co-author of the report and was then the chair of the Medical Research Council, to explain the problems with his approach. I suggested that applying MCDA might provide better, or even different results, and concluded, 'While judgement is always required in MCDA, it is a key feature of the approach that it separates data from judgement

---

1. The late Sir Colin Blakemore (1944–2022).

in a manner that is transparent and auditable, characteristics I'm finding is increasingly sought in various Government agencies.'

I heard nothing more, so assumed I had been presumptuous, until January 2007 when Professor Blakemore wrote apologising for the delay, explaining that preparing the paper had been very time consuming, but it was soon to be published in *The Lancet* (Nutt, King, Saulsbury and Blakemore, 2007). I replied asking for a copy and, figuring I had nothing more to lose, became even more presumptuous in suggesting that we meet so that 'in the event of press criticisms you could reply that work was under way to refine the approach.'

He sent the report, which showed that 20 psychoactive drugs were individually rated by experts on nine criteria using a four-point rating scale. These were circulated and discussed by all experts in a group meeting, where participants were invited to revise their initial assessments. These were subsequently averaged across the experts to provide a single rating for each drug on each scale, and those were then averaged again across the nine rating scales. The five most harmful substances were heroin, cocaine, barbiturates, street methadone, and alcohol, while the five least harmful were anabolic steroids, GHB (gamma hydroxybutyrate), ecstasy, alkylnitrates, and khat. These results showed very low correlation with their classifications according to the MDA 1971.

The paper was not published until March, so perhaps Professors Blakemore and Nutt figured they had nothing to lose in meeting with me. And meet we did, discussing the potential for expanding the 2007 analysis to accommodate a wider range of harm criteria beyond the original nine, along with a full explanation from me of what MCDA technical modelling can do when accompanied by the social process of decision conferencing, which engages a group of experts in contributing their knowledge and experience while constructing an MCDA model through a facilitated process of deliberative discourse.

The 2010 *Lancet* Paper

It took some time to raise the funding for a new project, but on 23–24 March 2009, the entire membership of the Advisory Council on the Misuse of Drugs (ACMD), one of the many groups of the Home Office that has a statutory duty to consider and advise on any matter referred to them by Ministers, gathered

An Application of Decision Conferencing and Multi-criteria Decision Analysis

in an off-site meeting to build an MCDA model, with myself and David Nutt facilitating, helped by my LSE colleague, Mara Airoldi. It took two days to agree what drugs were to be considered (slightly different from the 2007 study) and to identify and define the harm criteria against which the drugs would be evaluated, thus completing the structure of the model. At another half-day meeting on 19 June, the group slightly refined the structure and completed the evaluations. In July, the ACMD made public the structure of the MCDA model, which they agreed was useful, but they did not see fit to provide the model's results as concerns were raised about the evidence base for the evaluations.

As is mentioned in *Chapter 5*, in November, David Nutt, by then the chair of the ACMD, gave a talk at King's College London that was critical of the disjunction between the actions of Government Ministers and the recommendations of the ACMD, in particular the reclassification by the Government of cannabis from Class C to B (more harmful). This led to his dismissal by the then Home Secretary, Alan Johnson. Encouraged by the MCDA model's results, David Nutt promptly set up the Independent Scientific Committee on Drugs (ISCD) (later Drug Science) to pursue his goal of ensuring that scientific evidence about the harm of drugs could be made openly available and discussed in public.

Fourteen ISCD members, six of whom resigned from the ACMD, plus two invited outside experts, met on 7 June 2010 to further develop the ACMD model, with David Nutt and myself facilitating, helped by another LSE colleague, Gilberto Montibeller. After we briefed the new members on the structure of the MCDA model, the group set about scoring the 20 drugs on the 16 criteria and weighting the criteria. The final weighted scores showed that the five most harmful drugs were alcohol, heroin, crack, methylamphetamine, and cocaine, while the five least harmful were khat, ecstasy, LSD, buprenorphine, and, least harmful of all, magic mushrooms. For this model, the correlation between the final harm scores and the MDA classifications was zero. Published in *The Lancet* (D J Nutt, King, Phillips and on behalf of the Independent Scientific Committee on Drugs, 2010), the study has been cited over 1,700 times.

Both the 2007 and 2010 *Lancet* papers showed that although drug harm misuse is claimed to be the basis on which the substances are classified in the UK's MDA 1971, that cannot be the case. So, what did the 2010 approach contribute that was different from the 2007 research? Lacking hard evidence for most of the substances on nearly all the harm criteria, it was necessary to rely on expert judgement and experience to rate or score the drugs. Was this acceptable, given that a scientific approach relies on objectively obtained data? And is the approach replicable, the bedrock in science for establishing the validity of scientific inferences? To answer these questions, I will first describe the sound theoretical basis that has led to the applied technology of MCDA and show how the application of decision conferencing has created a socio-technical discipline that is particularly useful when objective data are sparse.

What is MCDA?

In 1926, a British mathematician, philosopher, and economist who was a Fellow and Lecturer at King's College at the University of Cambridge, published his musings on what an ideal decision maker would consider before choosing a course of action (Ramsey, 1926). His name was Frank Plumpton Ramsey and he recognised that the ideal decision maker's preferences would conform to a few simple ideas, for example, that if A were preferred to B, and B to C, then A should be preferred to C. This notion about the transitivity of preferences, along with just a few other assumptions about rationality, formed in his mathematical mind a system of axioms from which he could work out their logical consequences, or theorems.

The theorems identified two reasons for an ideal decision maker's preferences: the *value* (or *utility*) of the consequences to the decision maker, and the *probabilities* of those consequences occurring. A third theorem showed that multiplying the values or utilities by their associated probabilities gave numbers, known as *expected values* or *expected utilities*, that could serve as guides for choosing. Thus, a high-value outcome with a low probability of occurring, might be just as desirable as a low-value outcome with a high probability. The rational decision maker would consider both the value or utility of a decision's consequences and their likelihood of occurring.

Flash forward, past the further development of Ramsey's work, by the geologist Sir Harold Jeffreys (1939), the Italian actuary Bruno De Finetti (1974), the mathematician John von Neumann and his economist colleague Oskar Morgenstern (1947), the statistician Leonard 'Jimmie' Savage (1954), and we see the emergence by 1966 of an applied technology: *decision analysis* (Howard, 1966). Further development of the theory culminated in the 1993 Cambridge edition of *Decisions with Multiple Objectives: Preferences and Value Tradeoffs*, which stands today as a statement of decision theory and its application (Keeney and Raiffa, 1976). The authors state in the Preface to the 1993 edition:

> 'When a decision involves multiple objectives—and this is almost always the case with important problems—multi-attribute utility theory (MAUT) forms the basic foundation for applying decision analysis.'

They define *value* as the strength of preference for one consequence over another, which includes the judgement of trade-offs among the objectives considered. Together, the values associated with multiple objectives and the trade-offs among them is often referred to as multi-criteria decision analysis (MCDA); which is today emerging as the gold standard for guiding decisions in many fields, including healthcare (Phillips, 2017). Howard Raiffa described the approach as follows (Raiffa, 1968):

> 'The spirit of decision analysis is divide and conquer: decompose a complex problem into simpler problems, get one's thinking straight on these simpler problems, paste these analyses together with logical glue, and come out with a program of action for the complex problem.'

Raiffa's 'simpler problems' deal separately with elements of uncertainties and values, and with the connections between them. My decision analytic kit bag contains procedures for assessing probabilities and their connections with each other, methods for eliciting preference values and the trade-offs between values, along with my laptop computer whose 'logical glue' applies the simple expected value mathematics that puts the pieces together. Examples later in this chapter will show how this is done.

A final warning. Many ad hoc processes claim to be MCDA methods even though they are not based on MAUT. I don't use them because although they may be useful, they can give different results from the sound theoretical approach of Keeney-Raiffa. They are not accepted by the Decision Analysis Society or the Society of Decision Professionals.

What is Decision Conferencing?

The short answer is that a decision conference is a social process that enables a group of experts to be more rational than any one of us. Experts work together, face-to-face in a meeting or virtually, with an impartial facilitator who guides the group in decomposing the problem as the group works through the eight stages of constructing an MCDA model. Throughout, the experts bring their experience and knowledge to the discussion, considering alternative points of view and new information, as peer-review occurs in the here-and-now, stimulating creativity and providing new insights. Here are the stages, from Chapter 6 of *Multi-Criteria Analysis: A Manual* (Dodgson, Spackman, Pearman, and Phillips, 2000), illustrated with examples from the 2010 drug harm study:

1. **Context.** Establish the purpose of the MCDA. The 2007 paper was motivated by a sense that the classification of drugs in the MDA 1971, which is supposed to be solely based on the harm from misusing drugs, was not true in practice. The paper attracted media attention and public debate but was criticised for the choice of the nine criteria and the equal weighting system. The new analysis set out to provide a more scientific basis for the harm arising from misuse.

2. **Options.** Identify the options to be evaluated. The 20 substances from the 2007 study were slightly revised for the 2010 MCDA.

3. **Objectives and criteria.** Objectives are the aims or purposes that are to be represented, which were the extent of harms to the users and harms to others. Criteria are the standards for assessing the objectives, the four physical, three psychological, and two social harms to the users, and the seven physical, psychological and social harms to others, 16 criteria altogether, seven more than in the 2007 study. It took about two days to identify, discuss and define the 16 criteria, following my first question to the assembled experts at that initial meeting with the ACMD, 'What do you mean by harm?'.

4. **Scoring.** This is the process of eliciting preference values. The extent to which a drug is harmful was scored on a scale from 0 (no harm) to 100 (most harm) for a given criterion, shown as a percentage of the most harmful drug. That defines a ratio scale. For a group, the process of 'Think-Report-Discuss' was used. To minimise bias, the facilitator (1) asks all the experts to think but not verbally report a value, then when everyone has done so (2) verbally reports individual scores to establish the lowest and highest scores in the group, (3) asks those two experts to explain their reasons for their scores, and (4) invites discussion from the whole group to arrive at a single number or the median of a range. Finally, the facilitator initiates consistency checks, that is, comparisons of ratios of the harm scores among the drugs, which may lead to revisions of the scores, helping to establish their realism.

5. **Weighting.** This is the process of assessing what are known as 'swing weights,' which are scale constants that equate the units across all the criteria, as nine units on the Fahrenheit scale of temperature are equivalent to five units on the Celsius scale. They represent trade-offs, how many units on one scale equal how many on another scale, and once a common unit emerges, that justifies adding those units across the criteria. Swing weights of preference values compare the real-world differences on the scales *and* how much those differences matter, comparing two criteria at a time. Paired-comparisons of differences have long been known in psychology as a reliable method for creating subjective scales of values (Thurstone, 1959). For the UK study, the differences on the drug harm scales were always between no harm and the drug judged to be most harmful for a given criterion. Thus, swing weighting reduces to a comparison of the harms of the most harmful drugs themselves. Consistency checks, comparisons of sums of weights, usually result in reducing weights on some harms, ensuring their realism.

6. **Combine weights and scores.** A computer multiplies the scores for a given option by each option's weight, which creates the equal units of preference value.

7. **Examine the results.** Explore the results by engaging the computer's graphics to see the results from different perspectives. The figures show the gains from the 2010 results over those in 2007.

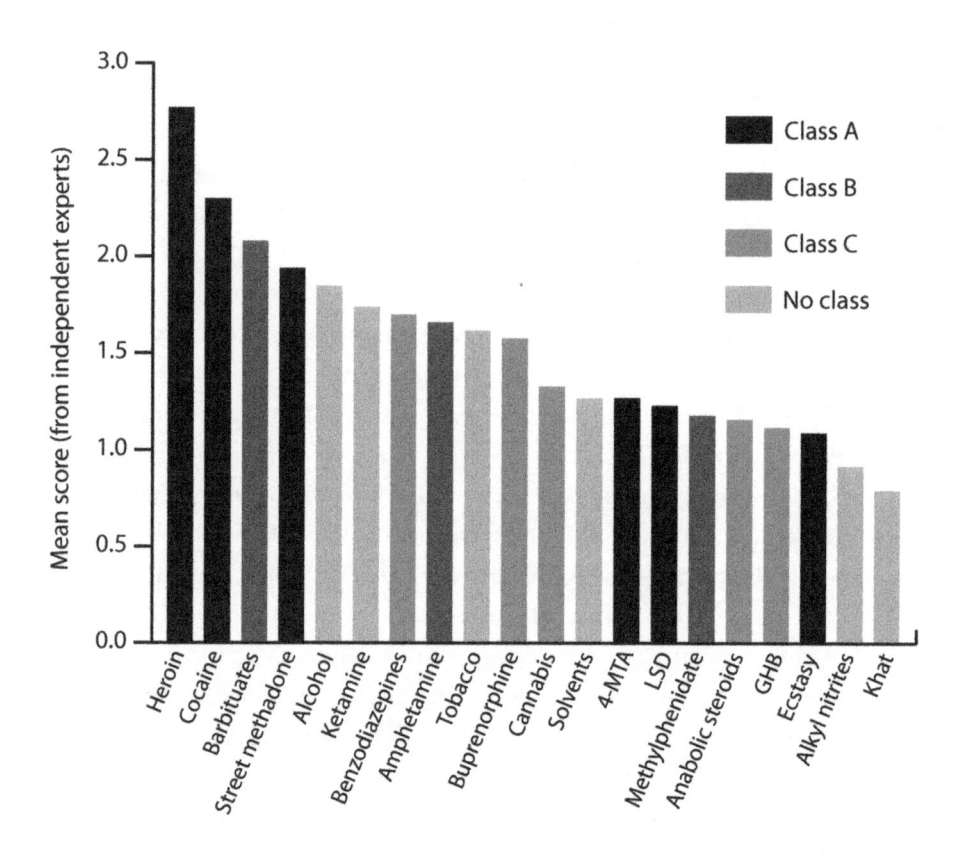

Figure 1: MDA classification of each drug (Nutt D, King L and Phillips L, 2010).

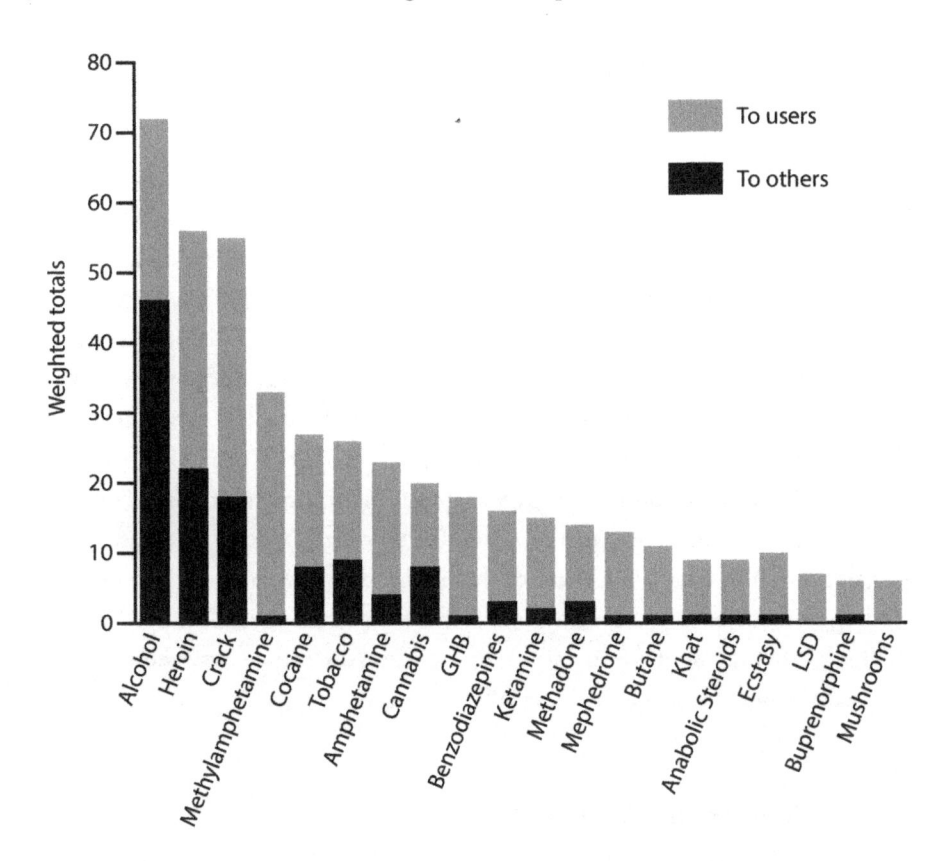

An Application of Decision Conferencing and Multi-criteria Decision Analysis

Figure 2: Drug harms to users and to others
(Nutt D, King L and Phillips L, 2010).

8. **Sensitivity analyses.** Change scores and weights to accommodate their imprecision and differences of opinion among the experts to see the effects on the overall results. Discuss and make changes until the group can agree the results. Changes to weights in the 2010 study showed that the relative weight on harms to Users compared to Others can change the ordering, but that is obvious from the relative lengths of the two sections in each bar.

A final but important note about decision conferencing. In part, the success of this approach to mobilising a group of experts is in the preparation. To plan the decision conference, the leader and facilitator must meet to ensure that the leader understands what a decision conference can accomplish. Preparation includes selecting a diverse group of experts, deciding what advance preparation, if any, would be desirable, and agreeing the outline of a calling note to be sent to each of them. The latter is particularly important as it establishes that this will be an active meeting in which everyone is expected to contribute. More details can be found in Phillips (2007).

Now, back to the question about what the 2010 approach contributed over that of the 2007 research. The purposes of a decision conference are to develop a shared understanding of the underlying issues that are to be addressed, develop a sense of common purpose, and gain commitment to an agreed way forward. By the end of the 2010 meeting, all participants had agreed to the final weighted preference values despite the imprecision of the input scores and weights, about which some disagreements remained, though they did not affect the final results. That justified the three named authors to include 'on behalf of the Independent Scientific Committee on Drugs.' It was gratifying to note that the correlation between the 15 drugs common to both the 2007 and 2010 studies was 0.70. As can be seen in the comparison of the bar graphs, it is evident that the 2010 study provided the experts with more scope for exercising their judgement, as the rank order of the drugs is more valid and the difference between the most and least harmful drugs is substantially increased.

Other Drug Harm Studies

Three years later, Drug Science initiated another harm study, this time for all of Europe. We met in Brussels with a new group of 40 experts representing 21 EU member States, who revised 27 of the 320 scores from the 2010 model and reassessed all the weights. The correlation between the final weighted scores of the UK and EU studies was 0.99. Comparing the ranks rather than the harm scores, showed five drugs were one rank higher and five one rank lower in the EU study, while one, methadone, was two ranks lower in the EU and khat was two ranks higher in the EU. The remaining eight drugs were identical in rank.

A final harm study carried out in Australia in 2019 with 24 experts from the country, facilitated by David Nutt, Patrick Sharry and Paul Gordon, scored 22 drugs on the UK's 16 harm criteria, adapted to suit the Australian context.

Correlations of the final weighted scores of the 15 drugs held in common with the other two studies were 0.89 with the UK study and 0.91 with the EU study. One outlier, crystal meth (methamphetamine), scored 66 in Australia, compared with 38 in the EU and 33 in the UK, which made sense as Australia had then the highest prevalence of use of methamphetamine of any country in the world.

The high correlations among these three studies, which engaged altogether 79 experts in three separate decision conferences, attest to the validity and replicability of the MCDA/decision conferencing approach. All of us are indeed more rational than any one of us.

Nicotine Delivery Products

In 2013, the ISCD convened 13 international experts in a two-day decision conference to create an MCDA model of the harms of 12 nicotine delivery products, including e-cigarettes, on 14 of the original 16 criteria that are relevant to nicotine. Not surprisingly, the results showed cigarettes to be most harmful. Published online in April 2014, little more was heard about the study until Public Health England (PHE) used the study's results to report in 2015 that 'e-cigarettes are around 95% safer than smoked tobacco.' That claim launched a furious attack in health journals and the media on PHE, the MCDA/decision conference process, and individual participants in the study (McKee and Capewell, 2015), including an unsigned editorial in *The Lancet* (2015), which suggested that the 95% figure was based on an 'extraordinarily flimsy foundation.'

We replied to these criticisms in a Correspondence piece (D J Nutt et al, 2016), as did one of the experts in the study (Polosa, 2015), who suggested that the furore was ideologic, 'with harm reductionists versus precautionary principle supporters presenting opposing views on e-cigarettes.' Although I had immediately responded to PHE saying that the phrase '95% safer' was unfortunate and should be replaced with '95% less harmful,' which they did, it was too late. We learned to take better care of our language in describing harm.

Drug Policy

So far, this chapter has established that the classification of drugs in the UK's MDA 1971 is not based on scientific evidence and that the process of arriving at this conclusion by the process of decision conferencing/MCDA modelling is a valid and reliable methodology. So, one might ask, could the process be used to build better drug policies?

It was two economists from Norway, Ole Rogeberg and Daniel Bergsvik, who asked that question of David Nutt. It took two decision conferences to provide an answer. In a pre-meeting, the four of us developed a policy table whose six columns were the issues to be addressed in any drug harm policy, while the cells below each column were alternative policy solutions unique to that issue. We presented the policy table to the group in the first decision conference and solicited their help in making revisions and additions. The group then chose one solution from each of the six issues to define four overall policy options: (1) Absolute prohibition, (2) Decriminalisation, (3) State control, and (4) Free market.

The group then developed 27 criteria, grouped into seven thematic clusters (Health, Social, Political, Public, Crime, Economic, Cost). Over the first and second meetings, participants evaluated the four policy options against the 27 criteria, creating separate MCDA models for three drugs, alcohol, cannabis, and heroin, each with different scores and weights.

To the surprise of most participants, State control for each of the three models came out as overall the most preferred policy, though it would, of course, be realised differently for each of the three drugs. Development and application of the model for alcohol and cannabis is reported in Rogeberg et al (2018), and for heroin in Rolles et al (2021). This has shown that the MCDA/decision conferencing approach is sufficiently flexible to be used for constructing new drug policies, hopefully a new Misuse of Drugs Act for the 21st century.

Dr Lawrence D Phillips is an Emeritus Professor of Decision Sciences in the Department of Management at the London School of Economics and Political Science. He developed, taught, and applied decision conferencing as a socio-technical discipline, and has published many papers about its application: see www.lawrencephillips.net

References and Extra Reading

de Finetti, B (1974), *Theory of Probability: A Critical Introductory Treatment, Volume 1*, Translated by Antonio Machi and Adrian Smith from Teoria Delle Probabilità, 1970 (Volume 1), London: Wiley.

Dodgson, J, Spackman, M, Pearman, A and Phillips, L (2000), *Multi-Criteria Analysis: A Manual*, London: Department of the Environment, Transport and the Regions (republished 2009 by the Department for Communities and Local Government).

Howard, R A (1966), Decision Analysis: Applied Decision Theory in D B Hertz and J Melese (eds), *Proceedings of the Fourth International Conference on Operational Research*, 55–71), New York: Wiley-Interscience (reprinted in *Readings in Decision Analysis*, 2nd edn, Decision Analysis Group, Menlo Park, CA, 1977).

Jeffreys, H (1939), *Theory of Probability* (3rd, 1961 edn), Oxford: Clarendon.

Keeney, R L. and Raiffa, H (1976), *Decisions With Multiple Objectives: Preferences and Value Tradeoffs*, New York: John Wiley (republished in 1993 by Cambridge University Press).

Lancet (2015), E-cigarettes: Public Health England's Evidence-based Confusion, *The Lancet*, 386: 829.

McKee, M and Capewell, S (2015), Evidence About Electronic Cigarettes: A Foundation Built on Rock or Sand? *British Medical Journal:* BMJ 2015;351:h4863. DOI: 10.1136/bmj.h4863

Nutt, D, King, L A, Saulsbury, W and Blakemore, C (2007), Development of a Rational Scale to Assess the Harm of Drugs of Potential Misuse, *The Lancet*, 369: 1047–1053.

Nutt, D J, King, L A, Phillips, L D and on behalf of the Independent Scientific Committee on Drugs (2010), Drug Harms in the UK: A Multicriteria Decision Analysis, *The Lancet*, 376: 1558–65.

Nutt, D J, Phillips, L D, Balfour, D, Curran, H V, Dockrell, M, Foulds, J and Sweanor, D (2016), E-cigarettes are Less Harmful Than Smoking, *The Lancet*, 387: 1160–1161.

Phillips, L D (2007), Decision Conferencing in W Edwards, R F Miles and D von Winterfeldt (eds), *Advances in Decision Analysis: From Foundations to Applications*, Cambridge: Cambridge University Press.

Phillips, L D (2017), Best Practice for MCDA in Healthcare in K Marsh, M Goetghebeur, P Thokala and R Baltussen (eds), *Multi-Criteria Decision Analysis to Support Healthcare Decisions*, 311–329, Springer International Publishing AG.

Polosa, R (2015), E-cigarettes: Public Health England's Evidence Based Confusion? *The Lancet,* 386(10000): 1237–1238. DOI: 10.1016/S0140-6736(15)00042-2

Raiffa, H (1968), *Decision Analysis.* Reading, MA: Addison-Wesley.

Ramsey, F P (1926), Truth and Probability, published 1931 in *The Foundations of Mathematics and Other Logical Essays, Ch. VII* (156–198), R B Braithwaite (ed.), London: Kegan Paul/Trench, Trubner & Co, New York/Harcourt, Brace and Company 1999 electronic edition.

Rogeberg, O, Bergsvik, D, Phillips, L D, Amsterdam, J Y, Eastwood, N, Henderson, G and Nutt, D (2018), A New Approach to Formulating and Appraising Drug Policy, *International Journal of Drug Policy,* 56: 144–152. DOI: 10.1016/j.drugpo.2018.01.019

Rolles, S, Schlag, A K, Measham, F, Phillips, L, Nutt, D, Bergsvik, D and Rogeberg, O, (2021), A Multi Criteria Decision Analysis (MCDA) for Evaluating and Appraising Government Policy Responses to Non Medical Heroin Use, *International Journal of Drug Policy,* 91: 103180. DOI: 10.1016/j.drugpo.2021.103180

Savage, L J (1954), *The Foundations of Statistics* (2nd, 1972, Dover edn), New York: Wiley.

Thurstone, L L (1959), *The Measurement of Values,* Chicago: University of Chicago Press.

von Neumann, J and Morgenstern, O (1947), *Theory of Games and Economic Behavior* (2nd edn), Princeton, NJ: Princeton University Press.

CHAPTER 17

The MDA 1971: Missteps and Misunderstandings

Rudi Fortson KC

The MDA 1971: A Regulatory Regime

The Misuse of Drugs Act 1971 received Royal Assent on 27 May of that year. It repealed the Drugs (Prevention of Misuse) Act 1964 and Dangerous Drugs Acts of 1965 and 1967.[1] Forerunners to those pieces of legislation included the 'Dangerous Drugs' Acts of 1920, 1925, 1932 and 1951. Then, as now, other pieces of legislation applied to various drug substances and drug products (depending on context and purpose) such as — but not limited to — the Food and Drugs Act 1955 (now repealed),[2] the Pharmacy and Poisons Act 1933 (repealed),[3] and the Medicines Act 1968 (of which many measures have been superseded by the Human Medicines Regulations 2012). Some drugs may constitute a 'noxious thing' for certain provisions of the Offences Against the Person Act 1861.[4]

The emergence of new psychoactive substances (NPS) that are produced and distributed for non-medicinal human consumption, have been difficult to control under the framework of the MDA 1971. The 'temporary controlled drug' (TCD) regime,[5] by which drugs had limited status as a 'controlled drug'

---

1. Schedule 6. All law stated in this chapter is as of the time of writing: 3 November 2021.
2. Food Act 1984; see now the Food Safety Act 1990.
3. Repealed by a series of enactments: the Statute Law Revision Act 1950, Pharmacy Act 1954, Medicines Act 1968, and Poisons Act 1972.
4. See, e.g. *R v Cato* [1976] 1 All ER 260.
5. Inserted by the Police Reform and Social Responsibility Act 2011.

by virtue of a 'temporary class drug order' (TCDO),[6] was not very successful. It took time to decide whether a TCDO should be made and, thereafter, to fully assess a drug's medical and societal harms (if any). This was one consideration that lay behind the enactment of the Psychoactive Substances Act 2016 (PSA 2016) (which, for most purposes, came into force on the 26 May 2016). The PSA 2016 catches any non-exempted substance which 'is capable of producing a psychoactive effect in a person who consumes it.'[7] A 'psychoactive effect in a person' is one that, 'by stimulating or depressing the person's central nervous system,' 'affects the person's mental functioning or emotional state.'[8] 'Trafficking'[9] in a substance that is caught by the 2016 Act is an offence (penalties are set out in section 10). Exempted substances include a 'controlled drug' (MDA 1971) or a 'medicinal product.'[10]

This short overview illustrates the fact that laws that regulate the production, distribution, possession and use of various drug substances and drug products operate as a package of measures that are capable of being enforced under the civil and/or criminal law. Those measures may or may not overlap in respect of the same drug. The relationship between the MDA 1971, the PSA 2016, the medicines legislation, and other drug legislation (including, e.g. consumer protection laws) is complex.

The MDA 1971 has been described as an instrument of prohibition, but Parliament intended the Act to function as a regulatory mechanism that could be adjusted in line with developments in science (including social science) and with social/behavioural changes. Earlier legislation was framed in the language of 'dangerous drugs.' By contrast, the MDA refers (for the most part) to the 'misuse' of drugs. It created the Advisory Council on the Misuse of Drugs (ACMD) 'to keep under review the situation in the UK with respect to drugs' which are being (or appear to them likely to be) misused 'and of which the misuse is having or appears to them capable of having harmful effects *sufficient to constitute a social problem*' (emphasis added).[11] The wording appears to recognise that

---

6. Section 2(1)(c) MDA 1971.
7. Section 2(1)(a) PSA 2016.
8. Section 2(2) PSA 2016.
9. Exportation, importation, supply, possession with intent to supply. Other than in a custodial setting, the simple possession of a psychoactive substance is not an offence under the PSA 2016.
10. 'Medicinal product' has the same meaning as in Regulation 2 of the Human Medicines Regulations 2012 (SI 2012/1916).
11. Section 1(2) MDA 1971.

non-medicinal drug-taking will occur; that it was not Parliament's intention to adopt a 'zero tolerance approach'; that Parliament would keep the situation under review, and that Parliament could intervene if the harmful effects of a particular drug (or family of drugs) had attained the threshold of being sufficient to impact adversely on society.

The MDA 1971 introduced a three-tier classification of drugs (Classes A, B and C), principally to assist in the determination of penalties (specified in the Act in respect of MDA 1971 offences) but also to make 'so far as possible, a more sensible differentiation between drugs':[12]

> 'It will divide them according to their accepted dangers and harmfulness in the light of current knowledge and *it will provide for changes to be made in classification in the light of new scientific knowledge*... Schedule 2 has been drawn up on the basis of the lists of drugs controlled by the 1965 and 1964 Acts in order, *and no more than this*, to provide for a smooth transition to the new system of control.' (Author's emphasis added)

While legal certainty is important, drug classification was not intended to be 'set in stone'. Like many regulatory regimes that are enforced with administrative and/or criminal sanctions, the intensity of legal control exerted under UK drug laws will differ depending on context (e.g. food safety, or unlicensed drug trading).

The MDA 1971 is an example of this approach. It imposes a number of 'restrictions' (e.g. on the production, possession and supply of controlled drugs), and it also imposes 'prohibitions' (e.g. relating to opium, and the supply of articles for administering or preparing controlled drugs). The use of the word 'restriction' was presumably deliberate given that each restricted activity is expressly subject to regulations made under the Act (notably, the Misuse of Drugs Regulations (MDR) 2001).[13] The regulations are broadly permissive. Thus, the relevant Secretary of State 'may' make regulations that exempt specified drugs from restrictions on importing or exporting them,[14] or producing,

---

12. Secretary of State for the Home Department (James Callaghan); *Hansard*, vol.798: 25 March 1970 col.1453.
13. It will be seen that various provisions under the MDA 1971 use the words 'subject to any regulations under [the Act]' (e.g., sections 3, 4, 5 and 6, of the 1971 Act).
14. Section 3(1)(a) or (b) MDA 1971.

supplying or offering to supply them,[15] or possessing them.[16] Again, the Secretary of State may make 'such other provision as he thinks fit for the purpose of making it lawful for persons to do things which under ... sections 4(1), 5(1) and 6(1), it would otherwise be unlawful for them to do' (section 7(1)). The range of activities, which specified persons or entities are permitted to carry out differ or vary in respect of each of the five schedules to the 2001 Regulations in which controlled drugs are listed.

There is one situation in which the Secretary of State *must* make regulations, namely, for the benefit of specified medical practitioners (e.g. doctors, dentists, pharmacists and veterinary practitioners) who may then lawfully produce, supply and possess particular controlled drugs (when acting in their capacity as such[17]). However, this mandatory duty is qualified if (in the Secretary of State's *opinion*) it is in 'the public interest' for the production, supply and possession of specified drugs to be 'wholly unlawful,' or 'unlawful' *except for* 'purposes of research or other special purposes'; or unlawful *unless* 'practitioners, pharmacists and persons lawfully conducting retail pharmacy businesses' are acting under the terms of a 'licence or other authority issued by the Secretary of State.' Such drugs are often styled 'designated drugs' and they appear in Schedule 1 to the MDR 2001 (and in the Misuse of Drugs (Designation) (England, Wales and Scotland) Order 2015).[18]

'Designated Drugs' May Have Medicinal Value

It is often said—typically by politicians—that designated drugs have 'no recognised medicinal value.' In fact, there is nothing in the legislation to this effect. Another statement (sometimes voiced) is that it is necessary to designate particular drugs in order to meet the UK's international obligations under three UN Drug Conventions.[19] This overstates the position. First, the conventions are not of direct legal effect on the UK. Secondly, the provisions of each

---

15. Section 4(1)(a) or (b) MDA 1971.
16. Section 5(1) MDA 1971.
17. Section 7(3) MDA 1971.
18. SI 2015 No. 704 (as amended).
19. The 1961 UN Narcotic Drugs Single Convention, the 1971 UN Convention on Psychotropic Substances; and the 1988 UN Convention Against Illicit Traffic in Narcotic Drugs and Psychotropic Substances.

convention are more nuanced than is often supposed. For example, the Commentary to the 1971 UN Convention points out that '[one] cannot foresee at present whether a substance [in Schedule 1] may in the future be found to be very useful in the treatment of frequently occurring diseases.'[20] This statement has importance in relation to psilocin, and fungus containing psilocin (and, indeed, cannabis[21]) which are drugs 'designated' under the MDA 1971. The assumption that, by virtue of inclusion in Schedule 1 MDR, cannabis has 'no medicinal value' has long been unsustainable—a fact supported by the 1968 'Report on Cannabis,'[22] which recommended that legislation should permit the continuance of cannabis prescribing by doctors:

'99. At present cannabis can be prescribed by doctors in the form of extract of cannabis and alcoholic tincture of cannabis. Until very recently the demand for these preparations has been virtually negligible. In recent months however, there has been a striking increase in the amounts prescribed. Our enquiries, supported by what we were told by our witnesses, indicate that there are a number of doctors who are beginning to experiment with the use of cannabis in the treatment of disturbed adolescents, heroin and amphetamine dependence and even alcoholism. Whilst we do not expect cannabis prescription will ever become standard medication in the treatment of these conditions, it is quite likely that the amount dispensed on medical prescriptions will continue to increase and that this process may be accelerated when synthetic cannabis derivatives, properly standardised, become available. We see no objection to this and believe that any new legislation should be such as to permit its continuance.'

The 1973 MDR[23] put an end to cannabis prescribing (see, now, the 2001 Regulations, Schedule 1). It is submitted that the likely reason why cannabis became a 'designated' drug was because that drug, like certain other substances,

---

20. Para.3, p.138, Commentary to the 1971 UN Convention.
21. Other than a 'cannabis-based product for medicinal use in humans': see the Misuse of Drugs (Amendments) (Cannabis and Licence Fees) (England, Wales and Scotland) Regulations 2018 (SI 2018, No.1055).
22. *Report on Cannabis* ('Wootton Report') (1968): prepared by the Hallucinogens Sub-Committee of the Advisory Committee on Drug Dependence.
23. SI 1973, No.797. Note that the most restrictive schedule in the 1973 regulations was Schedule 4, and not Schedule 1 as is currently the position under the 2001 regulations.

was not of irreplaceable therapeutic value[24]—alternatives were, or might be, available. The same discussion is now being heard in relation to *psilocin*[25] but the Home Office has, commendably, granted licences to certain persons to conduct clinical trials in relation to that substance.[26]

A Flexible Regime — Subject to the Will of Government

It follows from the above discussion that much legislative change could be achieved (and is) by way of secondary legislation under the MDA 1971 regime (following a consultation process) and not by way of primary legislation (that involves a far more complex and protracted process). In theory, where there is political will to bring about a result, there is a legislative way of achieving it under the MDA 1971 framework. The licensing regime is a particular mechanism by which certain activities can be rendered lawful that would otherwise be prohibited or restricted.

However, there have been instances when political considerations appear to have prevailed over science, damaging the reputation of the MDA 1971. The classification of cannabis is one example. The Independent Inquiry into the Misuse of Drugs Act[27] was firmly of the view that, on the evidence then available to it, cannabis was 'wrongly placed' in Class B and that it should be transferred to Class C along with cannabinol and its derivatives.[28] The ACMD made a similar recommendation in a report dated March 2002.[29] The Home Secretary accepted the report on the basis that rescheduling cannabis would reflect more accurately the relative harmfulness of drugs, and that it would give the misuse of drugs legislation greater credibility and indicate the Government's priority

---

24. Report on Cannabis, para. 6.
25. Psilocine, psilotsin 3-[2-(Dimethylamino)ethyl]indol-4-ol; Psilocybine 3-[2-(Dimethylamino) ethyl]indol-4-yl hydrogen phosphate, appear in Schedule 1 to the 1971 UN Convention. Schedule 1 of the Misuse of Drugs Regulations 2001 includes 'Fungus (of any kind) which contains psilocin or an ester of psilocin', and psilocybin; both drugs are Class A controlled drugs under Schedule 2 to the MDA.
26. www.imperial.ac.uk/psychedelic-research-centre/trials/ and www.kcl.ac.uk/research/psilocybin-trials
27. Drugs and the Law, Police Foundation, 2000: www.police-foundation.org.uk/2017/wp-content/uploads/2017/06/drugs_and_the_law.pdf
28. Drugs and the Law; Ch.7; and Ch.3, para.28.
29. The Classification of Cannabis under the Misuse of Drugs Act 1971 (2002), ACMD (March).

to tackle Class A drugs. Cannabis, cannabis resin, cannabinol and cannabinol derivatives were therefore reclassified as Class C drugs on January 29, 2004.[30] On the same day, the maximum penalty (on indictment) for 'trafficking' in Class C drugs was increased from five years imprisonment to 14 years (matching the maximum penalty for cultivating cannabis which, from the date of enactment, was 14 years imprisonment).[31] However, in July 2007, the then Home Secretary asked the ACMD to review again the classification of cannabis. The latter recommended that cannabis should remain Class C on the basis that it more closely equates with other Class C substances than with those in Class B.[32] The Government rejected that recommendation. Consequently, from 29 January 2009, cannabis in all its forms reverted to its Class B status.[33] However, there was no associated reversion of the maximum penalties on indictment (from 14 years to five) for 'trafficking' in Class C drugs.

Psilocin was controlled from the date that the MDA 1971 came into force, but fungus containing psilocin became a Class A drug in 2005.[34] This move was strongly criticised by the House of Commons Select Committee on Science and Technology (HCSCST) Fifth Report (18 July 2006) which stated that it had encountered 'a widespread view that the Class A status of magic mushrooms does not reflect the harms associated with their misuse.' The committee cited a RAND Report that concluded that the Government's decision 'was not based on scientific evidence,' noting that 'the positioning of them in Class A does not seem to reflect any scientific evidence that they are of equivalent harm to other Class A drugs.'[35] The Government's stance (which it stated robustly in is official response[36]) differed markedly from that of the HCSCST.

As for the proper classification of drugs as Classes A, B and C, there have been attempts to construct a more reliable index of relative drug harm[37] but,

---

30. MDA 1971 (Modification) (No.2) Order 2003 (SI 2003/3201).
31. Criminal Justice Act 2003, Schedule28 (from 29 January 2004).
32. Cannabis: Classification and Public Health (2008), ACMD.
33. SI 2008/3130; and see *Hansard*, 7 May 2008, cols. 705–718, HC; 6 November 2008, HC, cols.4–28; and 25 November 2008, cols.1378–1415.
34. Drugs Act 2005. See King, L A, *Forensic Chemistry of Substance Misuse*, 2nd edn, Royal Society of Chemistry, 2022.
35. https://publications.parliament.uk/pa/cm200506/cmselect/cmsctech/1031/103107.htm#note101
36. Drug Classification: Making a Hash of It? CM 6941, p. 12.
37. *The Lancet* 2007 (Professor David Nutt, Professor Colin Blakemore, William Saulsbury, and Dr Leslie King, Development of a Rational Scale to Assess the Harm of Drugs of Potential Misuse, 369 at 1047; and see Fortson R, *Law on the Misuse of Drugs and Drug Trafficking Offences* (6th edn, 2012), ch.1–079, Sweet & Maxwell.

to date, the Government has not undertaken a comprehensive review of the existing classification. That said, some of the suggested alternative indexes have problems of their own — especially as drug classification is currently linked to maximum statutory penalties for drug offences. Sentencing is not an exact 'science' and the sentencing process might not be assisted by an overly complex index of harms — especially if the index were to be contentious. It is unlikely that every MDA 1971 controlled drug (or variant) could be ranked accurately in a comprehensive scale of harm, especially as an increasing number of drugs are controlled by way of generic definitions. The number of drugs that would be caught by those definitions may be impossible to state precisely, and it does not necessarily follow that all variants are equally harmful or harmless.

The ACMD performs a most important role and it has a statutory duty 'to consider any matter relating to drug dependence or the misuse of drugs which may be referred to them by any one or more of the Ministers' and to give advice to Ministers when it is sought by them (section 1(3) MDA 1971). There is no doubting the commitment or the industry of its members. The 1971 Act makes no pretence that the ACMD is intended to be wholly autonomous, but the council 'may determine their own procedure.'[38] As originally enacted, the 1971 Act made provision for the constitution of the ACMD to be determined by the Secretary of State who, 'after consultation with such organisations as he considers appropriate,' was to include persons with expertise in the fields of medicine, dentistry, veterinary science, and the practice of pharmacy. There was also a statutory obligation to include persons who appear to have 'wide and recent experience of social problems connected with the misuse of drugs' (paragraph 1(1)(b), Schedule 1, MDA 1971). As a result of amendments made by the Police Reform and Social Responsibility Act 2011, the original wording was substantially pruned. The Secretary of State is now vested with the power to appoint members of the ACMD ('of whom there shall be not less than twenty') 'after consultation with such organisations as he considers appropriate.' According to the Explanatory Notes to the 2011 Act, the revision was said to 'allow for greater flexibility in the membership of the [ACMD].'[39] This, however, can cut both ways. It is clearly in the public interest that a wide and diverse range of skills and experiences of social problems connected with drug

---

38. MDA 1971, Schedule 1, para.3.
39. Explanatory Notes, para.18.

issues should be reflected in the constitution of the ACMD. In practice, there is an evidence-based selection process for membership, and thus appointments are not determined solely by the Secretary of State. However, there may have been merit in retaining the wording of paragraph 1(1)(b) to Schedule 1 (mentioned above).

The MDA: An Enduring Regime

There have been many calls for the repeal of the MDA 1971. Alternative regulatory models and 'blueprints' have been proposed. However, when references are made to the 'legalisation' or 'decriminalisation' of conduct concerning drugs (e.g. supply) there needs to be clarity as to what each expression is intended to convey and the context in which the expression is being applied. Neither expression is a legal term of art, nor is there a generally accepted meaning of each.[40]

Even if the MDA 1971 were to be repealed, other statutory drug-control measures (enforced by coercive sanctions) would remain. The MDA 1971 has survived for 50 years and there are no clear signs yet that the Act is 'retiring' any time soon.

Rudi Fortson KC is an independent practising barrister who is noted for his work in relation to serious crime, including fraud, confiscation, asset-recovery, money-laundering and drug law. He is a Visiting Professor of Law at Queen Mary, University of London. He is the author of *Misuse of Drugs and Drug Trafficking Offences*, 6th edn (Sweet & Maxwell, 2012).

---

40. See, e.g. R. Fortson, *Law on the Misuse of Drugs and Drug Trafficking Offences* (6th edn, 2012), ch.1–042a, Sweet & Maxwell. Contrast with the definitions used by the European Monitoring Centre for Drugs and Drug Addiction, PERSPECTIVES ON DRUGS: Models for the Legal Supply of Cannabis: Recent Developments — www.emcdda.europa.eu/system/files/publications/2720/Legal%20supply%20cannabis_update%202016.pdf

PART V
CHANGING POLICY

CHAPTER 18

Regulating the Legal: Minimum Unit Pricing of Alcohol in Scotland

Eric Carlin

This chapter considers lessons to be learned for public health from the battle to implement Minimum Unit Pricing (MUP) for alcohol in Scotland. Just as drug cartels control the illicit drug trade, leading to enormous health and social harms, public health has been damaged by sustained opposition to evidence-based regulatory controls on alcohol by its global producers. In Scotland, the global alcohol industry, fronted by the Scotch Whisky Association, used its resources to block the implementation of MUP for six years. In so doing they acted against the will of the Scottish people who had elected a Government in 2011 which had MUP explicitly in its manifesto as a crucially important and evidence-based tool to reduce harms due to alcohol consumption and to reduce health inequalities. Advocates for drug reform, who wish to achieve more effective protection for health and human rights, need to learn from the alcohol experience, here and elsewhere, in shaping their demands for legal change. Such change needs to be accompanied by national and international strategies to reduce social and economic inequalities, ensuring that economic operators are excluded from the policymaking process.

Alcohol — No Ordinary Commodity

Advocates for evidence-based drug policies who argue for a review of the legal system, including an update of the international drug conventions (United Nations, 1961, 1971, 1988) and in the UK the MDA 1971 (UK Government, 1971), would do well to consider the case of the drug alcohol for lessons about what to do and what not to do. Arguments for decriminalisation and/or legalisation of currently illicit drugs often focus on a number of areas considered problematic within the current legal framework, including:

- the breach of human rights implied by preventing people by law from ingesting substances that they wish to consume for pleasure, often embedded in social norms, and with the impact of marginalising further already disadvantaged groups and young people in particular, including increasing health inequalities;

- the harmful economic and social impacts of policies, so that the 'war on drugs' (Drug Policy Alliance, 2021) has led to the development of a multi-billion dollar and deadly global industry, disrupting economies and societies;

- the health harms that continue and that may be made worse by policies that lead to unnecessary disease and deaths, including by overdose or as a result of chronic long-term conditions, including viruses caused by sharing drug-using equipment.

Public health advocates are rightly concerned about the harms due to use of many substances, as well as of inefficient policies, to the health of populations and individuals. It is estimated that illicit drug use is — directly and indirectly — responsible for more than 750,000 people dying every year (Ritchie and Roser, 2018). However, despite its legality and social acceptance, the benefits connected with the production, sale and use of alcohol also come at an enormous cost to society. Alcohol is 'no ordinary commodity,' causing medical, psychological and social harm due to its physical toxicity, the impacts of intoxication and of dependence, with impacts for individuals, families and communities (Babor et al, 2010). Alcohol is a class one carcinogen and responsible for more than 200 diseases, health conditions and injuries (WHO, 2021). Many experts consider alcohol to be a more dangerous drug than many currently illicit drugs in the UK (inter alia, Nutt et al, 2010).

Economic operators in the alcohol industry wield enormous power, which has massive impacts on the health and wellbeing of individuals and society. Moreover, whereas there are few politicians who would openly align with global drug gangs, most mainstream politicians consider alcohol to have an important place in our cultural landscape. The alcohol industry is often considered as a respectable partner for economic growth as well as having an important contribution to offer to the implementation of alcohol policy to reduce harm (WHO, 2010). The industry's abuse of this privileged position, especially in low- and middle-income countries, has been well documented (McCambridge et al, 2018; Van Beeman, 2019); they have undermined public health policy efforts that are grounded in evidence. Arguments they have presented include that a 'whole population' approach uses ineffective 'blunt instruments' which punish the 'responsible majority' for the moral failings of a minority (McCambridge et al, 2018). From this perspective, MUP, setting a floor price below which units of alcohol cannot be sold, has been opposed as an illegal, ineffective and counterproductive measure that unfairly targets moderate and less wealthy drinkers (McCambridge et al, 2018). Despite such opposition, in the small country of Scotland, in the face of alarming alcohol health statistics, MUP, based on a growing body of evidence, was selected as one of a suite of policies, to reduce harm due to alcohol. This chapter considers this case study, including how the implementation of MUP was delayed because the global alcohol industry flexed its corporate muscles and financial power to block its implementation, with little regard for the evidence, for the human consequences of delay or non-implementation, the democratic legitimacy of their actions or their public reputation.

Population-level Measures, Including Pricing Policies to Reduce Harm Due to Alcohol Consumption

It is difficult to overestimate the impact of *Alcohol No Ordinary Commodity* (Babor et al, 2003, 2010)[1] in vitalising the public health awareness that alcohol harms are preventable at international level by implementation of evidence-based population level measures. Alcohol consumption and harms that emerge from it are considered in the book as social determinants of ill health and health inequalities. Accumulating evidence is reviewed in relation to several areas of alcohol policy, including actions to reduce affordability and to restrict availability and marketing. These areas have now become the foundation of the World Health Organization's recommended evidence-based and cost-effective alcohol policies (WHO, 2010) and alcohol 'Best Buys' to reduce NCDs (Non-communicable Diseases) (WHO, 2013).

Pricing policies and MUP — the evidence

A WHO review of pricing policies for alcohol highlights various reviews of the scientific evidence that have concluded that pricing policies are very effective in reducing alcohol-related harm (WHO Regional Office for Europe, 2020). The WHO review highlights what it describes as 'A huge body of economic literature' that indicates that policy approaches that increase the price of alcohol are likely to reduce alcohol consumption and harm. WHO has concluded that, of all alcohol policy measures, the evidence is strongest that reducing the affordability of alcohol can lower alcohol consumption and alcohol-related harms (WHO Regional Office for Europe, 2021). As well as this, the costs of implementing pricing policies are typically low, so that such policies should be considered cost-effective, especially when costs to health and public services due to alcohol consumption are considered (WHO Regional Office for Europe, 2020). Pricing policies have great potential as tools to improve public health, generate revenue, and redress the external costs of alcohol use to individuals, families, and wider society (WHO Regional Office for Europe, 2021). The health harms that accrue due to alcohol consumption are more serious for poorer

---

1. A new edition is anticipated in 2022.

populations. A policy approach to reduce the availability of cheap alcohol is likely to reduce health inequalities (WHO Regional Office for Europe, 2020).

Despite the evidence that alcohol pricing policies are among the most effective and cost-effective to reduce harms due to alcohol consumption, they are also among the least utilised. The WHO has made clear that there is potential for minimum prices to be used in combination with other complementary policies, including taxation, to reduce harm, as well as increasing government tax revenue. Minimum prices should therefore be considered as complementary to taxation (WHO, 2022).

Alcohol in Scotland

Alcohol consumption as a social norm is embedded in Scotland's national consciousness, though with a wide variation of what that means. There are different perceptions about different groups of consumers and their drinking practices, imbued with wider judgements about different groups in society, related to notions including class and gender (Emslie et al, 2015, 2013; Lennox et al, 2018). Scotch whisky is so integral to the nation's sense of self that the new Scottish Parliament building that was opened in 2004 has a main chamber with whisky bottles engraved in the wood panelling displays. The alcohol industry is estimated to contribute around £46 billion per year to the UK economy, equivalent to around 2.5% of Gross Domestic Product (GDP) (Institute of Alcohol Studies, 2017). However, whereas whisky evokes cosy and morally approved cultural sensibilities, the consumption of other products is often associated with behaviours deemed to be antisocial, including football violence. Such products include spirits, especially vodka, beer and in the late-twentieth and early-twenty-first centuries, cheap ciders. There is also a recurring moral panic in Scotland (Cohen, 2011) about Buckfast (a fortified caffeinated wine) with the opprobrium attached to this linked to the people who drink it—predominantly working-class West of Scotland males—and their behaviours.

The public health response in Scotland

The period following the publication of the first edition of *Alcohol: No Ordinary Commodity* (Babor et al, 2003) coincided with the highest level of alcohol consumption in Scotland and linked to this the highest number of hospitalisations and deaths due to alcohol (Beeston et al, 2016). Between 1987 and 2007, alcohol had steadily become more affordable (Beeston et al, 2016). Leon and McCambridge's (2006) review of the rates of alcoholic cirrhosis or end-stage liver disease was one of the key pieces of evidence that woke up health advocates and policymakers to the scale of that problem. Total recorded alcohol consumption in Britain had doubled between 1960 and 2002, giving rise to a need to examine and assess cirrhosis mortality trends. Between the periods 1987–1991, and 1997–2001, cirrhosis mortality in men in Scotland more than doubled (104% increase) and in England and Wales rose by over two-thirds (69%). Mortality in women increased by almost half (46% in Scotland and 44% in England and Wales). These relative increases were the steepest in western Europe, and contrasted with the declines apparent in most of the other 14 countries examined, particularly those of southern Europe. Figure 1 (from Leon and McCambridge, 2006, p.53) provides a visual representation of the story.

The Scotland Act 1998 allowed for the establishment of the Scottish Parliament and Scottish Government, with the omission of most health policy from Schedule 5 of the Act giving the Scottish Government the authority to legislate on many, though not all, health matters (UK Government, 2013). Within that novel context and with the election of the first Scottish Nationalist Party (SNP) Government in 2007, advocates, notably from the medical professions, via the newly-established Scottish Health Action on Alcohol Problems (SHAAP) partnership (www.SHAAP.org.uk), began to argue for population-based policies, including focusing on price (SHAAP, 2007). There was increasing recognition not only of the health costs of inaction but also of the economic costs. By the time the first Scottish Alcohol Framework *Changing Scotland's Relationship with Alcohol: A Framework for Action* ('the framework') had been instigated (Scottish Government, 2009), it included 41 different components, including a commitment to introduce legislation for a Minimum Unit Price (MUP) for alcohol, setting a floor price for alcohol products based on ethanol content. The framework also contained measures to expand provision of alcohol screening and brief interventions and treatment, with increased funding for these.[2]

---

2. Legislation related to the framework includes the Licensing Act (2005), implemented 2009; the Alcohol etc. (Scotland) Act 2010, implemented in October 2011; and the Alcohol (Minimum Pricing) (Scotland) Act 2012, which was delayed by one year as it did not command a Parliamentary majority support till then—more detail is available at www.healthscotland.scot/health-topics/alcohol/monitoring-and-evaluating-scotlands-alcohol-strategy-mesas

Figure 1: Time trends in age-standardised mortality rates for liver cirrhosis per 100,000 by age-group, sex, and country between 1950 and 2002. Reproduced by kind permission of *The Lancet*.

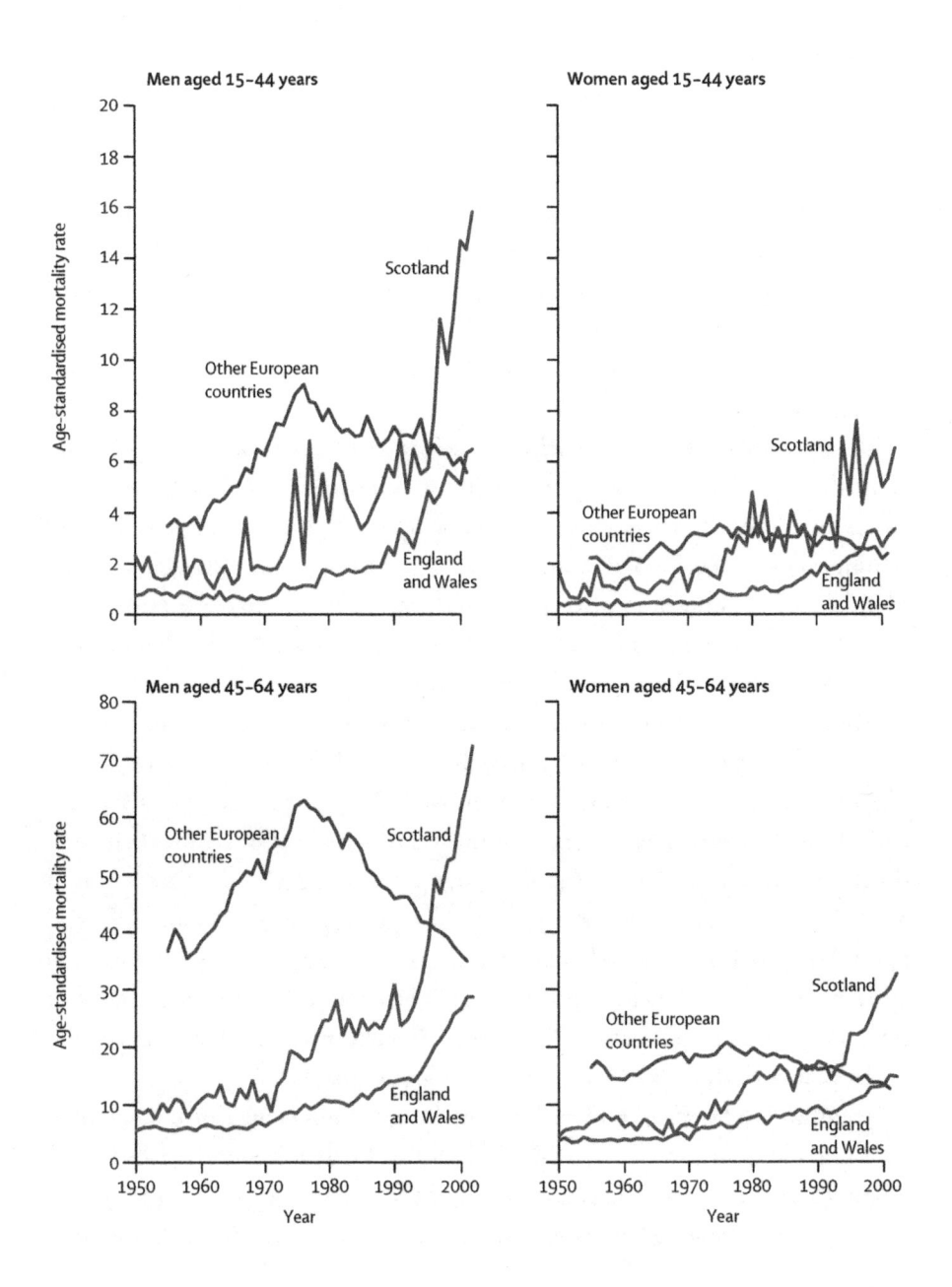

Scottish MUP policy drew largely on research from British Columbia that found that as minimum alcohol prices increased, there was an associated decrease in population consumption, hospital admissions, deaths, and crimes related to alcohol. Policymakers in Scotland also considered experience in Saskatchewan, where a 10% increase in minimum price reduced consumption of all alcohol by 8% (Beeston et al, 2020). The alcohol research model developed at Sheffield University was instrumental in shaping policy in Scotland (Katikareddi et al, 2016). Other evidence for MUP has since also been gained from the Russian Federation, which introduced a limited version of MUP for vodka and other spirits in 2010, along with a wider range of policy measures (Neufeld et al, 2020). The Scottish policy differs from the regulation in these other contexts as it sets a floor price for all alcoholic products, based on ethanol content, whereas other MUPs had varied for different products (Katikareddi and Hilton, 2014).

The Alcohol (Minimum Pricing) (Scotland) Act 2012 was passed by the Scottish Parliament on 24 May 2012, with no opposition, and it received Royal Assent on 29 June 2012 (Scottish Government, 2012). The Act specifies that the minimum price of alcohol is to be calculated according to the following formula MPU x S x V = minimum price at which the alcohol can be sold (where MPU is the minimum price per unit, S is the percentage strength of the alcohol, and V is the volume of the alcohol in litres, with the MPU being set by Scottish Ministers). A minimum price of 50 pence was set (but see later comments).

The 2012 Act requires a thorough evaluation of the impact of the novel legislation. It is specified that the provisions would expire at the end of a six-year period unless Scottish Ministers after five years were to provide for their continuation. To inform that decision-making process, the Ministers are required to lay before the Scottish Parliament a report on the operation and effect of the MUP provisions during that period. This includes paying attention to characteristics including age, gender, social and economic deprivation, alcohol consumption levels and patterns and other characteristics considered appropriate by Scottish Ministers (Scottish Government, 2012).

According to Sheffield University modelling (Angus et al, 2016), based on a 2012 starting point, in year one MUP would be likely to reduce deaths by 60, hospital admissions by 1,600 and crimes by 3,500. As a novel policy and dependent on people changing behaviours, medium-to-longer-term impacts are more important however than the short-term. The Sheffield model suggested that a 50p MUP would lead to 2,036 fewer deaths and 38,859 fewer hospitalisations during the first 20 years of the policy, with 121 fewer deaths and 2,042 fewer hospital admissions per year (Angus, 2016). Consumption reductions with a 50p MUP are estimated to be largest for those who drink the most, with the smallest effects among more moderate drinkers (Angus et al, 2016). It is estimated that reductions in mortality will be largest for the heaviest drinkers in the poorest sections of the population.

Table 1: The battle to implement MUP in Scotland, 2012–2018 — Key events.

Year	Event
2012	Alcohol (Minimum Pricing) (Scotland) Act passes with no opposition and receives Royal assent. Scotch Whisky Association announces it will launch legal challenge. European Commission seeks member States' views. European Commission offers opinion.
2013	Outer House of the Court of Session (Scotland) rules in favour of the Scottish Government. Scotch Whisky Association announces it will appeal.
2014	Inner House of the Court of Session (Scotland) refers to European Court of Justice.
2015	European Court of Justice Advocate General provides advice. That court lays down some specific requirements and refers back to Inner House (Scotland).
2016	Inner House rules in favour of Scottish Government. Scotch Whisky Association announces it will appeal to the UK Supreme Court.
2017	UK Supreme Court rules unanimously that the legislation is valid.
2018	MUP is implemented on 1 May 2018.

The legislation was passed in 2012 but implementation was delayed till 2018, due to legal challenges by global alcohol producers, fronted by the Scotch Whisky Association; among their arguments was that the legislation infringed UK (including the 1707 Act of Union) and European Union (EU) single market law (Hawkins and McCambridge, 2020). The Scottish Government committed not to implement until all legal challenges had been exhausted. Table 1 above highlights key milestones in the legal process. The UK Supreme Court finally decided the case in favour of the Scottish Government in 2017, exhausting all legal avenues (Hawkins and McCambridge, 2020).

Impact of MUP in Scotland — What is known so far?

The Monitoring and Evaluating Scotland's Alcohol Strategy (MESAS) programme, led by Public Health Scotland, is an extensive set of independent research studies that are considering both intended and unintended consequences of MUP. The Final Report is due to be published in late 2023, to inform decision-making about whether to continue the policy. The evaluation is gathering evidence in four key areas:

- Implementation and compliance.
- What happens to the market.
- Alcohol consumption.
- Impacts on health and social harm.

The evaluation is also considering other aspects that might impact on alcohol consumption and related harms — clearly the Covid-19 pandemic has disrupted what might have been expected.[3]

Among its findings, the first report on licensing and compliance in 2019 found high levels of compliance, with no impact on the on-trade or increases in illegal trading of alcohol or cross-border purchasing in England (Dickie et al, 2019). Although a qualitative study commissioned as part of MESAS (Iconic Consulting, 2019) suggests that the policy had negligible impact on some young people's drinking behaviours, a range of population level studies in the year following MUP implementation suggested far more promising signs of impact. O'Donnell et al (2019) examined shopping data in the 34 weeks immediately

---

3. For full information on the MESAS evaluation, see www.healthscotland.scot/health-topics/alcohol/evaluation-of-minimum-unit-pricing-mup/overview-of-evaluation-of-mup/why-we-are-evaluating-mup

following MUP implementation from a large and representative panel of British households to see whether there had been any changes in level or pattern of purchases. Purchases over the equivalent period before MUP implementation were used as controls and purchases in the north of England were also analysed.

The clearest finding across multiple studies is that MUP has been successful in reducing alcohol consumption in Scotland (WHO, 2022). Immediate reductions of up to 7.6% in purchases were more than double the Sheffield modelling-based estimates, confirming the authors' conservative assumptions, and highlighting that health benefits could be much greater. Immediate reductions were notable, most substantially for beer, spirits, and cider, including own brand spirits and high strength white ciders. The largest changes were for households who were purchasing the most alcohol each week and lower income groups. The policy appeared to be having a greater impact among those who were purchasing the most alcohol, as well as for lower income groups, confirming the policy's effectiveness in encouraging those who are most likely to be harmed by cheap alcohol to reduce their consumption (Mooney and Carlin, 2019).

The population level MESAS studies also showed very promising results in the first full year following MUP implementation. Alcohol sales in Scotland in 2018 included a 3.6% reduction in off-trade sales in the first year of MUP, compared to a 3.2% increase in England and Wales for the same period, making this the lowest level of alcohol sales in Scotland in 25 years. The gap between population levels of consumption in Scotland and England and Wales reduced from 14% in 2017 to 9% in 2018. Consumers were also switching to smaller packs, lower-alcohol, and more premium products and some products, notably high-strength cider were disappearing from supermarket and off-licence shelves (Giles et al, 2019). Related to this, there were 1,020 alcohol-specific deaths registered in Scotland in 2019, 10% fewer than in 2018 and the lowest annual total since 2013 (1,002). This was the first substantial decrease in recent years, after a period of general increase since 2012, representing 28% fewer deaths than the peak of 1,417 registered in 2006 (National Records of Scotland, 2021).

Although an annual decrease of this magnitude was notable, further time would be required to see if the reduction would continue, so as to conclude that this was to be a sustained shift in alcohol-specific deaths in Scotland. Notably disrupting the real-life experiment of MUP in Scotland of course was the Covid-19 pandemic which emerged early in 2020. It is as yet too early to assess the full impact of this on alcohol consumption and harms, with one MESAS-related study suggesting that in the early months of the pandemic in Scotland overall population reduced but some sub-groups increased their drinking (Stevely et al, 2021). There was also a significant impact on access to alcohol treatment services, with some treatment services being requisitioned for Covid-19 and drugs services arguably being prioritised over alcohol. Alcohol deaths increased again in Scotland in 2020 and 2021, with alcohol-specific death rates in the most deprived areas 5.6 times that of the least deprived areas in 2021 (National Records of Scotland, 2022).

Overall, studies that have considered the potential unintended negative consequences of MUP have found very limited evidence of the negative consequences that were hypothesised before the policy was introduced (WHO, 2022). There may have been some negative impacts in populations of homeless and street drinkers (Elliott et al, 2022). One important study, part of the MUP evaluation suite of studies, found evidence that the introduction of MUP increased financial strain for a minority of those in economically vulnerable groups with alcohol dependence (Holmes et al, 2022). An important lesson is that pricing policies do not stand alone. There need to be other strategic initiatives, including ensuring support for treatment and recovery from alcohol problems, as well as connection with the policies and programmes that are tackling some of the fundamental issues of our times, including but not limited to enabling and supporting positive mental health, reducing poverty and tackling inequalities at source, providing good quality housing and ending homelessness, reducing adverse childhood experiences, improving social connectedness, community cohesion and safety (Scottish Government, 2018).

Advocacy groups have called on the Scottish Government to uprate the MUP level so that it can have the intended impact of reducing affordability of the cheapest alcohol (BBC News, 2021). The 50p level was set based on 2012 prices but we know that minimum pricing policies set at a rate that is too low will be less effective as cheap alcohol will continue to be affordable. Wales introduced MUP in March 2020 and that experience will provide additional important evidence about the impact in another national context (Welsh Government, 2020).

Summing-up — Broad Lessons for Drug Policy

All psychoactive substances have potential to cause harms to the health and social functioning of individuals and communities, with higher risks to those who are multiply-disadvantaged, related to their social and economic contexts. Alcohol is no different in this regard from other drugs.

The potential power and influence of economic operators, whether a drug is licit or illicit, cannot be overstated. They should have no role in determining public health policies and should be restricted from obstructing or undermining them. International instruments, such as the Framework Convention on Tobacco (WHO, 2004), provide a useful model to support this.

Policy actions to reduce risks and harms must be evidence-based, with a public health focus and regulations and laws that support this. Evidence is constantly emerging for effective and cost-effective alcohol policies but, contrary to industry misinformation, WHO's policy 'Best Buys,' focusing on reducing affordability, marketing and availability, continues to have a robust evidence base to support them. Applicability of these principles to other drugs, should their legal context change, is important. As far as possible, actions to ban marketing should be global and comprehensive.

Real-life experiments, including MUP policy implementation in Scotland and Wales, as well as rigorous modelling, should inform future policy priorities and actions, while recognising the complexity and dynamism of the social world. Any legal changes in relation to currently illicit drugs need to be grounded in national and international strategies to reduce social and economic inequalities, so as to prevent harms as well as to support recovery for people who have drug (including alcohol) related problems.

Dr Eric Carlin was Director of Scottish Health Action on Alcohol Problems (SHAAP) from 2012 to 2021. Since July 2020, he has been a Consultant Public Health Expert, Alcohol Policies, with the WHO Regional Office for Europe. He is a Senior Honorary Research Fellow at Glasgow Caledonian University.

References and Extra Reading

Alcohol (Minimum Pricing) (Scotland) Act 2012: www.legislation.gov.uk/asp/2012/4/contents/enacted (accessed December 31, 2021).

Angus, C, Holmes, J, Pryce, R, Meier, P and Brennan, A (2016), Model-based Appraisal of the Comparative Impact of Minimum Unit Pricing and Taxation Policies in Scotland: An Adaptation of the Sheffield Alcohol Policy Model Version (3 April): www.sheffield.ac.uk/polopoly_fs/1.565373!/file/Scotland_report_2016.pdf (accessed December 31, 2021)

Babor, T F, Caetano, R, Casswell, S, Edwards, G, Giesbrecht, N, Graham, K, Grube, J, Hill, L, Holder, H, Homel, R, Livingston, M, Österberg, E, Rehm, J, Room, R and Rossow, I (2003, 2010, new edn anticipated 2022), *Alcohol: No Ordinary Commodity*, Oxford: Oxford University Press.

BBC News (2021) (November 19), Calls to raise minimum unit alcohol price to 65p in Scotland: www.bbc.co.uk/news/uk-scotland-59336255 (accessed December 31, 2021).

Beeston, C, McAdams, R, Craig, N, Gordon, R, Graham, L, MacPherson, M, McAuley, A, McCartney, G, Robinson, M, Shipton, D, Van Heelsum, A (2016), *Monitoring and Evaluating Scotland's Alcohol Strategy. Final Report*, Edinburgh: NHS Health Scotland: www.healthscotland.scot/media/1100/mesas-final-annual-report_5780_mar-2016.pdf (accessed December 31, 2021).

Beeston, C, Robinson, M, Giles. L, Dickie, E, Ford, J, Macpherson, M, McAdams, R, Mellor. R, Shipton, D, Craig, N (2020), Evaluation of Minimum Unit Pricing of Alcohol: A Mixed Method Natural Experiment in Scotland, *International Journal of Environmental Research and Public Health*, 17, 3394: 1–12.

Cohen, S (2011), *Folk Devils and Moral Panics* (3rd edn), Abingdon: Routledge.

Dickie, E, Mellor, R, Myers, F and Beeston, C (2019), Minimum Unit Pricing (MUP) Evaluation: Compliance (licensing) study, Edinburgh: NHS Health Scotland: www.healthscotland.scot/media/2660/minimum-unit-pricing-for-alcohol-evaluation-compliance-study-english-july2019.pdf (accessed December 31, 2021).

Drug Policy Alliance (2021), A History of the Drug War: https://drugpolicy.org/issues/brief-history-drug-war (accessed December 31, 2021).

Elliott L, Emslie C, Dimova E, Whiteford M, O'Brien R, Strachan H et al (2022), Minimum Unit Pricing: Qualitative Study of the Experiences of Homeless Drinkers, Street Drinkers and Service Providers. Edinburgh: Chief Scientist Office: www.cso.scot.nhs.uk/wp-content/uploads/HIPS1843-1.pdf (accessed August 17, 2022).

Emslie, C, Hunt, K and Lyons, A (2015), The Role of Alcohol in Forging and Maintaining Friendships Among Scottish Men in Midlife, *Health Psychology*, 32(1): 33–41.

Giles, L, Robinson, M and Beeston C (2019), *Minimum Unit Pricing (MUP) Evaluation. Sales-based Consumption: A Descriptive Analysis of One Year Post-MUP Off-trade Alcohol Sales Data*, Edinburgh: NHS Health Scotland: www.healthscotland.scot/media/2954/c-users-kims-desktop-sales-based-consumption-descriptive-analysis-of-one-year-post-mup-off-trade-alcohol-sales-data.pdf (accessed December 31, 2021).

Hawkins, B and McCambridge, J (2020), 'Tied up in a Legal Mess': The Alcohol Industry's Use of Litigation to Oppose Minimum Alcohol Pricing in Scotland, *Scottish Affairs*, 29(1): 3–23.

Iconic Consulting (2019), Minimum Unit Pricing in Scotland: A Qualitative Study of Children and Young People's Own Drinking and Related Behaviour Final Report (November), Edinburgh: www.healthscotland.scot/news/2020/january/first-study-published-into-under-18-drinkers-post-mup (accessed December 31, 2021).

Institute of Alcohol Studies (2017), Splitting the Bill: Alcohol's Impact on the Economy: www.ias.org.uk/uploads/pdf/IAS%20reports/rp23022017.pdf (accessed December 31, 2021).

Katikireddi, S V, Hilton, S and Bond, L (2016), The Role of the Sheffield Model on the Minimum Unit Pricing of Alcohol Debate: The Importance of a Rhetorical Perspective, *Evidence and Policy*, 12(4): 521–539.

Katikireddi, S V and Hilton, S (2014), How Did Policy Actors Use Mass Media to Influence the Scottish Alcohol Minimum Unit Pricing Debate? Comparative Analysis of Newspapers, Evidence Submissions and Interviews, *Drugs Education, Prevention and Policy* 22(2): 125–134.

Lennox, J, Emslie, C, Sweeting, H and Lyons, A (2018), The Role of Alcohol in Constructing Gender and Class Identities Among Young Women in the Age of Social Media, *International Journal of Drug Policy*, 26(5): 437–445.

Leon, D A and McCambridge, J (2006), Liver Cirrhosis Mortality Rates in Britain from 1950 to 2002: An Analysis of Routine Data, *The Lancet*, 367: 52–56.

McCambridge, J, Mialon, M and Hawkins, B (2018), Alcohol Industry Involvement in Policymaking: A Systematic Review, *Addiction* 113: 1571–1584.

Misuse of Drugs Act, 1971: www.legislation.gov.uk/ukpga/1971/38/contents (accessed December 31, 2021).

Mooney, J and Carlin, E (2019), Minimum Unit Pricing in Scotland: The Rest of the UK Should Follow Scotland's Lead, *British Medical Journal* (editorial September 25).

National Records of Scotland (2021), Alcohol-specific Deaths 2020: www.nrscotland.gov.uk/files/statistics/alcohol-deaths/2020/alcohol-specific-deaths-20-report.pdf (accessed December 31, 2021).

National Records of Scotland, (2022), Alcohol-specific Deaths 2021: www.nrscotland.gov.uk/files//statistics/alcohol-deaths/2021/alcohol-specific-deaths-21-report.pdf (accessed August 17, 2022).

Neufeld, M, Ferreira-Borges, C, Gil, A, Manthey, J and Rehm, J (2020), Alcohol Policy Has Saved Lives in the Russian Federation, *International Journal of Drug Policy* (June) 80: 102636.

O'Donnell. A, Anderson, P, Jané-Llopis, E, Manthey, J, Kaner, E and Rehm, J (2019), Immediate Impact of Minimum Unit pricing on Alcohol Purchases in Scotland: Controlled Interrupted Time Series Analysis for 2015–18, *British Medical Journal*, 366; l5274.

Ritchie, H and Roser, M (2019), Opioids, Cocaine, Cannabis and Illicit Drugs: https://ourworldindata.org/illicit-drug-use (accessed December 31, 2021).

Scottish Government (2009), Changing Scotland's Relationship with Alcohol: A Framework for Action: www.healthscotland.com/uploads/documents/9615-Framework%20for%20Action.pdf (accessed December 31, 2021).

Scottish Government (2018), Alcohol Framework: Preventing Harm www.gov.scot/binaries/content/documents/govscot/publications/strategy-plan/2018/11/alcohol-framework-2018-preventing-harm-next-steps-changing-relationship-alcohol/documents/alcohol-framework-2018-preventing-harm-next-steps-changing-relationship-alcohol/alcohol-framework-2018-preventing-harm-next-steps-changing-relationship-alcohol/govscot%3Adocument/00543214.pdf (accessed August 17, 2022).

Scottish Health Action on Alcohol Problems (SHAAP) (2007), Alcohol: Price, Policy and Public Health: Report On the Findings of the Expert Workshop on Price Convened by SHAAP: https://shaap.org.uk/downloads/59-price-report-summary-pdf/viewdocument/59.html (accessed December 31, 2021).

Stevely, A K, Sasso, A, Alava, M H and Holmes, J (2021), *Changes in Alcohol Consumption in Scotland During the Early Stages of the COVID-19 Pandemic: Descriptive Analysis of Repeat Cross-sectional Survey Data, Edinburgh,* Public Health Scotland: www.publichealthscotland.scot/media/2983/changes-in-alcohol-consumption-in-scotland-during-the-early-stages-of-the-covid-19-pandemic.pdf (accessed December 31, 2021).

UK Government (2013), *Guidance: Devolution settlement: Scotland*: www.gov.uk/guidance/devolution-settlement-scotland Misuse of Drugs Act, 1971: www.legislation.gov.uk/ukpga/1971/38/contents (accessed December 31, 2021).

United Nations (UN) (1961), Single Convention on Narcotic Drugs: www.unodc.org/unodc/en/treaties/single-convention.html (accessed December 31, 2021).

UN (1971), Convention on Psychotropic Substances: www.unodc.org/unodc/en/treaties/psychotropics.html (accessed December 31, 2021).

UN (1988), *Convention Against Illicit Traffic in Narcotic Drugs and Psychotropic Substances*: www.unodc.org/pdf/convention_1988_en.pdf (accessed December 31, 2021).

Van Beeman, O (2019), *Heineken in Africa: A Multinational Unleashed*, London: Hurst & Amp.

Welsh Government (2020), Minimum Unit Pricing for Alcohol: Summary Guidance: https://gov.wales/minimum-unit-pricing-alcohol-summary-guidance (accessed December 31, 2021).

World Health Organization (WHO) (2004), WHO Framework Convention on Tobacco Control, Geneva: WHO: http://apps.who.int/iris/bitstream/handle/10665/42811/9241591013.pdf;jsessionid=77385ACFDBFEA31A3C78C96E1D285E94?sequence=1 (accessed December 31, 2021).

WHO (2010), Global Strategy to Reduce the Harmful Use of Alcohol, Geneva: WHO: www.who.int/substance_abuse/msbalcstragegy.pdf (accessed December 31, 2021).

WHO (2013), Global Action Plan for the Prevention and Control of NCDs 2013–2020, Geneva: WHO: www.who.int/publications/i/item/9789241506236 (accessed December 31, 2021).

WHO Regional Office for Europe (2020), Alcohol Pricing in the WHO European Region: Update Report on the Evidence and Recommended Policy Actions, Copenhagen: WHO: https://apps.who.int/iris/bitstream/handle/10665/336159/WHO-EURO-2020-1239-40989-55614-eng.pdf (accessed July 4, 2022).

WHO Regional Office for Europe (2021), Making the WHO European Region SAFER: Developments in Alcohol Control Policies, 2010–2019, Copenhagen: WHO: https://apps.who.int/iris/handle/10665/340727 (accessed December 31, 2021).

WHO Regional Office for Europe (2022), Alcohol Pricing Policies in the WHO European Region: The Potential Value of Minimum Pricing for Saving Lives, Copenhagen: WHO: https://apps.who.int/iris/bitstream/handle/10665/356597/9789289058094-eng.pdf?sequence=1&isAllowed=y (accessed August 17, 2022).

CHAPTER 19

A Modest Proposal to Decriminalise the Simple Possession of Drugs

Kirstie Douse, Niamh Eastwood and Alex Stevens

In recent years, decriminalisation of drug possession has been recommended by international public bodies, including the United Nations Chief Executives Board (UNCEB, 2019) and the World Health Organization (WHO, 2017). In the UK, it has been backed by the Royal Society of Public Health, the Faculty of Public Health (RSPH and FPH, 2016), and both the Scottish Affairs Committee (2019) and the Health and Social Care Committee (2019) of the House of Commons. None of these bodies have specified how decriminalisation should be done; a question which has many possible answers (Greer et al, 2022).

Here we present a modest proposal to decriminalise the simple possession of drugs (without intent to supply) by repealing the sub-sections of the MDA 1971 that criminalise this activity.[1] This would leave substances controlled under the MDA in a similar position to those that are currently controlled under the Psychoactive Substances Act 2016 (PSA 2016); it would be illegal to import, produce or supply them, but simple possession would not be a criminal offence.

This proposal is modest in several ways. It does not require a new legal framework, but rather draws on that provided by the existing MDA 1971. It stops far short of the type of legal regulation of the production and sale of drugs that many call for. It would therefore do little to resolve problems that arise in the illicit market for these substances, such as violence and exploitation of

---

1. The chapter builds on a paper presented to the Criminal Law Reform Now conference in September 2021.

293

children and vulnerable adults. It reflects the existing moves away from criminalising people for possession of controlled drugs that are already being taken by police forces, who increasingly use out-of-court disposals for simple possession offences. Police would retain the power to search for and confiscate these substances when there are reasonable grounds to suspect importation, production, supply, or intent to supply.

The proposed change would, however, represent a significant step away from the failed punitive logic of UK drug policy. It would remove a law that has been used to create 2.9 million criminal records resulting from convictions and cautions in Great Britain in the last 50 years, so preventing the harms of criminalisation from being added to those experienced by many people who use drugs.

The Harms of Criminalisation

The harms imposed by the criminalisation of drug possession are multiple. Most obvious are the direct harms of arrest and punishment. Relatively small numbers of people are sent to prison for drug possession. In 2019, 899 immediate custodial sentences were given for such offences in England and Wales (Ministry of Justice (MOJ), 2020). Much larger numbers get a criminal record by being convicted of the offence at court or through being given a police caution, although these numbers have been dropping as police forces have made more use of out-of-court disposals, such as warnings, on the spot penalties, and more recently community resolutions, and as the use of stop and search has fallen significantly over the last decade. In 2010, there were 43,406 convictions and 36,007 cautions for drug possession, by 2019, these numbers had fallen respectively to 21,641 and 13,049, a still significant number of people criminalised every year (MOJ, 2020). A much larger number are harmed by the imposition of stop and search for suspected drug possession. In 2019, there were 558,973 stop and searches, of which 57% were carried out on suspicion of drug offences (Home Office, 2020). It is well documented that these harms fall especially hard on people from racialised communities (see *Chapter 12* in this volume by Akintoye, Amal and Stevens).

Beyond the direct and immediate harms of entanglement in the Criminal Justice System (CJS) are the less tangible, but longer lasting, harms to individuals and communities. Criminalisation leaves stigmata in the form of criminal records and the necessity to declare such offences in job and visa applications. For communities that are over-policed and under-protected, which are often those where large numbers of black people live, the disproportionate searching, arresting and criminalisation of young people is a barrier to the creation of trusting relationships with the police, and even with other agencies of the State.

The MDA 1971, as with previous Acts of Parliament that prohibited controlled drugs, sought to deter use of these substances through the threat of criminalisation. However, in the last 50 years the UK has witnessed huge growth in the consumption of controlled drugs. At the same time, there has been a significant increase in drug-related harms, not only the high rates of criminalisation but also record levels of drug-related deaths. Criminalisation has not reduced use by deterrence; use has increased. The legislative framework for possession of drugs appears to have little impact on a person's decision to use them, and so we should focus on models that reduce harms. Reforming the MDA 1971 to repeal the offences of possession is a first step in that process.

The Relevant Sections of the MDA 1971

The most relevant provision of the 1971 Act is section 5, specifically sub-sections 5(1) and (2). They make it a criminal offence to possess any of the substances which are defined as controlled drugs by the Act, unless that person or substance is exempted by other sections of the Act, including by the Misuse of Drugs Regulations 2001 (MDR). Section 5(3) makes it an offence 'for a person to have a controlled drug in his possession, whether lawfully or not, with intent to supply it to another.' Schedule 4 provides the maximum punishments available to the courts for those found guilty of an offence under the Act, including an offence under section 5(2).

It is worth noting here that Parliament recognised (in section 5(2A)) the limits to criminalisation of simple possession in 2011. When creating temporary class drug orders (TCDOs), legislators specified that section 5(1) and (2) would not apply to substances controlled under these orders. While simple possession of such substances was not criminalised under the MDA 1971, section 23A was also inserted into the Act to enable police officers to search for and seize substances that are subject to TCDOs.

For other substances, it is section 23 that gives a constable the power to search persons or vehicles and to seize substances if they have 'reasonable grounds to suspect that any person is in possession of a controlled drug in contravention of this Act or of any regulations.'

Comparison With the Psychoactive Substances Act 2016

The PSA 2016 is by no means a perfect piece of legislation. It includes a definition of psychoactivity that is scientifically absurd (Stevens et al, 2015). It does, nevertheless, provide an interesting comparison to the MDA 1971. Crucially, it does not create an offence of possession of the substances that it controls, except if there is intention to supply, or the possessor is in a custodial institution.

Sections 36 of the 2016 Act provides powers to stop and search if there are reasonable grounds to suspect a person of contravening sections 4 to 9 of the PSA 2016, which ban importation, production, supply and possession in a custodial institution (note: not possession outside a custodial setting). Section 37 gives powers to enter and search when there are 'reasonable grounds to suspect that there is relevant evidence in a vehicle.'

Section 43 of the PSA 2016 gives the power to retain any item found subsequent to a search carried out under sections 36 or 37, where that item can be used to determine an offence has been committed. An officer may also seize a psychoactive substance under section 43(5) regardless of whether it is relevant evidence. Essentially, section 36 or 37 allows for a search where there has been a contravention under the Act, but if a person is in possession for their own personal use then an officer, under section 43(5), can seize the substance. Sections 49 and 50 give powers to retain and dispose of seized substances.

Our Modest Proposal

In order to reduce the harms and costs of criminalisation, we propose removing the offence of possession by repealing sub-sections 5(1) and 5(2) of the MDA 1971. If these were repealed, but sub-section 5(3) was not, it would no longer be an offence to possess substances that are controlled under the MDA 1971, unless there was also intent to supply. The relevant part of Schedule 4 would also be repealed to remove the stated punishment for the offence.

This would also have the effect of limiting the power to stop and search under section 23 of the MDA 1971, as simple possession would no longer be 'in contravention of this Act.' We consider this to be a strong advantage of this proposal, as it would limit the harms imposed by disproportionate and ineffective stop and search practices. We see no powerful argument why search powers should be retained for simple possession if it is no longer a criminal offence. As we have already explained, Parliament did not believe it necessary to create a power to search on suspicion of simple possession of substances controlled under the PSA 2016.

Section 23(2) could therefore be amended to reflect the powers in the PSA 2016, whereby an officer can lawfully seize a psychoactive substance even if it is not evidence of an offence having been committed. Thus streamlining the system of policing for all substances, those controlled under the MDA 1971 and those, which by default and a poorly drafted definition of psychoactivity, fall under the PSA 2016.

This proposal is not limited to any particular substances, as has been the case with some previous alternatives to arrest and prosecution for possession, such as cannabis and khat warnings. It would follow other jurisdictions—including the Czech Republic, Spain, Portugal and the US State of Oregon—in applying decriminalisation to the simple possession of all controlled drugs.

This proposal does not, however, import some foreign innovation into UK law. It takes the current legal treatment of possession of substances that are controlled under TCDOs and the PSA 2016 and applies it to all substances controlled under the MDA 1971. Simple possession is not a crime in the PSA 2016, nor for TCDOs, and we see no good reason why it should be in the MDA 1971. Repeatedly Home Secretaries, and Ministers responsible for drugs, have rejected calls to decriminalise controlled drugs on the basis that the policy experience of other countries cannot simply be transferred into the UK context due to the difference in societal and cultural attitudes. In response to the 2019 Health and Social Care Committee's recommendation to consult on decriminalising possession of drugs, the Government stated they had

> '...no intention of decriminalising drugs...We are aware of decriminalisation approaches being taken overseas, but it is overly simplistic to say that decriminalisation works. Historical patterns of drug use, cultural attitudes, and the policy and operational responses to drug misuse in a country will all affect levels of use and harm.'
>
> *Home Office, 2021*

Yet, the UK has already decriminalised possession of some drugs through the PSA 2016 and the use of TCDOs. Repealing the relevant sections of the MDA 1971, as outlined above, would achieve policy consistence and clarity in the law, including for law enforcement.[2]

Counter-arguments

The main argument that is made against decriminalisation of drug possession is that it would increase harms by increasing use. It is often suggested that it would encourage drug use by 'sending the wrong message,' and by reducing the deterrence of drug use by the threat of punishment for possession. These mechanisms do not seem to operate in practice. Several international analyses and reviews have found little evidence to support the idea that decriminalisation causes drug use to rise. It seems that young people tend not to pay much attention to the messages they are being sent by legislators when deciding what substances to consume. Given the rarity of police detection, relative to the numerous incidents of use, it is unsurprising that laws that criminalise possession have little deterrent effect.

---

2. This argument for consistency between the MDA 1971 and PSA 2016 was also included in 2016 in a report to the Home Secretary by the ACMD on 'Interaction and Relationship Between the Misuse of Drugs Act 1971 and the Psychoactive Substances Act 2016'; a report that the Government has so far refused to publish.

The absence of any punishment from the proposed model may lead to claims of going 'soft on drugs,' or that it will be politically unpalatable to consider taking no action against drug-taking. As stated, the legal model and the threat of sanction has little impact on use, moreover countries such as Spain, Germany and Uruguay have, for decades, had systems where there is no punishment for possession of small quantities (Eastwood et al, 2016). There is a risk that inclusion of a sanction, such as civil fines issued by police, could lead to more people coming into formal contact with law enforcement (otherwise known as 'net-widening') or that failure to attend mandated treatment could result in a person being prosecuted for breaching an order (an example of 'mesh-thinning' (Cohen, 1985)).

Another argument made against decriminalisation is that it will make the job of police agencies harder when it comes to preventing, detecting and punishing the supply of controlled drugs. Current methods of controlling this supply are of doubtful efficacy, and may even be counter-productive by precipitating violence and other health harms. Some police officers, for example in Portugal, have reported that decriminalisation helps them to build better relationships with people who have drug problems, and so to improve the flow of intelligence, as well as the protection of this highly victimised group (Magson, 2014).

Additionally, it is sometimes argued that removing the power to search for possession of drugs would limit the ability of police officers to find other prohibited items, such as weapons. The law is very clear in this area. The MDA 1971 section 23 requires that an officer must have reasonable grounds that a person is in possession of a controlled drug. It does not provide a general power to search for any prohibited item. To use it as a pretext to do so is unlawful. Such an approach risks damaging legitimacy and trust in the police, and—as highlighted above—decriminalisation could in fact improve the public's view of law enforcement, especially amongst communities that are overpoliced (see *Chapter 12* in this volume by Akintoye, Ali and Stevens).

A counter-argument from a different perspective would come from those who want more radical reform. They will rightly point out that we need to go beyond decriminalisation of possession to the legal regulation of drug supply if we want to take the market for these substances out of the hands of organized crime. However, if legal regulation will happen substance by substance, we would still argue that we should decriminalise the simple possession of *all* substances.

Conclusion

We should note that our proposal relates only to decriminalisation. We have not made suggestions for increasing capacity for diverting people to education or treatment, as exists in Portugal and Oregon. This is largely because we believe that most people who use controlled drugs have no more need for education or treatment than the usual consumers of other drugs, such as alcohol or tobacco. If drug use is to be prevented, let us do it through measures that have evidence of positive effect, which criminalisation does not. If people need treatment, let that be provided to them in attractive, accessible and voluntary forms.

No doubt this proposal will be politically controversial. It will spark debates about how harmful drugs are, and the damage they can do to mental health, children and the developing brain. These arguments seem rather irrelevant to the question of whether to decriminalise possession, given the lack of evidence that it changes levels of drug use. Many substances that are controlled under the PSA 2016 are potentially more harmful than several of those listed under the MDA 1971 (including in Class A), but their possession is not criminalised. We see much stronger evidence that decriminalisation can reduce the harms of stop and search, arrest and criminalisation (Stevens et al, 2019), and so propose the repeal of sub-sections 5(1) and 5(2) of the MDA 1971 in order to reduce these harms.

Kirstie Douse is a Solicitor Advocate and Head of Legal Services at Release, the UK's centre of expertise on drugs and drug laws. She has co-authored a number of that organization's advice publications including 'Drug Possession Offences: A Guide to Help You Represent Yourself' and 'Sex Workers and the Law'.

Niamh Eastwood is Executive Director of Release. She has co-authored a number of that organization's policy papers including 'The Colour of Injustice: "Race", Drugs and Law Enforcement in England and Wales' (2018) and 'A Quiet Revolution: Drug Decriminalisation Policies in Practice Across the Globe' (2016). She is an Associate Member of the Drug and Alcohol Research Centre at Middlesex University, a member of the Scientific Committee of Drug Science and has been a technical advisor to the Global Commission on Drug Policy.

Professor Alex Stevens is Professor in Criminal Justice at the University of Kent. He was a member of the Advisory Council on the Misuse of Drugs (2014–2019) and President of the International Society for the Study of Drug Policy (2015–2019). He is currently a board member of Harm Reduction International and Chair of Drug Science's Enhanced Harm Reduction Working Group. His publications include *Drugs, Crime and Public Health* (Routledge, 2011) and *Drug Policy Constellations* (Policy Press, forthcoming).

References and Extra Reading

Cohen, S (1985), *Visions of Social Control*, Polity Press.

Eastwood, N, Fox, E and Rosmarin, A (2016), A Quiet Revolution: Drug Decriminalisation Policies in Practice Across the Globe: www.opensocietyfoundations.org/sites/default/files/release-quiet-revolution-drug-decriminalisation-policies-20120709.pdf

Greer, A, Bonn, M, Ritter, A, Shane, C, Stevens, A and Tousenard, N (2022), The Details of Decriminalization: Designing a Non-criminal Response to the Possession of Drugs for Personal Use, *International Journal of Drug Policy*.

Home Office (2020), Police Powers and Procedures, England and Wales, Year Ending 31 (March) (2nd edn): www.gov.uk/government/statistics/police-powers-and-procedures-england-and-wales-year-ending-31-march-2020

Home Office (2021), Drugs Policy: Government Response to the Committees First Report of Session 2019: https://publications.parliament.uk/pa/cm5801/cmselect/cmhealth/1178/117802.htm

House of Commons (2019) (Health and Social Care Committee), Drug Policy: First Report of Session 2019.

Magson, J (2014), *Drugs, Crime and Decriminalisation Assessing the Impact of Drug Decriminalisation Policies on the Efficiency and Integrity of the Criminal Justice System* (January), Winston Churchill Memorial Trust: https://media.churchillfellowship.org/documents/Magson_J_Report_2013_Final.pdf

Ministry of Justice (2020), Criminal Justice System Statistics: Outcomes by Offence 2009 to 2019, Pivot Table Analytical Tool for England and Wales: https://assets.publishing.service.gov.uk/government/uploads/system/uploads/attachment_data/file/1063880/outcomes-by-offence-2020-revised.xlsx

Royal Society of Public Health and Faculty of Public Health (2016), Taking a New Line on Drugs, RSPH/FSH.

Scottish Affairs Committee (2019), Problem Drug Use in Scotland: https://publications.parliament.uk/pa/cm201919/cmselect/cmscotaf/44/4402.htm

Stevens, A, Fortson, R, Measham, F and Sumnall, H (2015), Legally Flawed, Scientifically Problematic, Potentially Harmful: The UK Psychoactive Substance Bill, *International Journal of Drug Policy*, 26(12). DOI: 10.1016/j.drugpo.2015.10.005

Stevens, A, Hughes, C, Hulme, S and Cassidy, R (2019), Depenalization, Diversion and Decriminalisation: A Realist Review and Programme Theory of Alternatives to Criminalisation for Simple Drug Possession, *European Journal of Criminology*. DOI: 10.1177/1477370819887514

United Nations (2019), Summary of Deliberations, UNCEB: www.unsceb.org/CEBPublicFiles/CEB-2018-2-SoD.pdf

World Health Organization (WHO) (2017), Joint United Nations Statement on Ending Discrimination in Health Care Settings: www.who.int/news/item/27-06-2017-joint-united-nations-statement-on-ending-discrimination-in-health-care-settings

CHAPTER 20

The Legal Regulation of Drugs in the UK

James Nicholls and Steve Rolles

As many of the chapters in this book demonstrate, the MDA 1971 has failed to achieve its stated goals. However, it is one thing to identify the problem but another to develop viable solutions. Establishing workable alternatives to prohibition presents significant political and practical challenges, and there are many options on the table. Transform Drug Policy Foundation has played a leading role in setting out models for the future legal regulation of drugs. This chapter describes the principles behind that approach, and some of its essential components.

What is Legal Regulation?

There is a significant (but often misunderstood) difference between decriminalisation and legal regulation. Decriminalisation refers to the removal of criminal sanctions for low level or outdated offences. In relation to drugs, this is most commonly a reference to possession and use of drugs, but sometimes cultivation or low-level supply (see generally *Chapters 17* and *19*). There are various models of decriminalisation, and it is applied differently in countries across the world (Release, 2021). Legal regulation, by contrast, means the formal establishment of a legal market for drugs that is subject to the kinds of controls that currently apply to substances such as alcohol or pharmaceuticals. These include licensing regimes to regulate supply, fiscal controls, controls on production, and regulations to limit the nature and scale of marketing (Transform, 2020a). Critically, legal regulation accepts a role for the State in governing drug supply on the principle, more commonly applied to alcohol and tobacco, that psychoactive substances are not 'ordinary commodities' (Babor et al, 2010). This chapter works, therefore, from the principle that the alternative to prohibition is not only the removal of existing controls, but the establishment of alternative State powers which, ideally, produce more just and equitable outcomes.

Risk-based Models of Control

The regulation of drug markets can take many forms. Alcohol, for example, is regulated mainly, though not exclusively, through licensing systems that allow local authorities to place controls on hours of sales, the number of outlets, the layout of premises and so on. Licences are generally issued on the condition that certain requirements are met, and the primary means of ensuring compliance is the threat of licence removal. Additionally, alcohol is often subject to regulations on packaging and advertising, and fiscal measures—which aim to both generate State income and, as in the case of minimum unit pricing for alcohol (MUP) (see *Chapter 18*), influence consumption (Griffith et al, 2013; Angus et al, 2019; Anderson et al, 2021).

The licensing of retail, and controls on packaging, marketing and price reflect the fact that alcohol and tobacco are risky: they are (or contain) substances that can be associated with dependence, long-term health harms and potential negative consequences for people other than the consumer. We have, therefore, framework systems already in place for the regulated supply of risky drugs. The regulation of currently illegal drugs should be seen as an extension of these practices. Regulation is not about creating entirely new systems but adapting mechanisms that are routinely applied elsewhere.

Critically, the range and intensity of regulatory tools should reflect the risks of particular products in given environments. The MDA 1971 currently distinguishes between drugs in classifications A, B and C, largely reflecting schedules set out in the 1961 and 1971 UN Conventions (Transnational Institute, 2015). In this respect, the MDA 1971 at least recognises that risks vary. However, this is deployed to determine the degree of *punishment* applied for possession and supply, and to service the underpinning assumption that harsher punishments reduce consumption. By contrast, under a system of legal regulation risk assessment would determine the nature and intensity of regulations placed on production and supply. The riskier a drug preparation, or consumption behaviours in a given environment, the stricter the controls.

Intrinsic risk is not the only consideration, however. Political, social and cultural contexts matter too. Distinct models of cannabis regulation have emerged in Uruguay, Spain, Canada and different States in the US. These partly reflect 'objective' assessments of risk, but also political attitudes towards market competition, the balance between personal freedom and State intervention, or the influence of advocacy groups on the promotion of public health and social justice. In the UK, we have long-established systems for licensing both intoxicants and pharmaceutical drugs. While these are imperfect, they provide frameworks for a regulatory system that would be both politically amenable and practical in regard to established structures.

Types of Regulation

Transform has previously identified five types of regulatory control that are applicable to drug supply (Transform, 2009; 2020a).

Medical prescription
For people being treated for heroin dependency, the prescription of lower-risk substitutes such as methadone or buprenorphine is widespread. Where people do not respond to opioid substitution therapy (OST), there is strong evidence that the prescription of pharmaceutical heroin (diamorphine) is effective. Heroin prescribing is already allowed in the UK, and can involve take home prescriptions or consumption under supervision.

Specialist pharmacy sales
Pharmacists operate within a clearly defined legal framework. In the UK they are already involved in drug management, such as the supervised on-site consumption of methadone prescriptions. Pharmacies are not generally involved in providing drugs for non-medical use, although in Uruguay cannabis is retailed

through pharmacies (Transform, 2016). It may be impractical to expect pharmacists to add non-medical provision to their usual practice and would certainly be concerning for many operating in the field (Gittins and Rolles, 2020). As an alternative, Transform has proposed the establishment of specialist, non-medical drug pharmacies (Transform, 2009; 2020a). This professional specialism would be subject to similar training and codes of practice as conventional pharmacists but with additional specialist knowledge and qualifications. Under this model, trained health professionals would serve as gatekeepers: enforcing access controls such as restrictions on age, intoxication and amount purchased, while also offering specialist advice on risk, safer use, and access to services.

Licensed sale for consumption on the premises ('on-sales')

On-sales allow consumption only in the place where a product is purchased. This allows more control over consumption than is the case for 'off-sales'—to, for example, refuse service to drunken customers, or remove those who are behaving aggressively. It also allows licensing authorities to influence the environment in which consumption takes place, rather than just how products are sold.

A familiar example of on-sale drug supply is Dutch 'coffee shops' selling cannabis (*Chapter 10*). Although an example of tolerated supply, rather than full legal regulation, they show how the on-premises consumption of drugs can take shape. On-premises licensing could also be used for nightclubs which could tolerate, or be licensed to supply, stimulants such as MDMA. However, limiting supply *only* to on-premises consumption raises a number of questions. What about people who wish to take drugs at home, or in other locations? Do consumers need to be formally supervised in all cases? It seems unlikely that such a restrictive model would sufficiently meet the needs of those currently purchasing drugs illegally, and would therefore fail to effectively create a comprehensive alternative supply system.

Licensed sales for consumption off the premises ('off-sales')

Off-sales allow for consumption of products off the seller's premises (e.g. at home)—as is the case with the sale of alcohol or tobacco in shops and supermarkets. Most recreational cannabis retail in Canada and the US involves off-sales. Off-sales are licensed and, as such, carried out in accordance with licensing conditions. These may be applied on a premises-by-premises basis or more generally within a given jurisdiction. Licensing conditions can include price controls, requirements for vendor training, restrictions on advertising and promotion, age restrictions, requirements for provision of health-and-safety information, and not allowing sales in the same location as other substances.

As a newer form of off-sales, online retail presents additional challenges. In UK alcohol licensing, for example, the 'point of sale' for licensing purposes is actually the store or warehouse where the product is picked—not the 'doorstep' where it is delivered (Colbert et al, 2021). Therefore, age-access criteria are determined at point of sale rather than at delivery. There are no simple solutions to the problem of online age-controls, and any system of regulation would need to preclude online retail until such solutions emerged.

Unlicensed sales

Drugs of sufficiently low risk, such as coffee, require relatively few or no licensing controls. Under Transform's proposals, some mild products—such as coca tea—would not be subject to any of the licensing restrictions applied to stronger substances (Transform, 2020a). However, they would still be subject to conventional regulatory requirements concerning ingredients, labelling, etc.

Profit-making Versus Public Health

Drug regulation needs to manage the conflicting goals of commerce and public health. We know from experience that, especially when large-scale corporate entities are involved, business will prioritise profit over public health. There is also a long and well-documented history of alcohol and tobacco industry actors vigorously undermining efforts to restrict their activities, including research evidence that supports stricter regulation (e.g. Hawkins and Holden, 2014; Savell et al, 2016; McCambridge et al, 2018).

Effectively controlling commercial actors requires strong, coherent legislation that applies at all levels of the supply chain (Shover and Humphreys, 2018). It requires global commitments, modelled on the Framework Convention on Tobacco Control, that set out clear principles of health-led governance (World Health Organization (WHO), 2013). It also requires full transparency regarding the role of commercial interests in policymaking and research, and the guarantee that policy decisions will not be influenced by drug industries (Gomis, 2021). It also requires well-designed licensing systems to operate at the local level—learning from decades of experience in alcohol and tobacco—which prevent monopolisation, aggressive marketing and irresponsible retail practices.

Drugs require stricter controls than is the case for other consumables, and the protection of health should take priority. Commercial actors are eminently capable of promoting consumption; it is the job of Government to set the parameters for that activity, using the regulatory levers at its disposal. All of this is easier said than done, and we should not be naïve about what is possible. Advocates for regulation need a clear understanding of how difficult this can be, and the level of knowledge that is required to understand regulatory systems in detail. In the licensing environments, small details can be the difference between success and failure and industry expertise can exert enormous pressure on regulatory agencies (Nicholls, 2015). In order to actualise the principles of value-led drug policy reform, it is essential to engage with the fine grain of how regulation is implemented on the ground.

Supporting Previously Impacted Communities

While legal regulation may tackle one key instrument of social and racial inequality, it by no means guarantees that the alternative will be just. Left to itself, a legal market may quickly become the preserve of large-scale businesses that have little interest in the injustices of the past, and little incentive to promote fairness. Regulation needs to proactively shape the market towards more equitable ends.

Cannabis legalisation in North America has highlighted this issue. Some US States have addressed historical injustices through measures including the expungement of previous records for drug offences, reducing licence fees, limiting licences to prevent monopolies, and providing training for people from poorer, minority or previously impacted communities (Transform, 2020b). In the case of drug markets, where prohibition has led to decades of disproportionate criminalisation and economic exclusion, natural market dynamics cannot be left unconstrained. Rather, the regulatory system has to actively promote social justice and ensure that impacted communities are part of the policy-development process.

However, social equity measures can have trade-offs — especially if they are not carefully planned. For example, limiting the number of available licences in a given area may help prevent bigger operators from dominating; however, it may also have the opposite effect since scarcity increases licence value. If the cost of licences is too high, only those with deep pockets can afford to enter the market. This works against the interests of smaller, community-based retailers. This is partly a matter of balancing licensing costs with limitations on numbers of licences, but also ensuring proactive support for new market entrants, especially from poor or historically marginalised communities. Importantly, recent evidence suggests that the single most high-impact measure needed to support equity going forward is the expungement of prior convictions, so this needs to be a consideration in any reformed system (Kilmer at al, 2021). In the UK there is precedent for this. The Protection of Freedoms Act 2012, for example, allowed for historical convictions relating to homosexuality to be deleted and disregarded (Home Office, 2012).

Balancing Autonomy and Intervention

All regulation implies some degree of restrictions on individual freedom. Unless the goal is a market free-for-all, then the question is not *whether* to regulate but where to draw the lines of justifiable intervention. The classically liberal position is that the State should not intervene in private behaviours until, and unless, they demonstrably harm other people. The 'public health' position is that further constraint is justified if it protects citizens from health risks or the uninvited pressures of commercial influence. At the extremes of either side lie either the dereliction of Government duty (and the handing over of control to entities driven solely by profit) or the intrusion of a paternalistic State into aspects of private life where it may have no justifiable business.

But it is not only a matter of individual rights versus State intervention. Drug policy is social policy, and the challenges it needs to address include communities as well as individuals. Health harms, although they have an effect across populations, are usually — and to a significant degree — concentrated in economically and socially marginalised communities (Marmot et al, 2010). Therefore, when considering industry controls the aggregate effect of a given business on existing health inequalities is an essential consideration. In the UK, the aggressive marketing of very cheap, very strong alcohol has contributed to the enormous skew of alcohol health harms towards poor communities (Meier et al, 2016). There are now useful examples of ways that some of these harms can be mitigated. Early evidence from the introduction of MUP for alcohol in Scotland (*Chapter 18*), for example, has shown that it has reduced consumption of the kind of cheap, high strength alcohol which was associated with disproportionate health harms in poorer communities (O'Donnell et al, 2019; Robinson et al, 2021). These lessons need to be applied to other drugs in future.

Regulated Versus Residual Markets

Policy can always have unintended consequences. For example, strict controls on outlet density in cannabis retail have, in some cases, limited the extent to which regulated supply can penetrate illegal markets (Myran et al, 2021; Transform, 2020c). Elsewhere, over-burdensome controls have led to excessively high prices or unacceptably stringent barriers to market access, which have excluded people from marginalised communities (Worthy, 2021). On the other hand, excessively light-touch regulation allows aggressive, commercial markets to emerge, severely limiting the opportunity to minimise social and health harms. The limitations of theoretically sound policies are often exposed at implementation, which is why monitoring and evaluation are essential when new regulations are adopted.

Critically, this is not a battle of utopias (the 'drug-free world' versus a world where profit-seeking is wholly eliminated). It is a matter of developing systems that address the detailed issues of pricing, licensing and marketing controls in ways that achieve the best possible outcomes in the specific social and cultural circumstances where they are applied. Transform have set out detailed proposals elsewhere, and the evaluation literature on regions that have regulated is growing. We have moved beyond seeing the post-prohibition landscape as a distant vision, to a much more familiar, and pragmatic, policy landscape in which questions revolve around such issues as licence fees, outlet density thresholds, taxation frameworks, and the establishment of parameters for marketing content. These are all difficult problems, but they are the proper terrain for this debate.

Acknowledging the Limits of Regulation

The legal regulation of drugs is not a silver bullet. It will not eliminate problematic drug use or dependence and some people will continue to be harmed by their drug use, or as a result of the drug use of others. Furthermore, the social injustices currently exacerbated by drug prohibition will not disappear, though one significant instrument of their enforcement will be greatly reduced (Woolley, 2021).

Regulation would also not entirely eliminate illegal drug markets. As with alcohol and tobacco, there is always a residual illegal market that can be squeezed but never completely eradicated. Like all social policy, drug regulation will also only be as effective as its implementation — and the need to ensure a degree of local control over decision-making will invariably lead to a patchwork of implementation practices. However, variable implementation within a robust system is better than no control, no oversight and no effective means of enforcement. Even a partial reduction in illegal markets and prohibition-related harms still represents a net gain for society as a whole.

In any respect, such variability also exists under prohibition. In the UK, we have recently seen conflicts between devolved regions over the extent to which innovation is possible under the MDA 1971. In particular, the Scottish Government has been unable to introduce safer drug consumption facilities as it is limited by the provisions of the MDA 1971 (see *Chapter 18*). The heated political debate that has arisen around this issue is an illustration of both the need for flexibility across the devolved nations, and the extent to which uncertainty over the precise operations of the law stifle innovation and policy reform. Complexity, in this sense, is precisely the *reason* for action — not the justification for inertia. Prohibition not only creates and exacerbates a range of health and social harms, but additionally creates both conceptual and practical obstacles to addressing the very real health concerns around problematic drug use. The establishment of regulated supply has the potential — by redirecting resources and shifting political and ideological obstacles—to enable the adoption of a public health approach that would produce long-term benefits. It would facilitate a more rational and evidence-based policy making environment, which can only help in tackling the social conditions that underlie problematic use.

Dr James Nicholls is a Senior Lecturer in Public Health at the University of Stirling, and previously Chief Executive Officer of the Transform Drug Policy Foundation. He is a Trustee of the social justice and harm reduction charity Cranstoun. Dr Nicholls previously served as a Trustee of Adfam National and is a member of the Public Health England Alcohol Leadership Board.

Steve Rolles is a Senior Policy Analyst for the Transform Drug Policy Foundation, a UK-based charity, operating internationally, advocating for more just and effective drug policy and law. He is the author of a number of books on alternative approaches to the war on drugs.

References and Extra Reading

Anderson, P et al (2021), Impact of Minimum Unit Pricing on Alcohol Purchases in Scotland and Wales: A Controlled Interrupted Time-Series Analysis, *Lancet Public Health*, 6: e557–65.

Angus, C, Holmes, J and Meier, P (2019), Comparing Alcohol Taxation Throughout the European Union, *Addiction*, 114(8); 1489–94.

Babor, T et al (eds) (2010), *Alcohol: No Ordinary Commodity* (2nd edn), Oxford: Oxford University Press.

Babor, T et al (2019), *Drug Policy and the Public Good* (2nd edn), Oxford: University Press.

Burton, R et al (2016), A Rapid Review of the Effectiveness and Cost-Effectiveness of Alcohol Control Policies: an English Perspective, *The Lancet*, 389(10078): 1558–80.

Colbert, S et al (2021), Online Alcohol Sales and Home Delivery: An International Policy Review and Systematic Literature Review, *Health Policy*, 125(9): 1222–37.

DeWitt, S (2021), Achieving Social Equity in the Cannabis Industry, Ohio State Legal Studies, Research Paper 618.

Gittins, R and Rolles, S (2020), Pharmacists Can Help Put an End to Illicit Drug Deaths by Being at the Centre of a New Non-medical Use Market, *Pharmaceutical*

Journal (December 2): https://pharmaceutical-journal.com/article/opinion/pharmacists-can-help-put-an-end-to-illicit-drug-deaths-by-being-at-the-centre-of-a-new-non-medical-use-market

Gomis, B (2021), Cannabis Regulation: Lessons from the Illicit Tobacco Trade, International Drug Policy Consortium (IDPC) Briefing Paper: http://fileserver.idpc.net/library/Tobacco-lessons-for-cannabis-regulation.pdf

Griffith, R, Leicester, A and O'Connell, M (2013), Price-Based Measures to Reduce Alcohol Consumption, Institute for Fiscal Studies Briefing Note, BN138.

Hawkins, B and Holden, C (2014), 'Water Dripping on Stone': Industry Lobbying and UK Alcohol Policy, *Policy and Politics*, 42(1): 55–70.

Health Poverty Action (2021), A World With Drugs: Legal Regulation Through a Development Lens: www.healthpovertyaction.org/change-is-happening/campaign-issues/a-21st-century-approach-to-drugs/legal-regulation-of-drugs-a-development-lens/

Home Office (2012), Historic Convictions for Consensual Acts to be Deleted: www.gov.uk/government/news/historic-convictions-for-consensual-acts-to-be-deleted

International Drug Policy Consortium (IDPC) (2020), Principles for the Legal Regulation of Cannabis: http://fileserver.idpc.net/library/IDPC_Responsible_Leg_Reg_1.0.pdf

Kilmer, B et al (2021), Cannabis Legalization and Social Equity: Some Opportunities, Puzzles and Trade-offs, *Boston University Law Review*, 101(1003): 1003–41.

Marmot, M et al (2010), Fair Society: Healthy Lives. Institute of Health Equity: www.instituteofhealthequity.org/resources-reports/fair-society-healthy-lives-the-marmot-review

McCambridge, J, Mialon, M and Hawkins, B (2018), Alcohol Industry Involvement In Policymaking: A Systematic Review, *Addiction* 113(9): 1571–84.

Meier, P et al (2016), Estimated Effects of Different Alcohol Taxation and Price Policies on Health Inequalities: A Mathematical Modelling Study, *PLOS Medicine*, 13(2): e1001963.

Myran, D T (2021), How Has Access to Legal Cannabis Changed Over Time?: An Analysis of the Cannabis Retail Market in Canada 2 Years Following the Legalisation of Recreational Cannabis, *Drug and Alcohol Review*. DOI: 10.1111/dar.13351

Nicholls, J (2015), Public Health and Alcohol Licensing in the UK: Challenges, Opportunities and Implications for Policy and Practice, *Contemporary Drug Problems*, 42(2): 87–105.

O'Donnell, A et al (2019), Immediate Impact of Minimum Unit Pricing on Alcohol Purchases in Scotland: Controlled Interrupted Time-Series Analysis for 2015–18, *British Medical Journal*, 366: l5274.

Owusu-Bempah, A (2021), Where Is the Fairness in Canadian Cannabis Legalisation? Lessons to be Learnt From the American Experience, *Journal of Canadian Studies*, 55(2): 395–418.

Release (2021), Drug Decriminalisation Across the World: www.talkingdrugs.org/drug-decriminalisation

Robinson, M et al (2021), Evaluating the Impact of Minimum Unit Pricing (MUP) on Off-trade Sales in Scotland: An Interrupted Time-series Study, *Addiction*, 116(10): 2697–2707.

Savell, E, Gilmore, A B and Fooks, G (2016), How Does the Tobacco Industry Attempt to Influence Marketing Regulations?: A Systematic Review, PLOSONE, 9(2): e87389.

Seddon, T and Floodgate, W (2020), *Regulating Cannabis: A Global Review and Future Directions*, Oxford: Palgrave Macmillan.

Shover, C L and Humphreys, K (2018), Six Policy Lessons Relevant to Cannabis Legalization, *American Journal of Drug and Alcohol Abuse*, 45(6): 698–706.

Transform (2009), *After the War on Drugs: Blueprint for Regulation*, Bristol: Transform Drug Policy Foundation.

Transform (2016), *How to Regulate Cannabis: A Practical Guide* (2nd edn), Bristol: Transform Drug Policy Foundation.

Transform (2020a), *How to Regulate Stimulants: A Practical Guide*, Bristol: Transform Drug Policy Foundation.

Transform (2020b), Altered States: Cannabis Regulation in the US: https://transformdrugs.org/publications/altered-states-cannabis-regulation-in-the-us

Transform (2020c), Capturing the Market: Cannabis Regulation in Canada: https://transformdrugs.org/publications/capturing-the-market

Transform and St George's House (2020), Challenges for a World Where Drugs are Legally Regulated: https://transformdrugs.org/publications/st-georges-house-report

Transnational Institute (2015), The UN Drug Control Conventions: A Primer: www.tni.org/files/publication-downloads/primer_unconventions_24102015.pdf

Wilczek, T (2021), Corporate Cannabis at Home and Abroad: International Regulation and Neoliberal Legalization, *Journal of Canadian Studies*, 55(2): 244–78.

World Health Organization (2013), Framework Convention on Tobacco Control: www.who.int/fctc/text_download/en/

Worthy, R (2021), The Cannabis Industry is Booming, but for Many Black Americans the Price of Entry is Steep, *Guardian* 7 Sept: www.theguardian.com/society/2021/sep/07/cannabis-industry-black-americans

Woolley, S (2021), Our Drug Laws are Racist and Doctors Must Speak Out, *British Medical Journal* 2021;374:n2147: www.bmj.com/content/bmj/374/bmj.n2147.full.pdf

Index

5-HT2A *30*
12 step programmes *31*
#50YearsOfFailure *183*
1960s *183–192*

A

abstinence *29, 171, 237*
absurdity *xii, 186, 296*
abuse *89, 116, 123, 200*
accountability *43, 205*
acepromazine *134, 145*
acid house *56, 62*
ACMD. See *Advisory Council on the Misuse of Drugs*
Adam Smith Research Trust *154*
addiction *24–25, 90, 123, 131, 157, 215.* See also *Europe: European Monitoring Centre for Drugs and Drug Addiction*
  'pseudo-addiction' *123*
administrative offence *168*
adulteration *57, 59, 76–77, 150, 167*
advice *27, 91, 233*
Advisory Committee on Drug Dependence. See *dependency: Advisory Committee on Drug Dependence*
Advisory Council on the Misuse of Drugs *27, 39, 58, 69, 87, 225, 264*
  recommendation to reschedule cannabis *89*

sacking of David Nutt *58, 62, 91*
advocacy *212, 305*
age *113*
AIDS *23, 25, 102*
  UN AIDS Strategy *172*
Airoldi, Mara *251*
alcohol *23, 27, 95, 104, 117, 188, 215, 249–250, 276–292*
  alcohol dependency *30, 153*
  alcohol industry *275*
  'Best Buys' *278, 287*
  hospitalisation *279*
  minimum unit pricing *20, 28, 275–292*
    Alcohol (Minimum Pricing) (Scotland) Act 2012 *282*
  'no ordinary commodity' *279*
  Scottish Health Action on Alcohol Problems *280*
Alfie's Hope. See *Dingley, Alfie: Alfie's Hope*
alkylnitrates *250*
alpha2 *134, 138*
alternatives
  alternative approaches *78, 100, 135, 166–173, 211, 244, 260, 303*
  alternative drug narratives *99, 184*
  Alternative World Drug Report *245*
ambiguity *99*
amphetamine *25, 26, 166*

para-methoxy amphetamine *79*
anabolic steroids *250*
anaesthetic *131, 133–135, 141–142, 145, 151*
analgesics *117, 127, 131*
analogue control *43, 72*
animals. See also *veterinary matters*
    Animals (Scientific Procedures) Act 1986 *134*
    animal toxicity studies *62*
anorexia *28, 32, 153*
antagonists *29, 122, 134*
anxiety *28, 93, 113, 155, 201*
    end of life anxiety *30*
Anyone's Child *20, 211–224*
arbitrariness *90, 172, 215*
arrest *193–195*
arthritis *139, 147*
    arthritis in dogs *139*
Asians *195–196*
ataxia *136–138*
attachment *234*
audit *116, 250*
autonomy *309*
Avon and Somerset *195*
ayahuasca *28–29*

B

Baan Commission (Netherlands) *170*
Baker, The Rt Hon Norman *xi, 73*
bans. See *drugs: blanket bans*
barbiturate *40, 115, 138, 250*
Belgium *212*
benevolence *126*
benzodiazepine *27, 73, 77, 117, 137*
benzofuran *42, 46*

benzylpiperazine *27*
'Best Buys'. See *alcohol: 'Best Buys'*
Betts, Leah *57–58, 62, 213*
biology *25*
Black, Dame Carol *78, 156, 174*
'black mamba' *80*
black people *193–208, 295.* See also *race/racism*
    young black people and the police *198*
Black Sox *20*
Blair, Tony *214*
Blakemore, Colin *90, 249*
blame *216*
Blenkinsop, Arthur *187*
blood borne infection/virus *150–151, 171, 242*
BMA. See *British Medical Association*
'bohemians' *193*
brain *29, 300*
    brain disorders *25, 30*
branding *215*
Bristol Drugs Education Programme *78*
British Columbia *282*
British Medical Association *88, 92*
'British System' *172*
Brown, Gordon *90*
Buckfast wine *279*
bulking agent *150*
buprenorphine *117, 122, 134, 145, 157, 251, 305*
bureaucracy *44, 131*
butorphanol *134*

C

caffeine *117, 307*

Index

Caldwell, Billy *88, 155*
Caldwell, Charlotte *88*
Callaghan, James *185*
Canada *86, 212, 305*
Cancard *94*
cancer *113–117*
cannabis *27–29, 85–98, 104, 117, 169, 231, 249.* See also *tetrahydrocannabinol (THC)*
    BMA report *88*
    cannabidiol *139*
    cannabinoids *28, 70–71, 92, 231*
    'cannabis challenge' *189*
    cultivation *86, 245*
    medical cannabis *30, 85, 88, 91–93, 154–156*
        Centre for Medicinal Cannabis *154*
        costs of prescribing *155*
        Medical Cannabis Working Group *93*
    MORI poll of 2008 *89*
    recreational use *92*
    Report on Cannabis *267*
    rescheduling *88*
    'smell of cannabis' *194*
    trafficking *89*
    use in England and Wales *77*
    veterinary use *139*
carbon footprint *243*
care *31, 212*
    palliative care *124, 153*
carfentanil *135, 145*
'cat and mouse' scenario *72–73*
cathinones *70–73*
causative links *59*
cautioning *294*

CBT. See *cognition: cognitive behavioural therapy*
chemistry *39, 71, 80, 166*
    chemical restraint (animals) *133*
    toxic chemicals *245*
children *294, 300*
    child protection *217*
citizenship *191*
    second class citizens *214*
Clarke, Charles *87*
classification of drugs. See *drugs: classification*
Clean Sweep *242*
clenbuterol *139, 146*
clephedrone *76*
climate change *241–248*
clinical disorders *25*
coca *166*
    coca leaf cultivation *244–245*
    coca tea *307*
cocaethylene *150*
cocaine *25, 74, 150, 241, 250.* See also *coca*
    crack cocaine *151*
    crack pipe *152*
codeine *115, 117, 122, 135, 145*
'coffee shops' *170*
cognition
    cognitive behavioural therapy *31*
    cognitive impairment *25*
Coleridge, Samuel *117*
colonialism *193*
commerce *307*
    commercial sensitivity *44*
    corporate power *190*
Commission on Narcotic Drugs *172*

compassion *212*
confusional state *120*
consequences *108*, *119*
   negative consequences *117*
   unintended consequences *310*
consumer protection *72*, *264*
contamination *59*, *150*, *245*
Controlled Drugs (Supervision of Management and Use) Regulations 2006. See *drugs: controlled drugs*
Controlled Drugs (Supervision of Management and Use) Regulations 2013. See *drugs: controlled drugs*
Convention Against Illicit Traffic in Narcotic Drugs and Psychotropic Substances 1988 *166*
Convention on Psychotropic Substances *124*, *166*
Coon, Caroline *184*
cost-effectiveness *234*
counselling *108*
counterculture *183*, *190*
county lines *212*
couriers. See *drugs: couriers*
Covid-19 *25*, *77*, *194*
crack *251*
craving *104*, *123*
Crew *20*
crime *24*, *150*, *173*
   criminalisation *25*, *87*, *165*, *194*, *201*, *211*, *294*
      de facto decriminalisation *167*
      de jure decriminalisation *167*
      shift away from *78*

Criminal Justice and Public Order Act 1994 *56*
criminal justice approach *25*
Criminal Justice System *194*, *212*, *241*, *295*
criminal record *212*
   expunging convictions *309*
organized crime *150*, *212*, *299*
'soft on crime' *190*
Crown Prosecution Service *46*
cultivation of drugs *303*, *310*. See also *cannabis: cultivation*; *coca: coca leaf cultivation*
culture *298*, *305*
Curran, Val *59*, *62*
custodial institutions *80*, *296*
Czech Republic *297*

D

dangerous drugs. See *drugs: dangerous drugs*
DAT. See *diamorphine/heroin: diamorphine assisted treatment*
data reliability *60*
Davies, Dame Sally *92*
DCR. See *drugs: drug consumption room*
DCS. See *drugs: drug checking service*
Deacon, Hannah *88*, *89*
Deakins, Eric *188*
death *23*, *32*, *57*, *173*, *216*, *295*
   drug-related deaths *57*, *73*, *150*
   from alcohol (Scotland) *280*
   Portugal *168*
   Switzerland *171*
Decision Analysis Society *253*

Index

decision conferencing *254–259*
decriminalisation *107, 204, 271, 276, 303*
De Finetti, Bruno *252*
dentists *266, 270*
Department of Health *114*
depenalisation *86*
dependency *25, 114, 122, 125, 172, 270, 276, 304*. See also *World Health Organization: WHO Expert Committee on Drug Dependence*
depression *25, 105, 155*
   antidepressants *150*
deprivation *24, 114*
De Quincey, Thomas *117*
derivatives *39, 42, 51, 269*
detection *76, 78, 298*
deterrence *26, 70, 211, 295*
devices *149*. See also *drugs: drug paraphernalia*
diacetylmorphine. See *diamorphine/heroin*
diamorphine/heroin *28, 40, 104, 107, 115, 117, 121, 150, 172, 250, 305*
   diamorphine assisted treatment *167*
   heroin assisted treatment *167*
   pharmaceutical heroin *157*
diarrhoea *117, 135*
diazepam *104, 137, 143, 146*. See also *Valium*
dimethyltryptamine *30*
Dingley, Alfie *88, 155*
   Alfie's Hope *89*
disadvantage *276*
discrimination *19, 197, 211–213, 221*
disparity *203*

Dissuasion Commissions *168*
distribution *264*
diversion *78, 80–81, 124, 243*
Doblin, Rick *63*
driving *90*
drugs. See also *exporting, importing, manufacturing/producing, possessing, supplying illicit drugs*
   blanket bans *72–73, 81, 108*
   classification *18, 24, 26, 39, 48–49, 69, 88, 90, 149, 172, 200–201, 265, 279*
      cannabis *85, 154, 268*
      key events timeline *88*
      temporary class drug *116, 295*
   controlled drugs *149*
      Controlled Drugs (Supervision of Management and Use) Regulations 2006 *116*
      Controlled Drugs (Supervision of Management and Use) Regulations 2013 *114–115*
   couriers *200*
   dangerous drugs *188, 214*
      Dangerous Drugs Act 1920 *185*
      Dangerous Drugs Act 1964 *26, 172*
      Dangerous Drugs Act 1965 *263*
      Dangerous Drugs Act 1967 *263*
   dealing in drugs *26–27, 27, 104*. See also *supplying illicit drugs*
   drug checking service *152, 167*
   drug consumption room *33, 167*
   Drug Enforcement Administration (USA) *63*
   drug narratives. See *narratives*

drug paraphernalia *150–151*, *234*, *241–243*
drug schedules *26–38*, *44*, *55*, *63*, *85–98*, *92*, *115–126*, *135–147*, *153–155*, *166*, *172*, *194*, *265–271*, *295–302*
    Scotland *280*
Drug Science *30*, *62*, *91*, *249*
    Enhanced Harm Working Group *152*
    Medical Cannabis Working Group *156*
    Medical Psychedelics Working Group *154*
    Project TWENTY21 *30*, *89*, *93*, *156*
    Scientific Committee *18*, *91*
Drugs (Prevention of Misuse) Act 1964 *263*
Dutch Drugs Information Monitoring Scheme *58*
mood-altering drugs *153*
polydrug use *59*, *61*, *150*
'problem' drug use *100*
recreational drugs *153*
therapeutic drugs. See *therapy: therapeutic drugs*
UK drug policy *172–174*
dysphoria *121*

E

Eastwood, Niamh *183*
economics *24*, *277*, *280*
ecstasy. See *MDMA (ecstasy)*
education *107*, *225–240*, *300*
    Department for Education *228*
    Personal Social and Health Education *225*

Emafo, Philip *171*
EMCDDA. See *Europe: European Monitoring Centre for Drugs and Drug Addiction*
environment *24*, *241–248*
epilepsy *92*, *155*
equality *278*, *308*
ethanol *280*
ethics *126*
ethnicity *205*
etorphine *133*, *135*, *145*
euphoria *123*
Europe *43*, *47*, *72*, *107*, *113*, *134*, *171*, *280*
    European Monitoring Centre for Drugs and Drug Addiction *33*, *79*, *244*
    Trans European Drugs Information *79*
euthanasia (animals). See *veterinary matters: euthanasia*
eutylone *76*
evidence *32*, *69*, *80*, *89*, *90*, *93*, *152*, *154*, *171*, *190*, *225*, *276*, *312*
exclusion *25*, *201*, *308*
exhaustion *60*
exploitation *200*, *293*
exporting illicit drugs *114*, *149*

F

families *212–224*, *234*
fear *201*, *211*
    fear arousal *229*
Federal Drugs Administration (USA) *63*
fentanyl *28*, *117*, *121*, *134*, *140*, *145*, *151*
festivals *76*, *244*
flexibility *166*, *187*
Florida *58*

food *132, 265*
  Food and Drugs Act 1955 *263*
Foot, Lord *189*
forensics *79*
  forensic drugs examiner *39*
  Forensic Early Warning System *79*
  forensic science perspective *39–54*
  Forensic Science Service *45*
freedom *191, 309*
  Protection of Freedoms Act 2012 *309*
fungi *267*

G

gabapentinoids *114*
gas chromatography-mass spectrometry *45*
'gateway theory' *90*
GBL (γ-butyrolactone) *43*
generations of compounds *48*
generic drug control *39, 41–54, 72*
Germany *299*
GHB (gamma hydroxybutyrate) *27, 250*
globalisation *72*
Graham, Senator Bob *58*
Greer, George *63*
Guernsey *47*

H

hallucinogens *51, 115, 153*
Halpern, John *62*
harm *27, 39, 73, 99–110, 165, 213*
  harm reduction *23, 150–152, 171*
  health harms *276*
  hidden harms *108*
  index of drug harms *269–271*
  MDMA harm studies *62*
Harris, Rufus *184*
hashish. See *cannabis*
HAT. See *diamorphine/heroin: heroin assisted treatment*
'headshops' *71*
health *275.* See also *mental health*
  chronic health conditions *154*
  Faculty of Public Health *244, 293*
  Healthy Schools Programme *233*
  public health approach *25, 173*
  Royal Society of Public Health *293*
hedonism *211*
Henry, John *57*
hepatitis *23, 150*
  Portugal *107*
heroin. See *diamorphine/heroin*
HIV *xii, 102, 107–108, 150, 168–173, 171*
  Portugal *168*
Home Office *45, 72, 173, 194, 204, 250, 268, 298*
  Home Office licence *115, 149, 157*
Home Secretary *xii, 49, 69, 88, 89, 185, 204, 251, 268*
homologues *50*
homosexuality *309*
hopelessness *214*
House of Commons *186–192, 293*
  Advisory Committee on Drug Dependence *183*
  Health and Social Care Committee *173, 298*
  Home Affairs Committee *87*
  scheduling of cannabis *88*

Science and Technology Select
    Committee *90, 269*
House of Lords *92, 185*
    House of Lords report on medical
        cannabis *88*
    reports on medical use of cannabis
        88–89
    second review of medical use of
        cannabis *89*
Hughes, Charlie *155*
Hulsman Commission (Netherlands)
    170
Human Medicines Regulations 2012 *263*
human rights *165, 275, 276*
hydromorphone *135*
hyperalgesia *120*
hyponatremia *57*

I

Ibiza *63*
imaging *25, 29, 137, 143*
    neuroimaging *60*
importing illicit drugs *26, 72, 114, 149,*
    155, 157, 294, 296
impulsivity *60*
inequality *24*
infection *150*
information *233*
    Drugs Information Monitoring System
        80
injecting *151, 168*
    drug rooms *33*
insomnia *28*
intervention *78, 174, 225, 241, 280, 309*
    criminal justice intervention *104*

intoxication *25, 276*
Ireland *72*
Israel *72*

J

Jeffreys, Harold *252*
Johnson, Alan *251*
judgement *216, 249*
justice *191*
'Just say no' *213*
JWH compounds *48*

K

Kaleidoscope *20*
Kenya *212*
ketamine *27, 28, 30, 117, 135–136, 142–143,*
    145
khat *250, 258*

L

'laughing gas'. See *nitrogen: nitrous oxide*
LEAD UK *20*
League of Nations Convention *40*
'legal high' *70, 71–72, 78, 231*
legalisation *95, 271, 276*
legitimacy *203, 299*
Leshner, Alan *60*
licensing *44, 268, 303*. See also *Home*
    Office: Home Office licence
life skills *233*
lived experience *212*
London *193, 198*
Loop *58, 76*
lysergic acid diethylamide (LSD) *28, 30,*
    50, 166, 169, 251

M

magic mushrooms *27, 153, 251, 269*
Major, John *213*
manufacturing/producing illicit drugs
 114, 149, 244–245, 264, 265, 294
MAPS. See *psychedelics: Multidisciplinary Association for Psychedelic Studies*
marginalisation *214, 276, 309*
May, Theresa *xii, 204*
MBDB *45*
MCDA. See *multi-criteria decision analysis*
MDA 1971. See *Misuse of Drugs Act 1971*
MDMA (ecstasy) *27, 30, 55–59, 104, 106, 153, 213, 249, 250*. See also *therapy: psychotherapy: MDMA psychotherapy*
 classification *62*
 dehydration *57*
 euphoria, energy and empathy *60*
 historical timeline *62–63*
 USA safety study *63*
MDR. See *regulation: Misuse of Drugs Regulations*
MedCan *94*
media *87, 88, 92, 169, 214, 235–236, 249*
 media frenzy *62*
medicine *43, 64, 114, 149–162, 226, 264, 305*. See also *cannabis: medical cannabis*
 medical practitioners *266*
 Medical Research Council *90, 249*
 medicinal value *26*
 Medicines Act 1968 *263*
 self-medication *154*
memory *61, 101*
mental health *24, 32, 60, 88, 144, 150, 300*
mephedrone *45, 70, 73, 74, 76*

Merck *62*
mescaline *30*
'mesh-thinning' *299*
metaphedrone *76*
methadone *102, 115, 117, 122, 134, 145, 151, 157, 305*
 street methadone *250*
methamphetamine *27, 30*
methylamphetamine *251*
methylone *70*
Mexico *212*
midazolam *115, 137, 142, 146*
migrants *193*
minimum unit pricing. See *alcohol: minimum unit pricing*
Ministry of Justice *194, 294*
minorities *87, 204*
Misuse of Drugs Act 1971 *xi, 293*
 failure to control NPS *69*
 Independent Inquiry into the MDA 1971 *86, 89, 268*
 legal analysis *263–272, 303–314*
 'not fit for purpose' *17*
 Royal Assent *17, 88, 183, 263*
Misuse of Drugs Regulations *29, 85, 115, 265, 266–268*
Montibeller, Gilberto *251*
mood *60, 153*. See also *drugs: mood-altering drugs*
morality *167*
 moralising *183*
 moral panic *214, 232, 279*
morbidity *122*
Morgenstern, Oskar *252*

morphine *40, 115, 117, 120, 134, 145, 227.*
  See also *nitrogen: nitrogen morphine derivatives*
multi-criteria decision analysis *249–262*
Multidisciplinary Association for Psychedelic Studies. See *psychedelics: Multidisciplinary Association for Psychedelic Studies*
multiple sclerosis *93*
MUP. See *alcohol: minimum unit pricing*
myths *86, 90*

N

naloxone *124, 151*
narratives *99, 184, 213*
  false narratives about black people *201*
National Crime Agency *150, 241*
National Health Service *19, 93, 116, 232–239*
National Institute for Health and Care Excellence *93, 114, 155*
needles *242*
  needle and syringe programmes *151, 167*
  needle sharing *25*
negativity *60, 198, 213*
nervous system *264*
Netherlands (The Netherlands) *33, 61–63, 76, 90, 166, 169–171*
'net-widening' *299*
neuroscience *32*
neurotransmitters *29*
new psychoactive substances.
  See *psychoactives: new psychoactive substances*
New York *58*

NICE. See *National Institute for Health and Care Excellence*
nicotine *249, 259*
Nigeria *199*
nightmares *121*
nitrogen *46*
  nitrogen morphine derivatives *40*
  nitrous oxide *117, 174, 243–244*
nociception *118, 134*
normalisation *235*
'noxious things' *263*
NPS. See *psychoactives: new psychoactive substances*
NSP. See *needles: needle and syringe programmes*

O

OAT. See *opioids: opioid agonist treatment*
obsessive compulsive disorder (OCD) *32, 153*
Offences Against the Person Act 1861 *263*
online retail *307*
OPC. See *overdose: overdose prevention centre*
opioids *26, 117, 133, 140, 151, 172, 249, 265*
  epidemic *113*
  International Opium Convention *40*
  opioid agonist treatment *167, 171*
  opioid substitutes *157*
  Opium Act (1976) (The Netherlands) *170–171*
oramorph *115, 126*
Oregon *297*
outsiders *193*

overdose *121*, *216*
   overdose prevention centre *33*, *152*, *167*
oxycodone *115*, *117*, *121*, *125*

P

pain *28*, *93*, *101*, *105*, *133*, *212*
   chronic pain *113–130*, *155*
   End Our Pain *93*, *155*
   International Association for the Study of Pain *113*
palliative care. See *care: palliative care*
paracetamol *122*, *135*, *145*, *227*
paradox *76*
paraphernalia. See *drugs: drug paraphernalia*
Parke Davis Laboratories *135*
Parkinson's disease *60*
penalties. See *punishment*
'penicillin for the soul' *55*
pentobarbital *145*
pentobarbitone *138*
pethidine *117*, *121*, *134*
pharmacology *113*, *266*, *305*
   'non-medical pharmacies' *306*
   pharmaceutical industry *44*
   pharmacy *151*
   Pharmacy and Poisons Act 1933 *50*, *263*
   polypharmacy *114*
phencyclidine *135*
phenethylamines *40*
phenidates *47*
phenobarbital (phenobarbitone) *40*, *138*, *146*
Phillips, Geoff *50*
Philpott, Jane *219*

poisoning *50*, *77*, *263*
police *193*, *294*
   College of Policing *204*
   in schools *230*
   Police and Criminal Evidence Act 1984 *194*
   Police Foundation *86*, *92*
   police 'harassment' *201*
   Police Reform and Social Responsibility Act 2011 *270*
policy *79*, *172*, *287*
politics *99*, *211*, *266*, *305*
polydrug. See *drugs: polydrug use*
Portugal *33*, *107*, *167*, *297*
possessing illicit drugs *26*, *70*, *94*, *114*, *124*, *149*, *187*, *204*, *303*
   simple possession *293–302*
post-traumatic stress disorder *27*, *63*, *93*, *153*
poverty *102*, *105*, *286*
   poverty of policy *79–80*
powerlessness *199*
prejudice *211*
premises *124*
prescriptions *24*, *93*, *114*, *149*, *156*, *305*
   environmental impact *243*
   over-prescribing *116*
   paucity of in NHS *89*
prevalence *76*
prevention *232*
prison *81*, *90*, *104*, *196*, *294*, *296*
producing illicit drugs. See *manufacturing/producing illicit drugs*
prohibition *28*, *55*, *90*, *165*, *174*, *211*, *303*
   'proactive prohibition' *71*

Project TWENTY21. See *drugs: Drug Science: Project TWENTY21*
proportionality *27, 193, 297*
psilocin *267*
psilocybin *28, 30, 117, 153*
psychedelics *29, 166.* See also *psychoactives*
   medical use *153–154*
   Multidisciplinary Association for Psychedelic Studies *63*
psychiatry *23, 32, 91*
psychoactives *287, 304*
   new psychoactive substances *18, 43, 55, 69, 231, 263*
   Psychoactive Substances Act 2016 *48, 70, 117, 149, 173, 296*
psychology *25, 168*
psychosis *25, 90, 150*
psychotherapy. See *therapy: psychotherapy*
PTSD. See *post-traumatic stress disorder*
public interest *266, 270*
punishment *26, 172, 305.* See also *sentencing*
   'punitive logic' *294*
purity *74, 167*
'pushing'. See *drugs: dealing in drugs; supplying illicit drugs*

Q

quality assurance *151*
quinalbarbitone sodium (secobarbital sodium) *138, 146*

R

race/racism *190, 194, 201–205.* See also *black people*

Raiffa, Howard *253*
Ramsey, Frank *252*
raves *56, 62, 71*
receptors *71, 117, 121*
record keeping *149*
recovery *102*
recycling *242*
reform *185, 190, 205, 275, 297*
   All-Party Parliamentary Group on Drug Policy Reform *20*
   Conservative Drug Policy Reform Group *95*
regulation *29, 241, 303.* See also *Misuse of Drugs Regulations*
rehabilitation *215*
Reid, John *87*
relationships *234*
Release *20, 183*
remifentanil *120*
research *29, 149, 154, 266*
   funding *32*
respiration *118*
rhetoric *211*
Ricaurte, George *59–60, 63*
rights *191, 199*
   balancing rights *309*
risk *57, 229*
   managing risk *79*
   risk-based control models *304*
   risk factors (opioids) *118*
role models *235*
Runciman, Viscountess *86*
Russia *282*

S

safety *63, 90, 115, 126*
  safe spaces *244*
  unsafe sex *150*
Saskatchewan *282*
Savage, Leonard *252*
scapegoating *193*
scarcity *76*
scheduled drugs. See *drugs: drug schedules*
schizophrenia *90*
schools *226*
science *27, 58, 190, 238, 264*
Scotland *28, 102, 173, 275–292*
  Scotch Whisky Association *275, 283*
  Scotland Act 1998 *280*
  Scottish Nationalist Party *280*
SCRA. See *synthetics: synthetic cannabinoid receptor agonist*
scrutiny *205*
secobarbital sodium (quinalbarbitone sodium) *138, 146*
sedation *132, 140, 143*
seizures *94*
sentencing *62, 193, 270.* See also *punishment*
  Sentencing Council *196*
Serota, Baroness *185*
serotonin *30, 60*
  serotonin syndrome *150*
Sheffield University *282–284*
Shipman Inquiry *115, 126*
Shulgin, Alexander *55, 62*
Shulgin, Ann *55*
Single Convention on Narcotic Drugs 1961 *40, 124, 166*

skunk *88, 90*
sleep *119*
  sleep apnoea *119*
  sleep disorders *155*
Smith, Jeff *219*
social systems *25*
Society of Decision Professionals *253*
socio-economics *28*
sociology *184*
'soft on drugs' *299*
Spain *297, 299, 305*
spice *80, 90, 231*
stereotyping *213*
sterilisation *242*
stigma *25, 32, 86, 91, 154, 174, 211, 295*
  de-stigmatisation *156*
Stimson, Gerry *214*
stimulants *40, 74*
St John-Stevas, Norman *188*
stop and search *193, 294, 296*
  Best Use of Stop and Search *195, 204*
storytelling *184, 212*
strategy *32, 125, 169*
  Government Drug Strategy *78*
substance misuse *25*
  parental substance misuse *234*
substitutes *40*
suicide *23*
  veterinary surgeons *144*
'Summer of Love' *184*
'Superman' tablets *79*
supplying illicit drugs *26, 70, 114, 124, 149, 187, 244, 294*
surveillance *79, 174*
Switzerland *62, 171*

synthetics *70, 74*
   synthetic cannabinoid receptor agonist *42, 44, 47, 70, 71, 90*
   synthetic cocaine *245*
syringes *39.* See also *needles: needle and syringe programmes*

T

Talk ('the Talk') *199*
TCD. See *classification of drugs: temporary class drug*
teacher training *236*
technology *29, 31*
Teff, Harvey *186*
tetrahydrocannabinol (THC) *47, 50, 77, 90, 139, 231*
therapy *131, 153*
   Breakthrough Therapy *63*
   opioid substitution therapy *305*
   psychotherapy *32, 62, 64, 153*
      MDMA psychotherapy *62*
   therapeutic drugs *114, 133, 150*
   therapeutic index *136*
thiafentanil *135, 145*
tiletamine *137*
tobacco *23, 27, 95, 117, 188, 215, 249.* See also *nicotine*
   Framework Convention on Tobacco Control *287, 307*
toleration *63, 119, 170, 306*
toxicity *78.* See also *poisoning*
   alcohol *276*
   neurotoxicity *60*
trading standards *72*
trafficking *86*

tramadol *117, 122, 138, 146*
tranquillisers *166*
Transform Drug Policy Foundation *20, 212, 245, 303*
transparency *250, 307*
trauma *121, 212.* See also *post-traumatic stress disorder*
treatment *33, 152, 168, 300*
troublemakers *200*
trust *94, 201–205, 217, 237, 295, 299*
truth *220*
   truth serum *62*
   truth to power *218–221*
tuberculosis *117*
TWENTY21. See *drugs: Drug Science: Project TWENTY21*

U

understanding *212*
unemployment *102*
United Nations *31, 165–182*
   UN Conventions *89, 304*
      UN Convention Against Illicit Traffic in Narcotic Drugs and Psychotropic Substances *124*
      UN Convention on Psychotropic Substances *153*
   UN Office on Drugs and Crime *245*
Uruguay *299, 305*
USA *86, 305, 308*
   Controlled Substances Act *29, 48*
   Drug Enforcement Administration *63*
   'Ecstasy Anti-Proliferation Act' *59*
   US Army experiments *62*

V

Valium. See *diazepam*
vape liquids *77*
vegetable matter *39*
vehicle search *296*
veterinary matters *131–147*, *266*
  euthanasia *138*
  Royal College of Veterinary Surgeons *133*
  Veterinary Medicines Directorate *132*
  World Small Animal Veterinary Association *136*
violence *170*, *200*, *212*, *279*, *293*
vodka *282*
von Neumann, John *252*
vulnerability *214*, *294*

W

Wales *28*, *286*
  Welsh Emerging Drugs and Identification of Novel Substances *77*
warnings *168*, *294*
  early warning systems *79*
weapons *299*
West Midlands *195*
'whippets' *243*
whisky *279–283*
WHO. See *World Health Organization*
withdrawal *25*, *123*
women *193*
Wootton, Barbara *184*
Wootton Report *85*, *88*, *183*
World Health Organization *23*, *25*, *122*, *235*, *277*, *278–279*, *285*, *286*, *287*, *293*, *307*

WHO Expert Committee on Drug Dependence *89*

Y

Young, Jock *193*
young offender institution *81*
young people *212*, *276*. See also *black people: young black people and the police*

Z

Zeff, Leo *62*
zero-tolerance *31*
zolazepam *137*

A direct challenge to politicians and others by a world expert on drugs.

Nutt Uncut
by David Nutt

'Nutt's book achieves his goals, to "put into the public domain, in non-specialist terms, the truth about psychiatric disorders and their treatments" and to counter "extreme and unfounded claims" about drugs. It is also an absorbing read for clinicians who want to brush up on their psychopharmacology and to appreciate better the convoluted paths of government health policy decision-making.'—*BJPsych Bulletin*.

2021 | Paperback & Ebook | 256 pages | ISBN 978-1-909976-85-6

www.WatersidePress.co.uk